READING
BEHIND
BARS

Center Point
Large Print

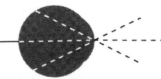

**This Large Print Book carries the
Seal of Approval of N.A.V.H.**

READING BEHIND BARS

A Memoir of Literature, Law, and Life as a Prison Librarian

Jill Grunenwald

CENTER POINT LARGE PRINT
THORNDIKE, MAINE

This Center Point Large Print edition
is published in the year 2019 by arrangement with
Skyhorse Publishing.

The text of this Large Print edition is unabridged.
In other aspects, this book may vary
from the original edition.
Printed in the United States of America
on permanent paper.
Set in 16-point Times New Roman type.

ISBN: 978-1-64358-321-1

The Library of Congress has cataloged this record
under Library of Congress Control Number: 2019943419

Contents

To Mom

Introduction

A man dressed completely in black snapped the steel bracelets around my wrists. "Don't worry," he said, taking a step back. The key to my freedom shone brightly in his oversized hand. "It's just for a minute."

Then he winked, a sly grin playing at the corners of his mouth.

What had I gotten myself into?

Prison. That's what I had gotten myself into. Not jail. Not a detention center, or a holding cell, or even the drunk tank. *Prison.*

The Clink. The Slammer. The Big House. The Pen. Lock up. Statesville. Sent up the river.

Not only had I landed myself behind bars, I'd *volunteered* for it. Well, volunteered might not be the best term. I was an employee of the prison, so I was at least being paid to be there; but still. Very few people make the conscious decision to enter a correctional institution of their own free will.

Against the backdrop of the cold, sterile warehouse, the man in black cut an imposing figure: that intimidating combination of advantageous genes that gave him both height and width. Not in the soft doughy kind of way, but in the "I could crush your head between my two bare hands without breaking a sweat" kind

11

of way. With two very large bear paw–sized hands. His broad shoulders indicated that he had probably played football in high school. He might even have been one of those burly men who entertained thoughts of playing college ball until an injury sidelined him and cut his dreams short. In one fell swoop, he may have been forced to trade a lifetime of slinging footballs for a lifetime of slinging handcuffs.

The pair he slung now slid into place around my wrists with an admittedly satisfying *click,* but even with their cool curves, the metal felt sharp against my skin. The cuffs dug into my wrists like knife blades. Even knowing it was futile, I still pulled my closed fists in opposite directions until the chain connecting them tightened.

Surrounding me was a sea of unfamiliar faces. There were roughly a dozen of them, mostly men, dressed in ratty sweats and torn t-shirts. A mixed bag of races and ages, their eyes studied me. Suddenly my black yoga pants felt too tight, the neckline of my t-shirt too exposed. As I took stock of the group, a blush crept up my neck and a sense of unease washed over me. Of everyone in that room why was I the one who was singled out? All I had done was show up at a warehouse on the appointed day at the appointed time, and look at what had happened. He might as well have sewn a scarlet "A" on my t-shirt and called it a day.

My eyes traveled over the group of strangers clustered around a long table in the corner and at that moment, I questioned every single life decision I had made in the past decade, all the way back to July 1999, the summer between my junior and senior years of high school, when I got an after-school job at the library in my hometown of Hudson, Ohio.

It had been the perfect job for me. I am, and have always been, a bookworm. Books are in my blood, the written word etched upon my bones. (Although, surprisingly, despite my love of books and knowledge and learning, I am not a Ravenclaw but, instead, proudly wear the green and silver of Slytherin.)

In elementary school, I spent recess holed up in the library, tucked into one of the window seats, devouring books that were way above both my reading and maturity levels. What I couldn't find on the shelves of McDowell Elementary School could usually be sourced from the stacks of the local public library (just as long as I tucked them between more age-appropriate reading material so my mom didn't see). Soon enough I started writing my own stories, scribbling away pages of high fantasy or historical fiction that were, once again, far above my maturity level; but that, of course, was part of the fun. At ten years old, my knowledge about the Vietnam War was gleaned almost entirely from a few paragraphs found in my elementary school's copy of *World Book*, but that didn't stop me from using it as the setting for my first novel.

So at seventeen years old, needing a job, the one thing I did *not* want to do was work another summer at the hamburger station of my local McDonalds. Because of my love of reading, I was eager to apply and get a job at the library. After all, what reader wouldn't want to hang around books all day?

So I was surprised when a few years ago, my mother told a group of people that the only reason I started working in the library was because of her. Say what now? According to my mother, I was lazy and unmotivated and needed to be dragged and nagged to apply.

One of us is clearly lying. Or, perhaps more accurately, one of us has a faulty memory. I don't want to make any bold declarations I may come to regret, but only one of us is writing a book and has the opportunity to set the record straight per our own memories. (Ah, see, there's that Slytherin pride: refusing to admit that perhaps I am indeed wrong.)

After getting hired, I spent the next seven years working at the Hudson Library & Historical Society. From the summer before my senior year of high school through every winter and summer break during college, I shelved books and checked out books and came to know every inch of that library like the dog-eared pages of a beloved, well-read novel. When I wasn't home on breaks, I was in school, getting my BFA in creative writing, with a minor in English literature. I practically lived and breathed books, so upon graduation I returned to my parents' house in Hudson and continued to work at the library while I decided what I really wanted to do with my life. As much as I wanted to spend the rest of my life writing books, that almost never pays the bills; I needed a Plan B.

Admittedly, it took me far longer than one would presume to realize that what I wanted to do and what I *should* do was become a librarian. For a year or two, I hovered on the periphery of adulthood, working jobs here and there, never finding that elusive "career." It was only in my mid-twenties that I reached a point where I wanted something with more of a stable trajectory and—light bulb moment—decided to go to graduate school to become a librarian. After graduating from the University of Kentucky with my masters in library and information science in December 2008, I once again migrated back to Northeast Ohio. Unfortunately, the economy had taken a huge downturn and jobs were scarce. Libraries—including Hudson's—were hemorrhaging money, reducing both hours and staff just to keep the lights on and the books available.

During our first semester of graduate school, my classmates and I had been sold the fairytale that by the time we graduated there would be a plethora of opportunities for us because all of those librarians who had been employed for decades would soon be retiring and their jobs would need to be filled. Eighteen months later, however, diploma in hand, I knew how overly optimistic that simple narrative was. Most of those old librarians couldn't afford to retire and even if they did leave, the libraries didn't have the funding available to hire replacements. Add to that the fact that library science masters programs were still producing graduates who needed jobs, which meant that there were hundreds of newly minted librarians fighting for and applying to the same handful of jobs.

And as 2008 sundowned into 2009, I was one of those newly-minted, job-seeking librarians. I added whatever creative writing flair I could to my resume while I put my internet searching skills to use looking for jobs. No part of the country was off-limits in my quest for gainful employment, although I hoped to remain in Ohio. But even well-established (and well-funded) institutions were struggling. More than once I applied to a position only to receive an email a few weeks later from the Human Resources department saying that they pulled the job ad. They just didn't have the money to pay someone.

One evening I was scanning the State of Ohio's government job boards when I came across a position for a Library Assistant at a correctional treatment facility. On a whim I applied, was interviewed, and was hired. (Only later would I learn what "correctional" actually meant.)

I was one of the lucky ones—I had a job. One of the very lucky ones, in fact, as many of my peers would still be searching after two years.

But now, looking down at the steel bracelets around my wrists, I didn't *feel* lucky. All those previous moments stacked on top of each other like a pile of books had brought me here, to this exact moment, and I *still* had no idea exactly how I ended up in the situation I was currently facing. Because when I had pictured my very first day as a professional librarian, it did *not* involve getting handcuffed.

Yet here I was. Even though I was a full-fledged librarian who had managed to find a job in a failing economy, I was getting handcuffed by one of my new coworkers. Evidently when it comes to picking an employee to use as an example, why *wouldn't* you take the newbie? Especially when she's the meek and quiet librarian who felt like a copy of *Macbeth* that had accidentally been shelved alongside the Florida travel guides.

Having worked in libraries in some form or another for twenty years, I was used to the many institutional rules that must be upheld, even in the face of frustrated and sometimes angry patrons: no food except in designated areas; no cell phone usage except in designated areas; a library card is required for all checkouts, no exceptions. I understand that it's your wife and you can provide her address, her birthday, her social security number, and her blood type, and I also understand she's been on hold for this book for quite a while, but without her library card, you are not leaving this library with the latest book in the sadistic saga of Christian Grey and Anastasia Steele. Rules are rules.

There are the same fairly standard rules in a typical library. But I wasn't working in a typical library now. I was working in a library within a men's correctional institution and, as I would soon learn, correctional institutions come with *a lot* of rules.

When an inmate first arrived at the facility, he sat through orientation where he learned all about how the facility worked—meal times, laundry (also known as quartermaster), and activities, including library services. He was also given a copy of the "Inmate Handbook." The handbook included some of the more nuanced rules related to the dress code, identification badges, recreation hours, commissary, and even how often inmates were required to shower ("at least three (3) times per week").

Included in the "Inmate Handbook" were the "Inmate Rules of Conduct," written into law via the Ohio Administrative Code. Inmates who violated any of the rules had a conduct report written up by staff and were subsequently punished. The breaches of behavior that inmates can violate are varied. The "Inmate Rules of Conduct" include some fairly innocuous items, like *(21) Disobedience of a direct order* and *(35) Being out of Place* but quickly escalate to more alarming things like *(57) Self-mutilation, including tattooing* and *(1) Causing, or attempting to cause, the death of another*, and a violation I would soon be intimately familiar with, *(14) Seductive or obscene acts, including indecent exposure or masturbation.*

Along with that, the employees also had their own set of rules to follow, which were set forth by the Ohio Department of Rehabilitation and Correction (ODRC). Ultimately, every rule had the exact same end goal: the safety and security of the facility and everyone inside of it. We all operated under the same premise: if, when we left the prison at the end of our shift, all persons inside were still alive and unharmed, then we had a good day no matter what other shit may have gone down.

This may seem like a low bar but it was not without precedent. Prison riots may be few and far between, but when they occur, they often are deadly affairs. Unfortunately, riots are an occurrence that the ODRC is intimately familiar with: on Easter Sunday 1993, over four hundred inmates at the maximum-security Southern Ohio Correctional Facility in Lucasville, Ohio, rioted and took control of the prison. Eleven days later, nine inmates and one corrections officer were dead.

Luckily, Lucasville is an extreme example and I had been hired at a minimum-security camp. Still, safety was paramount and while the most important rule for staff could be debated, the *first* rule for staff was that no employee was allowed around the facility unaccompanied unless they had passed the prison's unarmed self-defense course.

Which is how on a crisp February day in 2009, I stood in a small warehouse wearing sneakers I had just purchased a couple of days before, a ratty old t-shirt from the back of my closet, and a pair of black, coffee-stained yoga pants from my previous life as a barista.

I also now had a pair of handcuffs locked tightly around my wrists. The man in black, otherwise known as Correctional Officer Williard, turned me around the room, showing off his handiwork of proper handcuffing procedures to our colleagues.

"Welcome to the team, Miss Librarian," he said as he slipped the key into the lock and set me free.

I darted away from Williard and slipped into an empty seat at the table with my new coworkers. As Williard continued his presentation, I momentarily tuned him out as I gently rubbed my wrists.

Toto, I don't think we're in Kansas anymore.

PART I
THE VOICE OF
THE DOOR-KEEPER

He came to the prison. A bell-chain hung by the doorway and he pulled it. A panel in the door slid back.

"Monsieur," said the man, removing his cap, "will you be so kind as to let me in and give me lodging for the night?"

"This is a prison, not an inn," said the voice of the door-keeper. "If you want to be let in you must get yourself arrested."

—Victor Hugo, *Les Miserables*

Chapter 1
Out of the Frying Pan

It is the policy of the Ohio Department of Rehabilitation and Correction (DRC) to ensure a background investigation is conducted on each state employee, intern, contractor, and volunteer under primary consideration for employment or entrance into any of its offices/institutions unless otherwise exempted by this policy. The purpose of the background investigation is to identify offenses or behaviors that may impact job performance, volunteer participation, or internship work, or their ability to provide services.
—ODRC Policy 34-PRO-07

The small, dusty village of Grafton, Ohio (population 6,636) is located on the far western outskirts of Cleveland. So far west that it isn't really fair to even use Cleveland as a geographical reference point; but as a recent transplant in the opening act of 2009, that's all I had. Although transplant isn't the right term, either. "Prodigal Daughter" might be more appropriate. After high school, I—like LeBron James—had fled the quaint comfort of my Northeast Ohio hometown in an effort to find greener pastures, only to return after realizing Dorothy was right: there's no place like home. (Granted, LeBron left again, but he brought us home a championship title. Between stints in Miami and Los Angeles, I can't really blame the guy for escaping Cleveland winters.)

I had grown up not in the city of Cleveland but in the suburbs surrounding the city. Even then, Hudson was on the southeast side and I was far more familiar with the communities on the east side of the city than the west, where Grafton is located. Grafton was so far west from all familiar terrain it might as well have been in California.

As a town, Grafton offers its residents one industry of employment: corrections. It isn't a flashy field and it definitely isn't for everyone, but after the steel mills of nearby Youngstown had shuttered their doors, and the automobile industry was falling off the rails in Detroit, and the rest of the Rust Belt was struggling to survive, the prisons of Grafton could provide one thing very few employers could in the wake of the Great Recession: job security. Unless there was a major overhaul to our criminal justice system, prisons and the inmates housed in them weren't going anywhere anytime soon.

Over the past two weeks, since accepting the position of librarian at the minimum-security prison, I had gone through a barrage of tests that evaluated my ability to perform critical job functions as well as my ability to maintain the safety and security of the facility. Simple enough, right?

Not so much. I started with the drug test. This was immediately complicated by the fact that I can't pee on command. Ever. Whenever I have had to have x-rays taken (which, in my case, is about once every five years due a variety of very ungraceful moves that have resulted in multiple sprained ankles and broken bones), I'm that physically stubborn patient who, even after drinking water and/or purposely not using the restroom prior to the appointment, is encouraged to "just try" by the nurses even though I *know* I'm not pregnant. (How do I know you ask? Oh just little things called science! and cycles! and math! and just plain ol' abstinence!) Then, I always sit in the sad, sterile bathroom with its harsh yellow light and white walls unable to "perform." It often gets to the point where I just hand the nurse the empty cup and say I'll sign whatever they need me to sign in order to absolve them of all fault if I somehow magically am pregnant.

But prison pee tests can't be waived away with a signature and a "cross my heart, hope to die doc" because prison pee tests are looking for drugs. Nevermind that in my case this was an utterly pointless test as I am the least likely person I know to do drugs. I came of age during the "Just Say No" era, sitting through countless Drug Abuse Resistance Education (aka D.A.R.E.) programs throughout my childhood, while also witnessing Nancy Reagan on television warning of the dangers of drugs. I bought that party line and made it through high school, college, and even graduate school without ever once saying yes.

Of course, I had no way of convincing the lab assistant that I was drug free without filling the little plastic and very much empty cup in my hand. So I got prepared. While the lab shut down for an hour for lunch, I went to Walmart and bought the biggest bottle of water I could find. After chugging it down, I returned to the lab post-lunch and thankfully managed to produce the desired, if diluted, drug-free result. Check that one off the pre-employment checklist.

After the bladder blunder came a very extensive background check. I'd had background checks before but none of them involved driving out to the Lorain County Sheriff's Office to be fingerprinted. My unique swirls and whirls were sent not just through the county and state system but the FBI database as well. I wasn't very concerned about the background check (although suddenly every single unpaid parking ticket from my undergraduate years started to haunt me) but if nothing else, I knew that if I did pass this I'd never have to worry about another employment background check ever again. Seriously, nothing was going to top this.

Then there was the tuberculosis test. Or, as someone who grew up reading her fair share of tragic young adult novels set during the Victorian age, the *consumption* test. (This prompted much daydreaming: I was the anguished Fantine, desolate and destitute and dying without knowing the fate of my daughter Cosette. Or lovely little Helen Burns, leaving this world happy for the friendship of Jane Eyre.)

My knowledge of tuberculosis was so wrapped up in the fictional world I didn't even know tuberculosis was even a *thing* that people could still catch, let alone that Cleveland's MetroHealth hospital had an entire clinic dedicated to it that served all of Cuyahoga County.

Know what's not a good thing to give to someone who's mild OCD presents itself in the form of checking, checking, and rechecking things? A medical test that leaves a small bubble on the skin that needs to be examined two days later by a medical professional to see if it has changed. After getting injected I spent the next forty-eight hours checking the injection site with alarming frequency, my imagination crafting images of me coughing into lace, monogrammed handkerchiefs and producing spots of blood. (I also have a flair for the dramatic.) Spoiler alert: everything turned out fine.

The pre-employment process was long and arduous but I came out in one piece. Even the small bubble on my arm disappeared eventually. After also sitting through the required unarmed self-defense course, I now had permission to walk freely around the prison and fulfill the duties of a librarian. There was nothing to stop me now.

A few days later I was headed back to the prison, which stood on a long stretch of road flanked by its peer institutions. A month prior, when I made my first interview trip, Meredith Highland, head of HR, instructed me to look "for the one in the middle." Soon enough I would learn the layout of the four facilities that make up Prison Row in Grafton, Ohio.

State Route 83 is an almost entirely vertical fifty-mile stretch that begins in Avon Lake, Ohio, a small city lapping the shores of Lake Erie to the north, then cuts right through the heart of Grafton as it makes its way south to Wooster, Ohio. Wooster isn't exactly central Ohio, but it isn't too far from it either.

The Grafton section of the highway is nestled in a very rural area. On the east side of the road, standing alone, was Lorain Correctional Institution. In addition to being a multiple-level security prison, Lorain also acted as one of the state's two reception and distribution facilities for men. This essentially means that when an inmate who lives in the northern half of the state is sentenced, he is first sent to Lorain for processing and evaluation before making his way to his permanent prison. For the southern half of the state, there is a similar facility in Orient, Ohio. These intake centers only process male inmates: like most states, Ohio has gender-segregated prisons. Women, no matter the severity of their crime or sentence, are incarcerated at the Ohio Reformatory for Women, located in the center of the state near the capitol, Columbus.

Across the street from Lorain Correctional Institution are three other facilities. To the far left is Grafton Correctional Institution, a minimum-security prison similar in size to Lorain. On the far right was the Farm.

At nearly 1,200 acres, the Grafton Prison Farm functioned as both a prison and a working farm. While they were eventually all shut down in 2016, back in 2009 Ohio had ten prison farms, which historically offered inmates an opportunity to learn a skill they could take with them when they are released; another added benefit was that the farms also provided food for the prison. When it first opened, Grafton Prison Farm also operated as an honor farm: a facility that kept inmates there on their honor. This worked exactly as it sounds and worked about as well as you'd think, which is why, when I started working next door, it was no longer an honor farm but, instead, had a razor-wire fence that matched those of its neighbors.

Sandwiched between Grafton and the Farm, as promised, was my new employer.

Staring at my new work site, I felt like a fish out of water. I had neither intended nor set out to become a prison librarian. As a subject matter, prison libraries aren't exactly standard material covered in a graduate school curriculum (or at least it wasn't at mine) so I didn't know they were even a thing and I certainly didn't know what the term "correctional" meant within the context of a job ad found on a random website. Compound this with fact that I had an acquaintance who worked at a facility with the same name, only instead of "treatment facility" it was called "behavioral facility" and I conflated the two. It wasn't until Highland called to set up an interview that the other shoe dropped.

The day of my interview I almost flaked. I *wanted* to flake but desperate times called for desperate measures and, if nothing else I figured it would be good interview practice for all of those other job interviews I would hopefully have. Job interviews that wouldn't involve voluntarily stepping behind bars. But when Highland called me back with a job offer that included paid time off and benefits, well, I couldn't really say no.

I steered my car into the parking lot and pulled into an open space, opting to park beneath a tall light pole, a habit I had developed in graduate school when I had late night classes that required walking across campus in the dark. Gathering my personal items, I took my cell out of my purse and flipped it open to check for any messages. My friends and family knew I was starting today and a few had sent along well wishes. Closing the phone, I returned it to the glove box. Cell phones were considered contraband and not allowed inside.

A black SUV, helmed by Corrections Officer Lewis, was slowly patrolling the perimeter of the parking lot as I pulled in. Along with cell phones, guns were also not allowed inside the prison. Lewis, and the other COs assigned perimeter duty, were the only corrections officers who were armed. An inmate couldn't get shot while inside, but once he made it past that fence all bets were off. I had met Lewis a few days before at the unarmed self-defense course and as I got out of my car, she waved at me from across the parking lot. I returned her wave, took a deep breath, and headed up the long sidewalk to the main glass doors.

The lobby was quiet and empty. Nearly everything in the room was beige. Beige walls. Beige doors. Beige counters. The only things not beige were the brown lockers at the back of the room and several rows of brown chairs in the middle of the space, both reserved for visitors on visitation days. The chairs were worn from years of use, the faux leather cracked and split at the seams. Tufts of white stuffing poked out from the gaps.

A corrections officer, uniformed in the standard black, stood at the front of the room, and a metal detector separated us. He was the only other person in the lobby and his eyes followed me as I made my way to a tinted window in the far-right corner. Behind the window, shaded from my view, were the correctional officers working the security control room. They were the eyes and ears of the prison, safe, secure, and seemingly all-powerful behind reinforced steel walls.

"I'm the new librarian," I spoke a little too loudly into the call box. "It's my first day." Taking a step back, I cleared my throat, wondering if they could tell how nervous and out of place I felt.

At waist level, a metal box opened and a drawer slid out. "Identification, please," came a voice on the other side of the window. Squinting, I tried to make out any human shape behind the shaded glass, but the window was too dark to see anything. It felt almost like being in a noir novel. I was the plucky Girl Friday who had wandered into the villain's secret speakeasy and I needed the secret password to get inside.

I fished my driver's license out of my purse and dropped it in. The drawer disappeared until it was flush with the wall. I was allowed to proceed.

My shoes *click-clacked* against the also-beige tiles as I headed over to the officer. He waited patiently behind the counter as I piled my purse and lunch bag onto the end of the counter. On top of those items went my coat, incredibly heavy but very much required for Ohio winters.

I eyed the officer's ID badge. Ever the diligent student, I was determined to learn the names of all of my new coworkers as quickly as possible. *Schroeder, got it.* Behind him was a floor to ceiling, wall-to-wall window that looked out over the prison. To the left was a nondescript long concrete building and a large green yard. In the far distance I could see the three housing units that the prison's seven hundred inmates called home.

"First day, huh?" he asked, smiling. It was his attempt at making friendly conversation. I nodded, silent. My attention was focused on him as he searched my purse and lunch bag, going so far as to open the latter and peek at the food inside. I'm a leftover lover, the type of cook who prepares a casserole or soup on Sunday and then portions it out for the rest of the week's lunches. Today, however, not knowing what the kitchen would include, I had packed a paltry peanut butter and jelly sandwich with a side of potato chips and baby carrots.

Oblivious to my reticence, he continued, almost nonchalantly. "It's been kind of a crazy morning.

Had an incident down in seg earlier, so that's always fun." Schroeder bounced on his heels—he was excited by this.

"Incident," I repeated. The hairs on the back of my neck stood up. That didn't sound fun to me. The word "incident" sounded bad. Only bad things are incidents. You don't call good things or surprises incidents. You wouldn't call buying a puppy or winning the lottery "an incident." This was supposed to be a minimum-security prison. I had been *assured* this was a minimum-security prison. Most of the men were in on drug- or alcohol-related charges. These weren't violent men; or at least they weren't supposed to be.

Schroeder didn't elaborate further. "All set," he said with a grin. He pushed my items to the opposite end of the counter and waved me through the metal detector.

I held my breath as I passed beneath the gray arch. It remained silent.

At the end of the counter was a blue binder. I flipped open the front cover to an official looking lined piece of paper already partially filled out. On the next available line I wrote today's date, my name, and then *birth control*. Medications were a controlled substance behind bars and all medication inside the prison had to be accounted for, even that of the employees and even those medications that were of no use to the all-male inmate population. I had been warned in advance

36

that I was only ever to bring enough for that day's shift. As Tuesday was one of my late nights, that day's pack included the tiny blue pill I needed to take at 6:30 p.m. In anticipation of this, and to minimize the risk of losing a single pill, I had purchased a two-inch metallic cylinder with a screw top that now hung on my keyring.

After filling out the form, I reached over the counter for my coat. I slipped it back on, grabbed my purse and lunch bag, and waited expectantly for instructions.

A loud buzzer echoed throughout the room. On the other side of the large window I saw Dr. Harald, my new manager. Like CO Williard, Dr. Harald had been blessed both with height and width, only in his case, it was of the soft doughy variety. He was both taller and wider than Williard, measuring at least six-and-a-half feet tall and tipping the scales at around 450 pounds. His body composition required him to lumber more than walk, his weight shifting from side to side. His thinning, brown hair was starting to go gray. It was impossible to pinpoint his age— who knows how much the stress of working in a prison had aged him. He pulled open the outermost door and stepped into the glass and concrete box, waiting.

A former high school principal, Dr. Harald was now head of the Education department and all inmate education fell under his purview. The state even had its own school district within the Ohio Department of Rehabilitation and Correction: the Ohio Central School System (OCSS). Chartered in 1973, OCSS was started with the purpose of providing prisoners educational programs through both adult education courses, as well as vocational training. The library was more than just a place for the inmates to hang out for a few hours every day—it provided them with the opportunity to make choices and decisions that would better their lives and, hopefully, keep them from returning after they were released. Because this was a minimum-security camp, all of the inmates would be getting out eventually. For some it would be a few years, but for others, their stay with us was mere months. Part of my job was to contribute to their collective education and to prepare them for their eventual reentry into society, whenever that came.

A second buzzer echoed and Dr. Harald pulled open the heavy door closest to us. Entering the lobby, he shifted his clipboard into his other arm, and reached his hand out to shake mine. I returned it with vigor, wanting to make a good impression on my first day. We had met previously, when I had interviewed, but now he was officially my new supervisor. He turned his head towards the darkened glass of the control room and gave a nod.

The door behind him buzzed again and he

pushed it open into the enclosed box he had just been in.

Officially called a sally port, the alcove we now stood in had two strong, secure doors: the one we had just come through and the one still closed in front of us. Never were both doors allowed to be open at the same time. The doors were manually controlled by the corrections officers in the control booth and only after the door had closed behind us, did I hear the buzzer for the second door.

The exterior sally port door slammed shut behind us and I followed Dr. Harald a few feet to the control booth's other tinted window, this one facing out into the yard. This also had a call box and a small metal drawer set into the wall. We stood there and the drawer popped open at my waist. Sitting inside was my driver's license, a two-inch square black box with a button in the middle, and a ring of tarnished bronze discs.

"Those are your chits," Dr. Harald said, pointing to the discs. There were four in total, each slightly larger than a quarter but smaller than a half dollar. Each was engraved with the number sixty-four. "Those chits are tied to your set of keys, which is tied to you," he continued. "If you need to borrow a tool from another department, you give them the chit in return. It's like collateral."

"And this?" I asked, holding up the small black box with the gray button in the middle.

"Panic button. Push that and it will notify the security center here and guards will respond. Quickly. You don't want to push that accidentally, so be careful."

I gulped and stared at the full keyring in my palm: chits, panic button, and three keys. I had nowhere else to put them so I stuffed the entire keyring in my pants pocket, grateful the winter weather had forced me to opt for pants (and grateful that the pair I had worn that day was the magical unicorn of women's pants that came with working pockets).

Dr. Harald looked at me. "Ready?"

With a nod, I stepped out into the prison yard.

Chapter 2
And into the Fire

*It is the policy of the Ohio Department of
Rehabilitation and Correction to provide
for a qualified staff person to coordinate
and supervise library services within
each institution. Library staffing shall
be augmented through the selection,
training, and use of inmates as library
aides.*
—ODRC Policy 58-LIB-02

As Dr. Harald shuffled slowly down the walkway,
I strolled alongside him, taking everything in. I
had been inside when I interviewed a few weeks
back, but I had been so amped up with interview
nerves, combined with *Oh my God, I am inside
a prison* nerves, that I didn't really remember
anything from that first meeting.

The layout of the yard formed a semicircle with
buildings scattered along the perimeter. Starting
at the entrance and moving in a clockwise
fashion there was Administration, the Operations
building, and finally at the bottom of the loop,
three dormitory-style buildings where the inmates
slept. In the open area between was the yard,
an expansive green space that provided outdoor

41

recreation for the inmates. An asphalt path looped around, acting as a walking and running track.

Dr. Harald first led me to the Administration building. Included there was the Visitation Room, along with the offices for those in charge of the prison, including the Warden, the Major, the Fiscal Officer and, of course, Human Resources.

Inside Administration, I was reintroduced to Highland, head of Human Resources, and introduced for the first time to Warden Garcia, Deputy Warden Francis, and Major Torres.

Between the three of them, this trio kept the prison and everyone inside—both staff and inmates—safe. Warden Garcia was in charge of the entire camp and mostly dealt with any security issues that arose, while Deputy Warden Francis oversaw the operational side of things, including the Education department. Before I started, there had been a Deputy Warden of Prison Programs, which was the catchall for the non-security side of things such as recreation, education, and the library, but she had left and Francis was pulling double duty until a replacement was found.

Major Torres reported to Warden Garcia, and beneath him was a structured hierarchy that ranked the security team at the prison: Captain, Lieutenant, Sergeant, followed by all remaining Correctional Officers. There was only one Warden, Deputy Warden, and Major, but there were a couple of Captains and Lieutenants, a handful of Sergeants, and countless Correctional Officers who rotated their work shifts over the course of twenty-four hours.

Mixed in with these military-like folks were the civilian staff, like myself.

After signing all of the necessary papers with HR, I met Lieutenant Hall. He was the resident IT expert and he set me up with the username and password I would use to access my email from my library computer.

IT was the last stop on my introductory tour, and it was now time for me to get to work. I continued to follow Dr. Harald as he exited Administration and headed down the main pathway. A few yards past Administration, our feet stepped over a fading red line painted on the asphalt. I glanced over my shoulder and watched the security control center, and with it the entrance, getting smaller and smaller with each step. A sense of trepidation followed each step as well. This must be how Harry Potter and friends felt as they ventured into the Forbidden Forest. They had no way of knowing what lay beyond but they knew enough—I mean, it was called the *Forbidden* Forest for a reason—to know that they had to keep their guard up and that danger lurked under every bush and behind every tree.

As if to reconfirm my sense of unease, at that moment I noticed a sign posted beside the red strip. Walking out towards the yard, I could only see the back of the sign. Whatever was written on it was meant for those on the other side of the red strip. After walking over the strip, I peeked over my shoulder to read the big block letters: NO INMATES BEYOND THIS POINT.

It might as well have said ABANDON ALL HOPE, YE WHO ENTER HERE.

The line represented a demarcation between the levels of inmate interaction that happened among the staff. It was a little like Dante's *Inferno*, with the employees working in Admin being stuck in a weird sort of limbo. While the Warden and other security staff had reason to enter the yard and visit the inmates and other buildings, some staff had no reason to ever cross the red line, and so had very limited interaction with the inmates, if they had any at all. But they still worked in a prison, just like the rest of us, only they existed in a gray space between freedom and incarceration.

Yet, if the inmates decided to "storm the castle," (to quote *The Princess Bride*) the major prize would be winning Administration and the Security Control Room. In that regard they were possibly in a more dangerous position than the rest of us.

Right then, the yard was empty, partially covered with a blanket of snow, obscuring the baseball field in the distance. I had arrived during what is called "count." Several times a day, the inmates are counted, making sure all inmates were present and accounted for. Where I was now constituted an open yard, meaning as long as it wasn't count or meal times, the inmates could move around freely from their dorm to the library to recreation back to their dorm, etc. During count, when the inmates were in the dorms, and meal times were the only instance of controlled movement, when the correctional officers would herd the inmates like sheep. Other than that, the inmates were free to bounce back and forth across the yard into all permissible areas.

Following the curve of the semicircle, the next place up was Operations, the main hub of inmate activity, a long low building that ran parallel to the entire length of the yard. As we walked, Dr. Harald gestured to the other doors: Quartermaster, Commissary, Chapel, Segregation (ah! the mysterious "Seg" that Schroeder had mentioned), Recreation, Dining, Library, and, finally, Education.

Dr. Harald pulled out a keyring with a set of keys and chits that mirrored my own. He held a key up, showing me the number engraved on the head. "This one is for Education. The other one is for the library." He put the first key into the lock on the front of the wide set of double doors.

The foyer had the same dull beige hue as the lobby. Seems like that was standard issue. Two hallways ran perpendicular to the entrance, creating a backwards L. To my immediate left was the Education department office. At the very end of the hallway was a bathroom available only to staff with a key.

Opposite the Education office was a classroom with computers all around the perimeter. Set in the middle was a large set of tables. A small group of four people—three women and one man—were clustered around a table. As Dr. Harald led me down the long hallway, the women in the classroom peeked their heads out to watch.

Next to the computer classroom was another classroom, this one set in a more traditional style with all of the desks facing forward towards a whiteboard at the front of the room. Color punctuated the walls, bright posters with messages encouraging commitment and teamwork.

Beside the classroom was a large opening in the wall that showed the inmate restrooms. No doors or privacy here. In front of the restroom entrance was a standard-issued desk, now empty. A logbook sat open on top.

On the other side of the inmate restroom was another office. "This is our addiction treatment team," Dr. Harald said, waving absentmindedly at them. "They oversee the Alcoholics Anonymous and Narcotics Anonymous meetings here. Those are held in the empty classrooms in the far back corners back there." He gave another absentminded wave, as if to indicate whatever was down at the end of the hall wasn't important enough to be included on the tour.

So this was more than just a prison. *Well,* it was still very much a prison but it was a prison with a purpose: this particular minimum-security facility mostly housed inmates in on drunk driving charges and drug convictions. There was a smattering of other charges mixed in, but those two made up the bulk of the inmate population. This was not a coincidence; because of the strong focus on rehabilitation and addressing addiction, we were recognized as an institution where inmates could get the help they needed in those areas, in addition to serving their time. That's where the "treatment facility" part of the prison's full name came from.

Dr. Harald pointed out one more classroom, then circled back around and headed towards the front of the space, making a beeline for the computer classroom. "Everyone," he announced, entering the room, "this is our new librarian, Miss Grunenwald."

The three women and one man who had been sitting at the table when I first came in all stood up, smiling, and each reached out to shake my hand.

"I'm Mr. Hooper," the man said, pumping my hand up and down. He was short in stature with tufts of white hair surrounding his pale face, giving him a particular resemblance to Einstein. His large smile extended up to his eyes. "I'm one of the GED teachers."

Next to him stood an older woman with big round glasses. "Roberta Carson." She spoke in a clipped tone at a staccato pace, short and to the point. She kept her silver hair equally neat. It was short and spiky, standing up and out from her ivory skin. Roberta's brown eyes, enlarged by her thick glasses, held the same level of seriousness as her tone. "I'm the other GED teacher."

Beside her was a tall woman, her long blonde hair pulled back into a ponytail. "Nancy." When she smiled, her cheeks popped like ripe peaches. "I teach the computer classes."

Finally there was Kimberly, Dr. Harald's assistant. I had met her briefly during my initial interview. Her brown hair was clipped short in a pixie cut, eyes rimmed dark with heavy liner. She was as pale as water, which made the juxtaposition of her dark hair and eyeliner all the more stark, like a ghost from a gothic horror novel. "We're just getting ready to eat lunch." She pointed to an empty seat at the table in the middle of the classroom.

Stacked high in the center of the table was a tower of Styrofoam boxes. My new coworkers resumed their seats at the table and passed the boxes out. Roberta, like me, had brought her own lunch. My own lunch bag was a reusable, insulated Vera Bradley, in one of the popular and ever-stylish blue and white patterns. It was a recent birthday gift from my mom, chosen in colors that represented the University of Kentucky, my equally new alma mater.

I pulled my peanut butter-and-jelly sandwich, chips, and side of baby carrots from my bag. Nancy opened the lid of one of the Styrofoam boxes: spaghetti and meatballs, a small pile of peas, two slices of plain white bread, and an apple.

"Employees can have one meal during their shift," Kimberly explained. "Just call over to dining and they'll make you a box. It's the same as the inmates get."

"Oh." I gestured to my own lunch. "I'm a vegetarian."

"They make vegetarian meals, too! There's a whole process the inmates have to go through to get approval, but they'll make it for staff no problem."

Lunch progressed and my coworkers fell into what felt like a usual pattern of chitchat, often asking me questions about me and my life ("Where do you live?" "Downtown." "Married?" "Long-distance boyfriend." "Kids?" "No, but I have a cat."). After me, Hooper was the newest employee of the Education staff, Roberta the oldest. Nancy and Kim both fell somewhere in between. All had worked as teachers previously in both traditional and nontraditional school settings before coming to the prison. Even Dr. Harald had spent a decade or so as a vice principal in a local school district before moving up to what was essentially a principal at this branch within the Ohio Central School System.

While showing me around, Dr. Harald explained that just as I was going through an onboarding process as part of my new job here, the inmates also had an onboarding process. Part of that intake process included getting classified, or assigned, to a job within the prison. For some inmates this meant school. High-school graduation, or equivalent, was verified and inmates who did not have the required diploma were automatically put on the GED or pre-GED wait list to attend the classes taught by Hooper and Roberta. Priority was given to those inmates under the age of twenty-two who did not have a high-school diploma or GED.

For those inmates that already had their high-school diploma, there was Nancy's computer class. There they learned basic computer skills, keyboarding, and Microsoft programs with the aim to better prepare them for when they were released back into the real world and would be fresh on the job market. Having the necessary computer skills would, in theory, help mitigate the guilty conviction on their background check.

Kimberly glanced up at the clock on the

classroom wall. "Jill, come with me," she said, standing up. "Gotta go pick up the newspapers."

I stood up but Kimberly hesitated. "Did you call your keys in?" *Huh?*

She nodded at my blank stare and walked out of the room towards the Education office. I followed.

The office contained two smaller sub-chambers. The inner one belonged to Dr. Harald. His desk, presumably, was hidden somewhere beneath the piles of papers that covered it. Another smaller desk, belonging to Kimberly, was tucked into a corner.

Outside of that office was a space reserved for all of the employees. There was a shared computer available, a printer, a tiny dorm-room-sized fridge, and our individual mailboxes. I glanced at that. My last name was misspelled. Of course.

Kimberly directed me to a beige phone sitting next to the shared computer. "Every day," she said, picking up the handset and handing it to me, "you have to call up front and give them your panic button number."

I nodded and took the phone. She pointed to a piece of paper taped to the back of the desk with a list of extensions. I dialed the number for Security Control Center.

"Yeah?" a male voice answered gruffly.

"Yeah, uh, this is Grunenwald." I stumbled over

my words but Kimberly nodded encouragingly. "I'm calling my number in."

"Go ahead."

I flipped the panic button over to take a closer look at the white label on the back. "Twenty-four," I said hesitantly.

"Thank you," a voice answered perfunctorily. The line went dead.

Replacing the handset on the phone, I looked at Kimberly.

"Every day," she repeated. "Best if you do it right away. That way, if something happens and you have to hit the button, they'll know it belongs to you."

Panic rose inside of me like mercury in a thermometer. I hadn't even met any of the inmates yet and already my anxiety was running down a laundry list of worst-case scenarios. Sure, I'd gone through that whole unarmed self-defense class but I knew that if something happened, there was no way in hell I'd have the wherewithal to actually *apply* any of the techniques and moves I learned. Hell, it had been seventy-two hours since the unarmed self-defense course and I'd basically already forgotten every single thing I had learned. My flight-or-fight response would be to hide under my desk and keep hitting that panic button until someone who really knew what they were doing came to the rescue. I silently prayed that it would never come to that.

Kimberly and I bundled back up and stepped out into the crisp February air. A moving sea of dark blue passed in front of us. We pressed ourselves against the double doors of the Education building as men of all sizes, shapes, and ethnicities flowed past us and into the dining hall next to the library. They all were wearing the same standard-issue, dark blue, hooded winter coat. A few gave me the once-over, as I was new, like an exotic pet that needed to be tested and studied. Or a foreign species that had just landed on their planet, like in a science-fiction novel. The inmates craned their necks for a better view of this new creature that walked among them.

Once the path cleared, Kimberly began walking. I fell in step beside her.

"Brrr," Kimberly said, pulling her coat close. "I miss being able to smoke in here."

"I thought the ban didn't go into effect for another day or two."

Kimberly shrugged. "Might as well start early. Can't even smoke in the parking lot out there; I'd have to get in my car and drive off the property. I'm not wasting my lunch break doing that." She shook her head. "So dumb."

As I quickly learned, the Hollywood trope of inmates gambling with or trading cigarettes in lieu of cash is steeped in fact. But effective March 1, 2009, all areas of Ohio prisons were to be tobacco-free environments. That included, as

Kimberly said, the parking lot. Even as recently as a few years prior, smoking was permitted in the dorms. Just a few weeks before, when Dr. Harald was giving me a tour, he pointed out the clusters of staff and inmates standing around smoking. "Getting it in while they can," he had remarked.

At the time the ban was first announced last fall, it was thought that 70 percent of Ohio's inmates and 25 percent of the staff all smoked. Now, all tobacco products had been added to the long list of contraband. It wasn't just inmates who could get into trouble for having cigarettes anywhere on prison property—staff and visitors could, too.

When we reached the control booth, Kimberly leaned up to the voice box. "Just picking up the newspapers." To our right, the exterior sally port door buzzed open for us. She explained that technically speaking, we were supposed to turn our badge, keys, and chits in when we came through, but the guards made an exception for the newspapers.

Once inside, she led me around the desk to a door on the other side of the lobby I hadn't even noticed before. "Hey everyone," she called out as she entered the room. "This is our new librarian."

In the middle of the room was a cluster of smaller tables that had been pushed together to form one big one. Three middle-aged women, all in the same dark black uniform the other correctional officers I had seen wear, sat around the table opening envelopes. Kimberly pointed to each one as she introduced them. "Brown, Williams, and Jordan."

Brown and Jordan were both African American and wore glasses, but that's where the similarities ended. Where Brown was small and petite, Jordan was tall and large. Brown kept her hair pulled tight into a bun at the back of her head, giving her a severe look that extended to the aloof vibe she gave off just sitting there.

On the other side of the spectrum, Jordan had neatly curled hair that was as light and airy as her personality. She took up space, both literally and figuratively, with a bright charisma that radiated out.

Williams was white and older. I pegged Brown and Jordan as being in their thirties but Williams was probably closer to her mid-forties. Her brassy, blonde hair was held back in a ponytail with a scrunchie.

Kimberly turned and nodded to the tall, lanky man standing off to the side who was sorting newspapers. Up until that moment I had never fully understood the physical descriptor of beanpole before. "That's Sullivan."

Smiling, Sullivan used his elbow to gesture to a stack of newspapers and magazines that sat alone on a chair. "Those are yours."

In the center of the room, Jordan pulled some photographs out of an envelope. It was then that I first noticed they were all wearing latex gloves. "Ooh," she said, shaking her head. "I wonder if her mama knows she's sending pictures of all her bits and pieces."

Kimberly's cackle ricocheted around the room. "All incoming mail gets read." She was peering over Jordan's shoulder for a closer look at the photos but addressing me. "Certain pictures will get confiscated. Inmate never sees 'em."

"They get a note," Williams piped up. She had her gaze trained on a letter. Her bright blue eyes flickered quickly back and forth across the page. "So they can tell their girlfriend to, uh, tone it down."

"Do the women know their letters and pictures are getting looked at?" I asked.

Williams shrugged. She folded the letter and slid it back into the envelope. "They do and they don't care," she answered, reaching for another envelope from the pile.

Kimberly grabbed half the stack of newspapers reserved for us. I picked up the other half. Arms full, we walked to the door. Sullivan's long legs got him there first and he held it open for us.

"See you tomorrow, Miss Librarian," Williams said warmly, her bright blue eyes shining. She pronounced it *lie-berry-an,* her voice affecting a slight twang.

The control booth saw us exiting the mail room and, when we got closer, buzzed the interior sally port door open for us. Kimberly leaned into it with her back to push it open.

"Newspapers get delivered daily," she said. We were back on the main path, following it back down towards Education. "Monday through Friday. You can pick them up after lunch."

Meals moved quickly here and already men were exiting the dining room from lunch. A small cluster congregated outside the library doors, trying to hide from the correctional officers patrolling the sidewalk. "Keep it moving," one male officer kept repeating. In between commands, his mouth chomped loudly on a piece of gum. He walked with a slight swagger, like a cowboy off the cover of a Louis L'Amour western. All that was missing was a Stetson hat and a highly polished belt buckle the size of a fist.

Kimberly shifted the newspapers onto her hip, holding them like a small child, and unclipped her keys from her belt. She opened the library doors and ushered me in, then allowed one inmate to follow. Another inmate with a shock of red hair tried to join the line but she blocked his entrance. "Not until 12:30, Monroe. You know that."

"But—"

"Nope. Move it along back to your house." She shut the door and locked it before he could respond.

Darkness greeted us. The library's only window shared a wall with the main door but between the exterior awning and the mass of dark blue moving in front of it, all outside light was blocked out. Arms still full of newspapers, Kimberly used her elbow to switch on the overhead lights.

The room stretched back maybe twenty yards, forming a long narrow rectangle. At the very front, right near the entrance, was the librarian's desk. My desk. It was made of heavy wood with a high top. When I sat, only my head would peek out above, just visible to the inmates entering. On the floor, near the gap between circulation desk and my desk was another red line, this time made with duct tape. Its message was clear: No inmates beyond this point. More specifically, no inmates behind my desk.

Parallel to my desk was the circulation desk. This was where my inmate workers, known as porters, were stationed. Part of my job was to serve as a manager with a team of a dozen inmates. Like any library, the circulation desk is where the patrons would come to check out their books, magazines, and newspapers. Because of the strict no-computer policy, the library was still operating on a card system, just as it had been when I was in grade school. Every book had a pocket in the back with a card that the inmates used to check out the books. These days, card catalogs and the matching checkout cards are a nostalgic novelty. A relic from a forgotten time before the internet. Nostalgic librarians and readers stalk library sales and spend thousands of dollars to purchase one for their homes. But in 2009, fresh out of graduate school, where all focus was on the future of the field, I saw the checkout cards as antiquated and old-fashioned. There wasn't even a big wooden card catalog to go with them; it really was just the cards and pocket in the back of the books.

Kim pointed out a door across from the circulation desk, telling me it was my bathroom. Inmates were not allowed to use it. She pulled out her keyring to show me which key would open it. "You can't leave the library unattended," she continued. "If you need to use it, call the officer next door."

Beyond the desks was the library proper. The left half of the room was comprised of tables and chairs, all facing the front like a classroom. The right half of the room contained the stacks, filled to the brim with eight-thousand books.

Eight-thousand books sounds like a lot. Eight-thousand *anything* sounds like a lot. The reality, though, is that eight-thousand books makes for a very, very small library indeed. For comparison, at the other end of the spectrum, the main branch of New York Public Library houses several *million* books. The eight-thousand-tome collection I was now in charge of maintaining was indeed tiny for the library world.

Still, it was *my* library, and small or not, I was kind of in love with it. There were a grand total of four shelves crammed full of books. The library really needed more shelves, with books stacked sideways and on top of each other just to make room, but budget and space limited any kind of expansion. Two of the shelves were outward facing only, drilled into opposite walls. On the far left side of the room, over by the tables, was the library's reference section comprised of dictionaries, encyclopedias, and other general reference materials that were only to be used in the library. *Everything* was outdated. The copies of *World Book* were from the late nineties. The last time I had seen them was in high school, back when they were the latest edition. Along the bottom of the spines, the alphabetical letters indicated the collection of encyclopedias were out of order. I'd have to fix that as soon as I could but, if nothing else, it seemed to suggest the inmates were at least using the encyclopedias, which is more than I can say for my classmates and myself back in high school.

The shelf on the far right wall was our fiction section, housing authors A through K. Next to that was a freestanding structure with shelves on both sides. The left side held nonfiction, while the right side had fiction authors L through Z.

At the very far back of the rectangular room was the area designated as the law library.

Ohio Revised Code. Ohio Administrative Code. Federal Rules of Civil Procedure. Federal Rules of Criminal Procedure. Decisions from the United States Supreme Court, Federal Courts of Appeals, Ohio Supreme Court, and others. Aside from housing all these important tomes, the law library was also the only place in the prison where inmates had access to a computer. Two desktop computers stood on the desk. One was perpetually broken but they both had an open source word processing program and a limited access version to LexisNexis, a program for legal research. Computer usage was strictly verboten by the inmates, except for Open Office for typing and LexisNexis for research. The latter was a locked down version that didn't allow the inmates to visit any other sites and was designed for those inmates who didn't want to bother with the heavy law books.

When I had initially interviewed for the position, Dr. Harald had brought me to the library on my tour. We sat at one of the tables in the middle of the room and he talked about the importance of the library within the context of the prison. The library served several purposes; its main function was to serve the informational needs of the service population, like every other library in the world. In this case, that "service population" was the seven hundred or so inmates incarcerated at the prison. Like every other librarian in the world, my job was to develop and maintain a collection that met the specific needs of my patrons. Every library is unique because every library's user base is unique and this library was no different. However, different communities meant different needs meant different collections. For example, at graduate school, there wasn't a single fiction book in the entire collection of the library where I worked. All of it was nonfiction and research-based. Here, in the prison, the fiction titles outnumbered nonfiction two-to-one.

The other purpose of the library was just to provide a space for the inmates to go. "If they aren't busy," Dr. Harald expanded, "they get into trouble. The library is just one place they can go so they aren't sitting in the dorms bored."

Along with the library, when it came to spaces to keep the men entertained and out of trouble, the prison also offered the recreation center and—weather permitting—the baseball field right outside the library. What set the library apart from every other available space at the prison was that I had no guard with me. Oh, there was always a correctional officer next door in Education so they were always a phone call—or push on the panic button—away, but along with that, it meant they were *at least* a phone call or a push on the panic button away. If shit happened, there was going to be a delay in response time—both mine and the officer coming over. And that's assuming I can even get to my phone or panic button in time to alert the officer.

Suddenly I was wishing I had paid more attention to the unarmed self-defense class.

But while the library itself had no correctional officer and while the Education correctional officer did rounds every hour or so, the majority of the time it would be just me and because I didn't have a correctional officer in here, that also meant that the inmates didn't have a correctional officer in here.

This made the library a unique pocket of freedom within the confines of a prison. It was just an illusion of freedom to be sure: the men knew they were in prison, and I knew they were in prison, and we all knew the reality of the situation even if there were no bars; but for a few hours a day, they could come to the library and temporarily forget where they really were. With multiple newspaper subscriptions, including national and Ohio state news, they could sit quietly and pretend they were catching up on their local paper from the comfort of their own home.

There was one other benefit to this space: for those who worked there, known as "porters," the library was also one of the better-paid positions within the prison and there was a long wait list that was constantly being added to. There were two types of porters: regular library porters, those who handled the newspapers and circulation desk, and law library porters. Both had educational requirements for the job, with the law library porters requiring a higher level of education, for which they were compensated slightly above the regular library porter. It wasn't much, but in a place that paid six dollars a month on average, any extra money was good money. The man who had followed us into the library was one of these porters.

"This is Spencer," Kimberly said, introducing me. He was a tall African American with a full dark beard. "Spencer, this is Miss Grunenwald, the new librarian."

Spencer gave a short nod of acknowledgment. He shrugged off his heavy, dark blue coat and hung it on the single chair behind the circulation desk, then immediately went to work on the newspapers and magazines. A third-party service delivered all of the prison's newspapers, both for the library and personal subscriptions inmates had. Since we did not receive them directly from the newspaper itself, the papers were always a few days out of date. The inmates never seemed to mind, however, as any news from the outside was appreciated, and there were televisions and radios in the dorm rooms if they wanted to get their news in real time.

Behind the circulation desk was an expansive metal bookshelf that came up to my waist. Back issues of the newspapers were kept there while the latest editions hung on a free-standing wire rack right next to it. Above the metal bookshelf, on the wall, was a wooden magazine holder. The newest editions of each magazine went in front, with the last couple back issues stuffed behind it.

Spencer worked quickly and quietly, first sorting the newspapers and magazines alphabetically, then placing them into their appropriate slots.

Kimberly continued: "Inmates are supposed to go back to their dorms immediately following lunch and then wait to be released for the afternoon, but your porters will try to be waiting at the door around noon to help get the newspapers ready before you open for the afternoon." She pointed to a clipboard in the right-hand corner of my desk with a list of names and hours. "This is the porter schedule. They are all usually pretty good about showing up on time."

The desk was elevated like a single step of a staircase and on top of it was another clipboard. The page was full of scribbled names and yesterday's date. She removed the signed pages, exposing a fresh blank one. "Sign in and sign out pages," she explained. "Every inmate, no matter what, needs to sign in and sign out every single time they come in and then when they leave. Even if they keep leaving and coming back. Which they will. Multiple times."

"What do I do with them at the end of the day?"

She handed me the signed sheets she had pulled and pointed to a small filing cabinet I hadn't even noticed. "Save them. You have to submit a monthly report to the state librarian each month. Dr. Harald told you about the dress code?"

I nodded and recited: "Shirts tucked in, no hats indoors, ID badge visible."

Behind my desk was a pile of books, covers tattered and torn. A six-foot-tall metal bookcase tucked into the corner was also weighed down with even more books. I stepped behind the desk and started to pull them from the shelves to see the books tucked underneath and behind the ones on top. The titles were familiar, if a few years old. John Grisham's bestseller from a few years prior. The entire *Little House* series. Older selections from James Patterson, Janet Evanovich's respective number series, and Sue Grafton's letter series. The copies were worn and well-read.

"Those are donations," Kimberly said, catching my gaze. "Books that need to be input into the system. The former librarian didn't have a chance to finish."

"Gotcha," I said, attempting to sound casual. Inside, my stomach was doing flip-flops. It was like looking at the personal library of a hoarder, not the expected nice, neat organized personal library of a librarian. I had to catalog *all* of these books? I had taken a cataloging class over the previous summer, but could barely remember most of the finer details and nuances. Plus, where the hell was I going to fit all of them? The shelves were full beyond capacity as it was.

Kimberly bounced a little in place, anxious to leave. Training incoming employees apparently fell under "other duties as assigned" on her job description. "Any questions?"

I shook my head.

"If anything comes up, I'll be next door, but you should be fine." She beamed. "Good luck!"

She left before I had a chance to respond.

Suddenly, I was alone in the library with Spencer. The room was quiet except for the rustle of newspapers as he moved them around. "Don't be nervous," he said from his corner.

"What?"

Spencer turned to look at me. In his eyes, I read a mixture of kindness and, I think, pity. Pity for the new librarian who was *clearly* feeling way out of her depth. "Don't be nervous," he repeated. "Everyone loves the library, you'll see. Nobody wants to do anything stupid to fuck up their ability come here." Spencer glanced up at the clock that hung above the solitary window by my desk. "Time to open."

I went over to the door to unlock it, and saw a crowd of dark blue coats waiting to get in. Forcing a smile to hide my building anxiety, I settled myself behind my desk and waited for my first patron to enter the library.

The door creaked open. I looked up and was greeted by a dog.

Chapter 3
In the Doghouse

Institution library staff shall be responsible for ensuring that all non-security DRC policies are maintained and available to the inmate population in the institution library and/or law library.
—ODRC Policy 58-LIB-01

Not just any dog, but a St. Bernard.

And not just any St. Bernard, but a full-grown, 250-pound, slobbering, drooling mess of a St. Bernard. Only thing Cujo here was missing was a barrel collar.

The St. Bernard sat obediently at the side of an inmate. His slobbery mouth turned up into a grin as he stood there, slavering and drooling all over the tile floor of the library.

My library.

Now, dogs have never been my favorite animal. The clichéd stereotype of a crazy cat lady librarian? That's me. I had a cat at home, Chloe, who I adopted while in graduate school and I had plans to adopt more. I don't really *do* dogs. Cats, see, are self-sufficient. And independent and sassy; but, most importantly, they are small and manageable. Smaller dogs I can tolerate—like lap dogs, which are basically just needy cats. But this shaggy beast with paws the size of my cat? Nope. Nope. Nope. Nope. Nope.

The inmate attached to him—because, make no mistake, the dog was leading the man and not the other way around—was a slightly older gentleman in his late forties or early fifties. His olive skin, paired with a full head of dark hair and matching beard, marked him as Middle Eastern, making him, so far, the only non-Caucasian and non-black inmate I had seen in my, admittedly, short time at work. He gripped a leash and while the dog appeared to be under control, the dog also outweighed his human companion by at least a hundred pounds. But even if it were a different, smaller breed, that doesn't change the fact that there was still a *dog* in my library.

Outside, in public libraries, service animals are allowed. Was that what this was? Was that even a thing? Are there service animals in prison?

Silent, with no acknowledgment of the gigantic dog bumping him at the waist, the man signed his name to the sign-in sheet and, with his free hand, removed his identification badge and handed it to Spencer. Their exchange was so muted I couldn't hear it, but Spencer took the badge and clipped it to the side of the magazine rack. He handed the latest edition of the *Cincinnati Enquirer* to the inmate. Dog and master moved into the crowd in search of a table.

I picked up the phone that sat at my desk and dialed Kimberly's extension. "McIntyre," she said, introducing herself by her last name.

"Hey," I said. I kept my voice low. "Um, there's a dog in here."

"What?"

"There's a *dog* in the library," I repeated, emphasizing the middle word.

"Oh! Yeah, that's part of the puppy program. They have to take their dogs everywhere with them, even the library."

"Oh. Okay." I hung up the phone. I added "puppy program" to my growing list of things to ask Kimberly about further during the evening break.

When I looked up there was an inmate leaning over the desk. He peered at me inquisitively. I suddenly sympathized with animals at the zoo.

"You the new librarian?"

I nodded. "I am. I'm Miss Grunenwald. But you can just call me Ms. G."

"Yo!" He turned around and shouted to someone at the back of the line. "We got a new librarian!"

The queue at the door grew exponentially. Inmates jockeyed for their place in line, while others crammed themselves into the tiny foyer. Because the dining hall didn't have enough capacity for all seven-hundred inmates at once, meals worked in shifts, one dorm at a time

71

going down to eat. After, inmates were supposed to return to their dorms and wait until the yard opened for the afternoon. But the inmates knew if they ate slowly, walked slowly, and loitered just long enough, they could sneak into the library just as it was opening. It was important to get there early, as like every other library I've worked in, the materials—including the newspapers—were first come, first served.

The line cracked as an inmate forced his way to the front. His gaze gave me the once-over as he crossed the threshold and took his spot beside Spencer. I ran my finger down the porter schedule until I found Tuesday afternoon: Spencer and Childers.

Childers was Caucasian and gangly with unwashed, disheveled hair. Like Spencer, he was tall, although Spencer still towered over him. I clocked both of them to be around my age, somewhere between late twenties and early thirties.

The pair of library porters fell into the same rhythm: ID badge to porter, paper to patron. Badge to porter, paper to patron.

Another crack opened in the long line of incoming inmates and an older African American man came to the desk. His arms were full of manila folders, papers shoved into them every which way. He quickly pulled his hat, dark blue like his coat, from his head, revealing black hair sprinkled with white and gray.

"I'm Washington," he said hurriedly. "I'm one of the law porters. I'm sorry I'm late, lunch and Cooper out there and—"

Out of the corner of my eye, I saw the cowboy correctional officer walk past my window. I waved my hand. "It's okay."

Washington nodded. "I'll be in the back. If you need anything, let me know."

Already a crowd had formed back in the law library, waiting expectantly for Washington. He ignored them, carefully removing his jacket and hanging it on the back of a chair. His own stack of papers went onto a shelf beside the legal texts. Only after he had settled and situated himself did he turn to attend on the waiting inmates.

The circulation desk pulsed with activity. Enough time had gone by that the men who had gotten in at opening were finished with their first newspaper. Now, the process worked in reverse: Paper to porter, badge to patron. Paper to porter, badge to patron. When an inmate wanted to read another newspaper, the badge simply got moved to the appropriate spot.

I was impressed. This library was a well-oiled machine. Internally, I breathed a sigh of relief. Despite the location, it really wasn't that different than every other library I'd worked in over the years.

Lunch was over and the yard was open for afternoon recreation hours. Outside my window, I saw inmates and correctional officers moving up and down along the walkway. While the inmates moved in a lackadaisical motion, the correctional officers walked with purpose. They knew they had a job to do.

After a flurry of ten minutes of heightened activity, the crowd at the door and my desk thinned. With a deep breath, I settled back in my seat.

The library had opened in such a frenzy, I hadn't had a chance to examine my desk with any real focus. I essentially had two desks: the big, main one at the front of the room, and behind that, a small computer desk that held the desktop computer. Ready to get to work, I powered it up.

Tackling the donation pile, or piles as it were, seemed as good a place as any to start. At least to get a sense of what I was looking at. The donation pile was haphazard at best and a hot mess at worst. Books of every shape, size, and condition were piled on top of each other and shoved into every available nook and cranny of the metal bookcase. There was no organization, no sense of purpose. It was as if the boxes of books just showed up one day and the librarian, overwhelmed and short on both time and space, just did whatever it took to get the books out of the boxes and onto the shelf and out of the way.

Come to think of it, that's probably *exactly* what happened.

Once my computer booted up, I logged in with the username and password that Hall had set me up with earlier. I had been told that the previous librarian's files had all been transferred over, so I began poking around in different folders and documents. Eventually I came across an Excel spreadsheet marked "Catalog."

I clicked to open it. As I scrolled down the spreadsheet, my eyes widened in horror.

Before I continue, I feel it necessary to take a moment to show you the "man behind the curtain." Libraries cannot function without an accurate and up-to-date catalog. The catalog is basically what keeps track of the books owned by the library. How can a library know if a book has gone missing or has been checked out, or if they even own it, if they don't keep an updated list? Updating it means adding new books to the catalog and deleting books from the catalog if they are weeded, that is, removed from the collection.

Card catalogs were still around when I was a kid and I loved thumbing through the cards to discover a new book or author. When I was a page in high school, the library had transitioned to an online public access catalog (OPAC), which was a digital database of their books, but they still maintained a card catalog in the basement. When I assisted with weeding, I was tasked with finding the cards and removing them from the card catalog.

When a patron logs into their library's website and searches for a book, they are searching the catalog. They'll find out if the library owns the title, how many copies there are, the available formats (audiobook, physical book, ebook), and, perhaps most importantly, where to find it in the library. Each book is giving an accession number, which is a unique identifier tied to each individual book. That way, if a library owns five copies of a title, they know which four exact copies are sitting on the shelf and which copy Jane has checked out. That's what those barcodes represent on books.

Most library catalogs are databases. I was looking at a list. Literally.

Before me was a spreadsheet of all roughly eight thousand books that made up the prison library's collection. I had the title, the author, the subject, and . . . that was it. There were no unique identifying numbers, which meant I had no way of knowing if duplicates were intentional or accidental.

I couldn't remember much from my cataloging class, but I remembered enough to know that this was cataloging chaos.

This act of adding new books was going to be a much bigger project than I had originally anticipated, mostly because it was going to require dealing with the books currently in the library first. There was no way I was prepared enough to tackle this yet, it would have to be put on the back burner for now.

Catty-corner to my computer desk was a high freestanding drawer. Inside I found routine office supplies: three-hole punch, whiteout, and a pair of safety scissors, just like the kind I used in kindergarten when the teachers were worried our clumsy five-year-old fingers would slip and we'd hurt ourselves. *Ah.* They weren't afraid of the inmates hurting themselves, they were worried about the inmates hurting someone else. Specifically another inmate or, even worse, a staff member. Scissors—real scissors, with points and blades—could be used as a weapon. A deadly weapon, if a person was so inclined.

Beneath the drawer was a wire cart. I rolled it out and found hanging files, each marked with a series of letters and numbers. I pulled one out at random. Ohio Department of Rehabilitation and Correction logo was in the upper left corner. On the right-hand side of the page was a box.

Subject: Institutional Religious
        Services
Number: 72-REG-01
Page: 1 of 7

I continued reading. *It is the policy of the Ohio Department of Rehabilitation and Correction (DRC) to ensure that inmates, who wish to do so, may subscribe to any religious belief they choose. Inmate religious practices, as opposed to belief, may be subject to reasonable time, place and manner restrictions. Inmate participation in religious activities . . .*

My eyes lit up. This was a file cabinet's worth of prison policy. Here was *everything* I could possibly want to know, along with plenty of things I didn't want to know, and other things I didn't even *know* I wanted to know about how the prison was run. So much reading and research to be found in the dozens and dozens of hanging files.

Christmas had come early.

I'm naturally curious and as a librarian, my favorite tasks are those that make me feel like I'm Sherlock Holmes on my latest case. The game's afoot! I love playing the detective, digging in deep, searching for clues, reading up on a subject, garnering information. In grad school, I once tracked down a single missing page from a patent. This may not sound like a big deal, but the patent was from the 1970s and the scientist associated with the research facility where I worked was desperate. But every patent database brought back the incomplete patent and the intellectual property law firm that had filed it was no longer in business. Even the United States Patent Office didn't have the full patent, at least not unless I wanted to drive to Virginia to search their archives and hope it was there.

After weeks of searching I finally found a law firm in England that had previously been associated with the original firm. The association was tenuous at best; it was basically the fourth cousin once removed of law firms, but it was enough of an association that they had all the old files.

The day that single page showed up in my email as a PDF, I understood how triumphant Hercule Poirot felt at the end of every Agatha Christie novel.

Here before me was a treasure trove of information to be read and understood. To some this might seem boring; they were just administrative rules after all. But for me, it was the information and understanding that could be gleaned from such rules that excited and fascinated me. It was like cracking open a clock and seeing the intricate dials, the way the pieces clicked and locked into place. I replaced the file on religious services and went to grab another at random when I noticed a flash of black hovering to my left.

A female corrections officer leaned against the desk, her right arm propped on top. She smiled at me. "CO Scott," she said. I rolled my office chair across the small gap of linoleum and shook her hand. She nodded out towards the crowded library. "How's your first day going?"

I shrugged. "Okay so far."

She turned her head of strawberry blonde hair back out over the crowd. "I'm the Education officer today. If you need anything just call next door."

On top of the counter, in the corner nearest the window, was a thick, spiral-bound horizontal notebook. Scott removed a pen from her breast pocket and clicked it open. Consulting the digital watch on her wrist, she wrote her name, the time, and date on the next open line in the notebook. As she leaned down, I noticed the constellation of dark freckles that stood out across her nose.

"Actually," I said slowly, thoughtfully. My brain ran down the state of my body, weighing going now or waiting later and having to call. "Would you mind waiting just a second while I popped into the restroom?"

Scott nodded her affirmation and I stood up, pulling the keys from my pocket and finding the one that Kimberly had told me belonged to the bathroom. I walked across the small foyer between my desk and the bathroom and unlocked it. It was closet-sized, which seemed fitting as it clearly doubled as a closet: there were hooks on the wall, presumably for staff personal items. Beneath the hooks was a small two-shelf standing bookcase that held all manner of surplus office supplies like whiteout, sleeves of staples, and typewriter ribbon (*typewriter* ribbon?! Between the circulation cards for checkout and the typewriter ribbon, I was starting to think I'd entered some time travel portal). Alongside the office supplies were various cleaning supply spray bottles holding liquids of different colors.

Emerging from the restroom, I thanked Scott and resumed my post behind my counter and the afternoon progressed. The cogs in the library wheel moved steadily along. Inmates checked out newspapers and magazines and books. Scott came by on her hourly rounds. After 2 p.m., Scott was replaced by the evening officer, Womack. Other officers popped in to say hello and introduce themselves and see how I was doing.

As I sat at my desk and watched the inmates drift in and out, I realized Kimberly had been right: I saw the same inmates come in, stay for a while, leave, only to return again a short while later.

One in particular was Andrews, a lanky, young twentysomething who moved with the ease of a gazelle. He looked like one, too: his light skin carrying a slight tawny overtone. Andrews introduced himself during a pocket of calm. He repaired the books, he explained, clearly on a volunteer basis. His job assignment was Education, he was in the GED classes, and that took priority over any other job assignment, so he didn't have the option of working in the library. Miss Carol, however, the librarian before me, let him volunteer in the library by repairing the books. I'd already seen the state of some of the titles, so if he wanted to tape them back together, I was more than happy to allow him to continue.

As the hands on the clock made their 360-degree laps, the library started to thin out. After the rush of reading the afternoon newspapers, inmates floated in and out, popping in as they bounced between classes in the Education department or games in the recreation center.

At 3:30 p.m., I began ushering inmates out of the library, both so I could wrap up and they could all be back to their dorms in time for the 4 p.m. count. The porters were the last to leave, tidying up the law library and newspapers for the evening shift after dinner.

Washington stopped by the desk on his way out. "You did okay today," he said, nodding. He pulled the worn blue state-issued hat over his head. "You did okay today."

Behind him was Koch. Both of the law porters were on the older side, over sixty at least. Koch had tufts of wild gray hair that grew in all directions around his coke-bottle glasses. In a parallel life, he and Mr. Hooper, the GED teacher, could have been brothers.

When everything was done, I locked up and headed next door to Education.

"How was it?" Kimberly asked. She was filing papers in Dr. Harald's office.

"Okay," I replied. I turned my head to read the

labels on the files. TAB. ABLE. I recognized the combination of letters as tests that determined which of the Education classes an inmate would be put into. "Tell me about the dogs."

"Oh!" She temporarily stopped her filing and turned to look at me. "We get dogs from the Lorain County Humane Society. Inmates in the Puppy Program are assigned a dog to train, the dog stays with them and then goes back to the humane society who can adopt them out, saying the dog already knows basic commands."

"Ah." Dogs in prison. *Welp*. That explained that.

"The dogs are supposed to be trained. That's, like, the whole point, so if they get out of control you can ask them to leave." Kimberly turned back to her filing.

I wandered down the hall. Near the copy machine stood a woman. A brunette, she was about my height and, I guessed, close to my age. She turned at the sound of my footsteps and a smile bloomed against her pink skin. "Are you Jill? I'm Stephanie, one of the recovery counselors." Stephanie cocked her thumb in a gesture pointing towards the office in the back.

A gigantic man poked his dark, bald head out of the office. "Steph, you done with your notes?"

Stephanie pointed to the stack of papers sitting on top of the copier. "Almost."

He started to retreat, then stopped when our eyes met. "Kwame," he said, his mouth extending into a smile. Kwame pointed a finger at me. "You're the new librarian." Statement, not a question.

Before I could ask Kwame what he did, classroom doors opened on the either side of us, and inmates flooded out, followed by their instructors. For Roberta, Nancy, and Mr. Hooper, school—and thus, work—was done for the day. But the library was open late on Tuesdays and Wednesdays, meaning I had to stay for a few more hours to run the late shift.

On the correctional officer's desk near the Education restroom was a log similar to the one I had next door. Everyone signed themselves out as they bundled up in their winter coats, ready to face the cold walk up to the entryway.

CO Womack found me in the group. "I have to go help with count," he said, "but I'll be here this evening if you need me."

"One last thing," Kimberly said, wrapping her scarf around her neck. "The yard closes early during Daylight Savings Time. As soon as it starts to get dark, inmate movement stops. That means they can't leave the library until closing. Watch for the lights out there." She gestured to the lamp posts, like stadium lights, that dotted the perimeter. "When the library closes for the night, you have to call it in up front so they know inmates are leaving. Count the number of inmates so they know."

I made a mental checklist. Count inmates. Watch for lights. Call up front.

"See you tomorrow!" she said, brightly. A chorus accompanied her as the Education team and the recovery services team left the building and headed up front, their laughter lingering in the empty space.

I went back to the library after my colleagues left, sat down at my computer, and logged in. After checking for any new facility-related emails, I turned my attention to the small wire cabinet of hanging files to my right. Might as well get some reading done while I waited for the evening shift to start.

There was about an hour of downtime. I used the time to educate myself on the recreation center and Segregation. Then at 5:00, I unlocked the library door.

"Hey Ms. G.!" a few inmates called out with a wave as they came into the library after dinner. Word had gotten around. I nodded my hello, committing faces of repeat visitors to memory.

The evening shift was far more subdued, as many inmates opted to stay outside to take advantage of the limited sunlight while they could. Newspapers were read, but not with the same flurry of demand as before.

Moments after I unlocked the door, my evening porter, Jefferson, arrived. I was starting to think my predecessor had only requested tall inmates be assigned to the library because Jefferson was the tallest of them yet. He was dark as midnight and carried himself proudly, walking with deliberation as he took his seat behind the circulation desk and began checking newspapers out to waiting inmates.

Time ticked on. Outside my window, the sunlight began to fade to black as night encroached. As Kimberly said, out in the distance near the fence, the sky-high lampposts clicked on, blanketing the yard in artificial light.

During a lull, my evening porter rolled his chair over, closing in on my desk. "I'm Jefferson," he said with a smile. His hazel eyes were dazzling like gemstones.

"Hi Jefferson," I answered. "I'm Ms. G."

Jefferson's smile widened showing a row of pristine white teeth that gleamed against his dark skin. "I'll be here every Tuesday or Wednesday evening. If you need help with anything, just ask." He rolled his chair back to its spot and began organizing the checkout cards from earlier in the day.

My porter settled, I relaxed. Out of the corner of my eye I saw an inmate leaning over the counter. He was small, his oversized blue jacket drowning him.

Meeting my gaze, the inmate smiled at me and jerked his head up in greeting. It was like catching a cat mid-hunt. He started to look for an empty chair among the crowded tables.

"Wait! Make sure you sign in!"

He raised a single eyebrow in surprise then turned and came back to my desk. He didn't walk but sauntered, making a big show of it. The coat was so oversized he had to push the sleeves up, his hand hidden among the blue folds. He grabbed the pen with a flourish and signed his name. As he did, I snuck a peek at the ID Badge clipped to the outside of his coat. Jackson.

Name signed, he again used overly exaggerated gestures to put the pen back on the clipboard before turning to find an open spot.

About twenty minutes later, Jackson came back up to the front of the library and started to move towards the front door.

"Where are you going?"

"Restroom."

I shook my head. "Yard's closed."

"But I gotta go." He raised his voice slightly, catching the ear of every other inmate in the room.

I hesitated. Yard closed meant yard closed, which meant no inmate movement. Those were the rules and this was an institution that ran on rules. No rules, or disobeyed rules, meant chaos. It meant confusion and safety was at risk. I wasn't going to screw this up my first day.

The familiar flush of embarrassment started to creep up my neck, knowing I had twenty inmates watching me, waiting to see what my next move would be.

Power in prison is in constant flux. Oh, sure, at the end of the day, ultimately the staff and officers have all of the power. Our word is law here.

But inmates also have power, just of a different kind. There was a reason the library only offered inmates dull-edged safety scissors that required temporarily turning in their identification badge to use. The inmates had the power to inspire fear within the staff. And the thing of it was, we weren't even working with violent men. We were working with men who drank too many beers and kept getting behind the wheel of the car. We were working with men who could make a much better living selling drugs on the street corners of Cleveland than they ever could flipping burgers at McDonalds, so they kept doing it. The only violent men on my watch were in on domestic violence charges, so while they had exhibited violent behavior in the past, it had been directed at a specific person; they did not have an overarching violent tendency that I needed to watch out for.

And yet, all of them had to be kept from using real scissors and I needed to be on constant watch to maintain my own personal safety. "Constant vigilance!" as Mad-Eye Moody repeated through-out *Harry Potter and the Goblet of Fire*. (Or, well, I guess technically it was fake Moody, but whatever. Details.) At any time, someone could snap out of the carefully constructed drug-and-alcohol rehabilitation narrative the prison had devised and take us all down.

Because of this, some of the correctional officers wielded their own power with a heavy hand. They wanted everyone to know that they were in charge and acted accordingly, as if the black uniform didn't already give it away.

As a civilian staff member, I found myself at a crossroads. I was part of the staff, the people with the true power. But as a *librarian,* that wasn't my job. That wasn't even in my nature. I wasn't here to demand respect or flaunt what limited power I had just because I could. I was here to run a library. I was here to make sure the educational and recreational needs of the inmates were met. I was here to help.

There were two kinds of staff members here: those drunk on power, seeing the inmates in their care as beneath them, and those who were here to help, who saw the inmates as men just trying to do their time and get out. I knew which one I wanted to be, but which one was I going to be?

I picked up my desk phone.

"Womack," he answered from next door.

My eyes never left Jackson's face. "I have an inmate who needs to use the restroom. Can I send him over?"

There was a pause. In the background, I could hear the hustle and bustle of inmates joking and laughing as they attended that evening's Alcoholics and Narcotics Anonymous meetings.

"Yup," Womack finally answered.

I hung the phone up. "Next door and then back. That's it."

The corner of Jackson's mouth turned up in a slight smile as he exited the library. It's possible I had made the wrong choice, but only time would tell.

At 7:14 p.m., just a minute before closing, I counted the number of inmates remaining in the library. They made it easy for me, lining up in front of the circulation desk, ready to go.

"It's Grunenwald," I said into the phone. "I have twenty-six inmates leaving the library."

"Where are they going?" the guard up front in the control center asked.

"What?"

"I need to know where they are going."

Damn. That had not been part of Kimberly's instructions. Just count them she said. Just count them and call up front to let them know. And now, the inmates were pouring out of the library and into the closed yard, scattering like rings in a puddle.

The officer on the other end of the phone, perhaps realizing I was the new librarian and had no idea what I was doing, spoke again.

"Tomorrow, find out which dorms they are going to after leaving the library. 5 to A, 10 to B, that sort of thing." Grateful, I hung up the phone.

With a heavy sigh, I collapsed into the chair behind my desk. My day was officially over at 7:30 p.m., so I had fifteen minutes to sit and catch my breath and collect my thoughts and—

The door of the library opened. "We're closed!" I called out, wearily.

Two inmates walked in. "Yo," the shorter one said. "I'm Santiago. We're here to clean. Can we get into the closet?"

Right. The cleaning supplies. I stood up and went to the restroom, using the correct key to unlock the door. Santiago grabbed a spray bottle and rag, while his companion used the restroom sink to fill up the bucket.

I watched the two men work. Their work was haphazard and casual. This was not a professional cleaning crew, but I was so startled by their appearance I didn't know how to respond and, besides, I was so anxious to leave, to have my first day officially over, that I was happy to let them do whatever they needed to do to clean the library and be done.

"Thanks," Santiago said, as I locked the closet back up.

They left, and I quickly gathered my belongings, ready to get home. I locked the library door and headed up the path to the control center. A few yards beyond the library, the bright lights from inside the recreation center lit my path, and I was able to see a large, open space that had a variety of activities available. I spotted inmates crowded around a pool table, while others sat around a board game.

The yard was empty, except for a few second-shift correctional officers on rounds. They nodded in greeting and I hurried up the path.

At the control center, it was the reverse of the morning's routine. I gave the correctional officers behind the tinted windows my keys, chits, and ID badge at the exterior window. The outer sally port door buzzed open, then the inner sally port door. Once again, my bags were searched and I went under the metal detector. This morning, the concern had been me bringing things into the prison. Now the concern was me taking things *out*.

I walked around to the interior control room window, where my ID badge was waiting for me in the drawer.

I slipped it into my purse and walked to the main lobby doors, exiting into the fresh night air.

I had done it. I had survived both my first official day as a librarian and my first day as a librarian in a *prison*.

As I walked towards my car, searching for it among the others, the exact parking spot I'd picked long forgotten in the haze of the day,

I knew that this job was going to be far more challenging than I had anticipated. I always knew, or at least thought I knew, that this wasn't going to be like any of the previous library jobs that I had had, but I was so not prepared for what I *didn't* know about this job.

Chapter 4
The Hole

The institution library staff shall visit all special population areas of the institution at least once per week to determine inmate needs regarding legal and reading materials.
—ODRC Policy 58-LIB-01

BEEP BEEP BEEP!

The relentless sounds of my alarm clock jolted me awake. I opened one eye and stared at the blurry red digits through the pitch black of my bedroom. Outside my window, the Cleveland skyline stood silent and dark; even the city that I love was unwelcoming this early in the morning.

5:40 a.m.

I groaned internally. At least it was Friday, right?

Except for me, it wasn't the end of my workweek. Per state policy, the library was open six days a week, which obviously had to include weekends. Each prison was allowed to define their schedule, and for my library, Monday through Saturday hours were the norm. State policy also required the library be open two nights per week as well, all of which explains why my first day started on a Tuesday and I had to stay there late.

My colleagues in the Education department all had a standard Monday to Friday, 7:30 a.m. to 4:00 p.m. schedule. As the librarian, I was not so fortunate. My hours were much more erratic.

Tuesdays and Wednesdays, I arrived shortly before lunch and stayed until 7:30 p.m., which, you know, was fine. I got to sleep in on those days and maybe run some errands before driving out to Grafton. Then, on Thursdays, Fridays, and Saturdays, I worked 7:30 a.m. until 4:00 p.m. That was okay, as I got home at a reasonable hour despite the long commute. Sundays and Mondays comprised my weekend, which meant I got one traditional weekend day off and one weekday off, which was helpful for general errands.

The issue was that, of course, when my friends would want to go out to the bars Friday night, I'd have to beg off, or go home after only one drink. Cinderella here had an early alarm clock calling her name. Saturday nights were a bit more reasonable because I could sleep in the next morning, but after several days in a row of 5:40 a.m. wake up calls, I was exhausted and would still skip going out, or go home after only a drink or two.

Then again, I'm a somewhat antisocial introvert, so it honestly wasn't that bad of an arrangement to me.

My boyfriend at the time lived on the other side of the state so the only times I even attempted to pretend to have a social life was when he was in town. Otherwise, I was quite content with my 10 p.m. bedtime no matter what day of the week it was.

In my absence on Mondays, Kimberly worked in the library. It was a task, I was discovering based on the complaints from inmates, she only did because she had no way of getting out of it. She'd huff and puff her way through the day, putting off as much work as she could by telling the inmates to come back in on Tuesday when I returned.

I was starting to get into my groove of the new job, but after my first Thursday at work, I knew Thursday mornings were going to be the bane of my existence. With an hour commute each way, I got home at 8:30 p.m. Wednesday night only to have to turn around and leave the house by 6:30 a.m. Thursday morning. Again, as an introvert, there was almost no time to decompress from all the interactions I had done the night before and then I had to turn around and be back at it again.

This morning was still early, but it at least wasn't on the heels of a late night. So while today *was* Friday, that glorious end of most people's workweek, it wasn't *my* Friday, since I still had a 5:40 a.m. wakeup call tomorrow, too. And I only had the ridiculously early wakeup call because my apartment was so far away from work. I lived in a downtown Cleveland area known as The Flats. My loft-style apartment was in a converted warehouse that had previously been a sewing machine factory. Faded white letters were still visible in the brick, remnants of a past life. I loved it.

The only downside of my location was that it added a significant amount of time to my commute. I'd never before been envious of people who lived on the west side of the city, but now I imagined how nice it must be to wake up at a relatively normal time and have a nice, short commute to work. If nothing else, at least I was driving against the usual morning rush-hour traffic.

Aside from cutting into my sleep, commuting also made me sympathetic to the visitors who traveled to our facility several times a month to visit incarcerated friends and family. During the sentencing period, there are several factors that determine which prison an inmate is assigned to as their permanent institution. Incredibly, location of home and family is not one of those things taken into consideration, and inmates can end up very far from their support system back home, as well as any news from home.

That's why the prison had subscriptions to newspapers from all over the state of Ohio; to specifically meet the reading and informational needs of the inmates. Especially the informational needs of the inmates who didn't live in Northeast Ohio. Clevelanders had the benefit of also having access to local radio and television stations that would keep them up to date on the news from the area, but for those who lived elsewhere in the state, there were limited resources available, which is where the library newspapers come in. Everything came via Pony Express. Not really, but it sometimes felt that way. Outside the razor-wire fence, information was available instantaneously via broadband internet and Wi-Fi. Inside, however, there was no internet access. Everything had to come via the good ol' United States Postal Service. Neither rain, nor sleet, nor snow, nor prison bars either, it seems.

Family and friends were the inmates' other option for staying up-to-date. If the bustling mail room on my first day wasn't enough proof of the amount of letters that came in every day for the inmates, I also had inmates show me their mail. Letters from home sharing news clippings from their city, updates on family, new photos of the children they hadn't seen in months. Even books came in the mail, supplementing the limited offerings in the library. For example, I didn't have the budget to stock *The Help*, the latest *New York Times* bestseller that everyone wanted to read. I didn't have the budget to stock anything, really. The prison ran a tight, lean ship, and new books, especially new hardcover books that everyone wanted to read, were not an acceptable line item. And I do I mean *everyone* wanted to read it. Staff, guards, inmates—everyone. Several times a week I had inmates coming in asking if we had copies available. The library, however, didn't have it, but copies could be found floating around thanks to prisoners who had copies sent in.

Some inmates were also lucky enough to get their news in person with visits from family. Visitation happened twice a week, although the inmates were limited to a certain number of visits per month. All of these restrictions put a strain on relationships.

So even though it was less than a week in and I was already struggling with my commute, that was always put into perspective when I considered the struggle that family and friends of prisoners underwent. If nothing else, I could see my family whenever I wanted and sleep in my own bed every single night.

It was the end of winter and thus far Cleveland's weather had been rather mild, but I knew I might not always be so fortunate. The prison was quite literally in the middle of nowhere. There was nothing surrounding it for miles. I couldn't imagine what getting to work would be like when snow really started to take hold.

At least grateful for the mild weather, I shut my alarm off, dragged myself out of bed, and began my morning routine, which started with feeding my cat Chloe (who was loving the early alarm because it meant she got fed earlier in the day). That was followed by a shower, getting dressed, breakfast, and coffee. Lots of coffee. Before 6 a.m. levels of coffee. With sugar. Lots of sugar. Anything to keep me awake and alert, since today had the added bonus of being Inmate Orientation.

The prison had new inmates every single day. After arriving, the men were assigned their bunks and received their issued uniform, but they weren't officially considered integrated into the system until Orientation, which happened every Friday. It was a lot like onboarding or orientation at any new job. There they would learn about how meals worked, how laundry operated, that sort of thing. Included in the lineup of information was library services.

All week, I knew the days were leading up to Orientation. To me standing in front of a room of new inmates and explaining all about the library. I was dreading it.

Despite my years of theater in high school, I don't like standing in front of an audience. Theater, literally, required me putting on a mask of sorts and pretending to be someone else, but that's why I had so much fun doing it: I could pretend to be someone else, so I wasn't the person speaking in front of the crowd.

Now, though, I was the librarian and the only one at that. There was nobody else to get on stage for me; I had to do it all. It was certainly a big change from where I was ten years ago when I first started working at a library. My time as a page was mostly spent in the stacks shelving books. But every once in a while I would be tasked with covering the circulation desk while someone was at lunch. I hated it. Absolutely hated it. I hated being put on the spot, on having to deal with confrontation or unhappy patrons. The unpleasantness of it gave me panic attacks. As soon as the regular circ desk employee would return from lunch, I would immediately scurry back to the comfort and safety of shelving books.

What I didn't know and only found out later from my then-coworker is that our manager, Sue, knew I had this very visceral reaction to working the circulation desk and so she told the circ staff to not call me for assistance. It didn't matter if the desk was understaffed or lunches started late: Sue became a Mama Bear and decided that I was no longer required to work the circ desk. I was content and happy shelving books and that's where I belonged. Until my first job, I didn't know how grateful I should have been to Sue.

Now, with a podium and a room full of strangers looming large ahead of me, all those old anxieties were starting to bubble back up to the surface, ready to overflow.

• • •

"Kimberly will be by around 9:30," Dr. Harald told me as he went over the schedule for the morning. In the future I would facilitate the library portion of Orientation myself, but for the first one, he wanted me to sit in, listen, and observe. "It will only be about ten or fifteen minutes. And then after you close for the morning, we'll go to Segregation."

Right. Seg. In all my anticipation about Orientation, I had completely forgotten about the ominous-sounding Segregation.

"Okay," I said, nodding in an attempt to shake the nerves from my head. "Sounds good. See you in about an hour." As I went next door to open the library, I kept chanting to myself, *You can do this, you can do this*. I needed some reassurance, even if only from myself.

Like Tuesday and Wednesday evenings, the mornings at the library were quiet and far more subdued than the afternoon sessions. Afternoons brought the newspapers, and with the newspapers came the inmates. The papers always arrived rolled up, like messages that had been pulled out of a bottle. The inmates were Robinson Crusoes, castaways hungry for any information from the mainland.

At 9:30, right on time, Kimberly walked into the library. "Just go on next door," she instructed, taking my seat at the main desk. "It's in the classroom all the way in the back, on the right."

I went to the log book on top of the counter and signed myself out and headed next door. Then, (feeling *déjà vu* rather quickly), I went to the log book on the correctional officer's desk and signed myself in to the Education department. Like the inmates, staff movement around the prison was monitored.

Dr. Harald was waiting in the hallway outside of the classroom. "They are just finishing up, but we're up next."

The classroom door opened and a staff member I didn't recognize walked out. I followed Dr. Harald into the room and while he took a seat up front, I found an empty spot in the back, behind all the inmates. There was a healthy mix of black and white inmates, closely resembling the ratio that already existed inside the prison.

Most sat slumped defensively, or, well, as slumped as they could get in uncomfortable metal folding chairs. Almost every one of them had their arms crossed against their chests, feet sticking as far out in front of them as possible, which was a challenge for some of them, given their height and the cramped configuration of the room.

As Dr. Harald droned on about the offerings of the Education department, discussing the various levels of the GED program and computer programs, several inmates closed their eyes and tilted their head back, deciding it was nap time.

"The library is run by Miss Grunenwald sitting there in the back. She's new, just like all of you."

I sat up straighter in my chair as a dozen heads swiveled in my direction.

I hate being stared at. Even with my heightened emotions and anxiety, I can usually mentally hide in a fight-or-flight mode that overtakes me. My body, on the other hand, operates strictly on a compulsion to blush, causing my entire round face to match my red hair. I could feel my cheeks flaming just then, and more than one inmate gave me a sly smile. Once again, I understood how Red Riding Hood felt when she first met the Big Bad Wolf.

Dr. Harald continued on, going over the hours of the library and the services offered. I mentally took note, trying to remember everything he covered, while regretting not bringing a piece of paper and pen with me. Next Friday I would be doing this alone and notes would probably have been quite helpful. Unfortunately, I didn't have an opportunity to run to the library, grab some scrap paper, and do a quick mental brain dump of everything I remembered because it was time to head to the Segregation unit.

The exterior door of Segregation was a nondescript, stand-alone white door, and the only door in the building without an accompanying window. So nondescript, if it hadn't been pointed out to me, I would have walked right past it, which was probably the point of its stark design.

Dr. Harald was carrying a stack of books that he had to shift to his other arm in order to pull out his set of keys again. "Only a few of us have a key for Seg," he explained, putting a key into the outer door. "If I'm not over here, you can ask one of the captains."

The door opened to reveal a long hall with a second door several yards ahead of us. Dr. Harald shut the exterior door behind us, then walked up to the second door. He pointed to a camera high in the ceiling.

A loud, familiar buzz ricocheted around the space and Dr. Harald pushed open the door in front of us and the hallway extended.

In Hollywood prisons, Segregation is often referred to as "the hole": a deep dark dungeon of a room barely large enough for a grown man to sit, let alone stand. I had a feeling the reality would be a little less dramatic. Or at least I hoped it would be. If nothing else, the white walls gave it a lighter, brighter feeling than I had expected. In reality, instead of being a single dank, dark cell, Segregation is a prison within a prison. Its cells are reserved for those inmates that need to be removed from the general population. Sometimes it is for safety reasons—the inmate in question is a victim, or likely victim, of violence—while other times, inmates are sent there for punishment purposes.

(In case you're wondering: The old adage regarding how perpetrators of certain crimes, like rape or anything involving children, will basically get fed to the wolves once they arrive? In truth, often those inmates are segregated immediately, and are never even given the opportunity to mingle with the general population.)

At the end of the hall was another locked door, this one with a small window. On the right-hand side of the hallway was a tiny office with a high desk. Behind it sat a large white woman with cropped gray hair. She leaned forward across the high desk, squinting, clearly in need of a pair of glasses. I learned that this was Donnor, the head of the Rules Infraction Board, or RIB. The board operated as a panel that had the authority to administer punishment, up to and including time spent in Segregation.

Dr. Harald ushered me in. "Donnor, this is Miss Grunenwald. Our new librarian." Donnor gave a pleasant wave and a bright smile. "Guess I'll be seeing you on Fridays!" she said. With that, Dr. Harald and I stepped back out into the hall and the door into Segregation buzzed open.

The gray floor stretched out several yards in both directions. Lining the walls were heavy-duty doors, each sporting its own porthole window. At the back was what appeared to be a two-story cage with a freestanding basketball hoop. The cage reached high into the sky, marking the outdoor recreation area for Segregation inmates. Catty-corner to it was a room with a table: indoor recreation for the Segregated inmates. Aside from their allotted two hours a day in these places, the rest of the time, Seg inmates were in their cells.

Dr. Harald stopped at the desk that sat at the front of the room. Upon seeing me, the two correctional officers perked up.

"Who do we have here?" the one on the right asked. He was rotund and bald. The overhead fluorescent lights provided a glare off his pale head. His name badge read *Michael Bolton.*

I cocked an eyebrow at the nametag. Bolton noticed and laughed. "Trust me, I've heard it all before."

His partner was a tall, graceful African American woman of Amazonian stature. Her thick, black braids were coiled and piled atop her head like a crown.

"I'm Davis," she said, shaking my hand. "You're the new librarian?"

"I am. I just started this week."

"Welcome to Seg," Davis continued, taking her seat back at the desk she shared with Bolton.

A white dry-erase board hung on the wall behind the desk. I craned my neck up to read the columns of inmate names and numbers, each assigned to a bunk, followed by the infraction number and the reporting staff member. It went so high up on the wall, I came to the conclusion

Bolton and Davis were probably forced to stand on the desks just to update it.

Dr. Harald was walking around to the different doors along the perimeter of the room. I hurried over to catch up to him.

"Mr. Masterson?" He put his voice close to the door. "I have your books for you."

Movement began to stir from the far side of the room. Standing on my toes and peering in, all I could see was a metal bunk bed. A round white face came into view in the porthole window.

"I was sleeping, man." Masterson rubbed his eyes and blinked a few times then ran a hand through his blonde hair. He looked past Dr. Harald and locked on to me.

"I brought your books," Dr. Harald repeated. He looked to the correctional officers' desk. Bolton pushed himself off his chair and came over.

I hadn't noticed before, but at Bolton's hip hung a gigantic key ring. It swung with each step across the room. He found the appropriate key and put it into a key hole in the middle of the door. A slot pulled open, revealing a gap just wide enough for a couple of books.

Dr. Harald slipped the books into the slot, and they disappeared into the room along with Masterson. Bolton slammed the fold-out door shut.

I followed Dr. Harald as he went around to each

cell, asking inmates if there were any books they would like brought back the next day.

Dr. Harald finished up at the last cell and headed back towards the main door.

"Nice meeting you!" Davis said, nodding in my direction, as I followed Dr. Harald out.

As Dr. Harald pushed the heavy steel door out into the sunshine, he handed me the piece of paper he had been carrying around. I opened it up, attempting to decipher what could only politely be described as chicken scratch. "These are the requested books you'll need to bring back tomorrow," he explained. Fridays were for requesting books, Saturday for delivering them. He elaborated, saying most inmates weren't specific about titles; they would usually just request authors or genres, and it was up to me to pick the books to bring back the next day.

The only rule was no hardback books. None. Under no circumstances were hardback books allowed into Segregation—paperbacks only. The weight and flat, hard cover made the hardbacks too dangerous.

Books are considered dangerous for all sorts of reasons: content, language, violence. There is also a philosophy of arming oneself with books and knowledge, as if preparing for a battle of wits. But this was the first time I realized they could be used as literal weapons.

Since this was a minimum-security prison, I

knew most of the inmates were in on nonviolent charges. I also knew that my porter Spencer had been right: nobody was going to do anything dumb enough to get themselves into trouble and risk extending their stay. Still, there was a room full of gentlemen tucked behind steel doors that proved otherwise, and visiting them was now on my weekly task list.

Since our initial meeting, Andrews had been in every day to repair books, most often with tape, glue, or some combination of both. "Hey, Miss G, can I get the box?" he asked, leaning across my desk.

With a nod, I stood up from my desk, went to the supply closet, and pulled out a blue shoebox that rested on top of the pile of surplus office supplies. Inside were dedicated safety scissors and a collection of tape varieties.

Stepping out of the closet, I handed Andrews the box with one hand while locking the door with my other. He turned on one heel and disappeared into the crowd, headed for the law library.

I scanned quickly. Tattered books lined the walls of the library. Covers torn, pages missing. With his collection of tape, Andrews did what he could to revive them to a passable condition again. Without a budget for buying new books, we had to make do with what we could.

Koch appeared at my desk as soon as I sat back down. I had recently learned that Koch had been an engineer before prison. I had worked with engineers in graduate school, when I worked at a science research library. Admittedly, my privilege had made me naïve enough to paint a very inaccurate portrait of the kind of guys I was working with in here. "Miss G.," he started, "I don't want to complain . . ."

I clasped my hands together on top of my desk and waited.

"Well, it's just." Koch shifted his weight back and forth between his feet. "Andrews, ma'am."

"Yes?"

"He's always back there in the law library with them books and he's not a law porter. He's not even a library porter!" Koch's eyes grew larger behind his oversized glasses, horrified at this minor infraction.

"I know, but the books need to be repaired and he's willing to do it."

Koch stared at me, silent. His eyes magnified through the thick glass. Finally, with a resigned nod, he turned and went back to the law library.

Andrews walked up to the desk, the blue shoebox tucked under this left arm. He separated himself from the mass exodus and politely waited until there was an opening before coming over to where I stood waiting.

I outstretched my hand, ready to take the box

111

back, when he spoke: "Y'know, Miss G., there's a lot of books back there that need to be repaired."

I did know, plus the pile grew every day. Books were returned with covers half torn off, if not missing all together. Not just single pages, but complete sections were often pulled clean from the spine. My porters removed the ones in the worst condition but were forced to keep everything else until they were too far gone to be circulated.

"Miss Carol," Andrews said, referencing my predecessor, "well, she let me repair books back in the dorm."

"She did?" I failed to minimize the uptick in my voice.

His blue eyes flickered brightly and he continued in a rush. "Oh yeah. Y'know, I can only be here a few hours a day and I got my own job I gotta do. In the dorms I can repair them even when the library isn't open."

This seemed an unusual practice in the realm of library science, but so much of what I had learned before had been thrown out the window the minute I stepped foot in the prison. Beyond that, what reason would Andrews have to lie? I mean, if he wanted to tape and repair books in his free time, on top of whatever job he already had, who was I to stop him? The pile of books in need of attention was never ending, and if his ability and desire to do it outside of regular library hours helped us stay afloat, well, okay then. Especially if my predecessor had already agreed to it.

"Okay," I said slowly, drawing out the first vowel. "I suppose that's alright then." From the book repair supplies box I removed a roll of tape and pair of safety scissors and handed them over.

"The thing of it is," Andrews continued, ducking his head apologetically as a lock of strawberry-blonde hair fell into his eyes. "This stuff isn't really allowed in the dorms. It's contraband, see, so, if you could just, like, write a note saying it's okay that I have it that would be great."

I narrowed my eyes. I had a niggling feeling in the back of my brain that something about this just wasn't right, but I kept coming back to my initial question: *Why would Andrews lie?*

At this point in the night, the library was nearly empty except for a few stragglers who were slowly making their way to the exit, and my porters, who were all finishing up their tasks and cleaning up their work areas. Count would be starting soon and the inmates needed to get back to the dorms.

Andrews hadn't moved. He waited expectantly, eyes scrutinizing me, impatient to leave but not wanting to leave empty-handed.

I felt my skin flush. I didn't know what to do, but I was anxious to just get him out of the library, so I nodded and sat down. I pulled a piece of blank computer paper from the printer and dashed off a quick note: *Andrews has my permission to have the scissors and tape in the dorms.* I signed and dated it and handed it over to him.

His eyes lit up. "Thanks, Miss G.!" he exclaimed. He grabbed the scissors and tape and stuffed them into the pockets of his winter coat. Turning on his heel, he bounced out of the library and back to the dorms.

Within the next few minutes, the inmates all left and I fell back into my seat, body deflating. Now, sitting alone in the empty library, a sense of unease washed over me. Had I reacted too hastily with Andrews? He was antsy to leave and I was ready to close up the library, but in my impatience had I made a misstep?

There was nothing to be done about it now, though. My days off were in sight.

Chapter 5
Weekend Reading

In an attempt to most efficiently use the resources available within the Department, every effort shall be made to redistribute surplus library materials prior to discarding these materials. Any library material in such physical condition as to render it unusable shall be disposed of with regard to institutional library procedures.
—ODRC Policy 58-LIB-03

"Z675.P8 C55. Z675.P8 C55. Z675.P8 C55."

Muttering to myself, I referenced the scrap of paper in my hand again, then peered at the tiny letters and numbers printed on the spines of the books in front of me. When the alphanumeric combinations began to resemble something vaguely familiar to the one in my hand, I slowed my pace. My finger walked along the white line of labels before stopping at the one that matched my piece of paper.

I pulled the book off the shelf. *Library Services to the Incarcerated* by Sheila Clark and Erica MacCreaigh. At only 250 pages, it didn't seem large enough to contain all the nuances that came with prison librarianship, but as I thumbed through, the chapter headings caught my eye: "Facilities and Equipment," "Understanding the Patrons," and "Understanding Yourself," among others.

Now that I'd found one, I turned to the second call number on my piece of paper and my finger traced the books until I found its match. *Down for the Count: A Prison Library Handbook* by Brenda Vogel. This was an even slimmer volume, less than 200 pages, but seeing chapters with such intriguing titles as, "Prison Libraries: How They Came To Be" and "Collection Management and Corresponding Woes," appealed to both my personal love of gathering information and my professional struggle with our physical collection of books.

Yes. Both of these would do just fine.

I tucked the books under my arm and climbed down the narrow metal steps to the main reading room floor. It was Monday, essentially the Sunday equivalent of my workweek. Having a regular weekday off afforded me more freedom than I had anticipated. I could run errands with lines that were so short when compared to a busy weekend. To my delight, Cleveland's iconic West Side Market was practically empty (at least when compared to the Saturday suburban surge) on Mondays, so I had now decided to add the Cleveland Public Library to my routine as well.

I'd been at the prison for a week and in all of my interactions with staff and inmates, I was beginning to see the entire experience as a shining beacon of opportunity. And not just in terms of what books and materials I provided—this was the kind of job I had gone to library school for, the kind of position where I could both encourage reading and literacy and make a positive impact on others. Five days in, though, and I also knew that there were opportunities for me to learn more. If I wanted to be effective at my job, I needed to do a little research.

Contrary to popular belief, librarians don't have all the answers. But we do know how to *find* the answers, which is how I ended up deep in the stacks of the main branch of CPL.

Built in 1925, the historic main branch of Cleveland's library is a stunning example of Renaissance architecture in the heart of downtown, a palace of marble among the busy city streets. While I had a local branch that was slightly closer to my apartment (and with far better parking), that location didn't have the books I was looking for. The Main Branch downtown did, however, which is how I ended up tucked into the far reaches of the library's collection retrieving them.

With my books safely in tow, I headed out of the reading room and towards the sweeping marble staircase that would take me downstairs to the lobby. I was so absorbed in the hallway's mini art gallery that I didn't notice the tall blonde gentleman until he was nearly right in front of me.

"Jill?"

I forced my gaze from the painting. I was so startled it took my brain a second to catch up with my vision.

Standing before me was Anthony, former assistant director of the library in my hometown. Several years ago he had taken a job in the literature department of Cleveland Public, and I had not been in touch with him since.

Of all the libraries in all the world, why'd I have to walk into his?

Anthony furrowed his brow. "You . . . emailed me a while back, didn't you?"

Indeed I had, since Anthony was part of whatever limited library network I belonged to. As I recalled, Anthony had not responded. Forcing a smile, I nodded. "Yes, I had just graduated with my MLIS and moved back to town. I had emailed to see if you knew of any job openings."

"Ah." He shifted the stack of books in his hands and walked a few steps up, closer to me on the staircase. "Unfortunately not."

"Oh," I waved my hand. "That's okay. I got one. I'm working as a prison librarian on the far west side."

Anthony's eyes widened. He again shifted the

118

stack of books in his hands and leaned against the wide marble handrail. "You know, I had considered doing that decades ago."

"Really?" I had a hard time imagining Anthony wrangling inmates. Then again, he probably was thinking the same thing about me.

"Well," Anthony said with a nod, "I've got to get these books back upstairs. It was nice seeing you."

I waved and took my books down to the circulation desk to be checked out. As I watched the Cleveland Public Library employee scan my books, I realized how far I had come. Ten years ago, I started working at the public library as just an after-school job, not really expecting it to go anywhere. But now, I was a librarian, in charge of my very own little library. All of the people I had worked with back then, including Anthony, had been instrumental in showing me what a library could be, inspiring me to take this path. Running into Anthony here seemed like serendipity.

My new work schedule took some adjusting. In college I worked the front desk of a dorm and would occasionally work weekends and for at least one semester worked the overnight shift, requiring me to arrive at work at 4 a.m., but now I was working *early* every Saturday. Waking up before six on a Saturday meant Friday nights out with friends would be few and far between: going

119

to work in a prison on a mere three or four hours of sleep would not be wise.

The Saturday before my own personal visit to the library had broken as bright and early as all the other days preceding it. I stumbled around my kitchen, willing myself to wake for the last day of my first week at the prison. Coffee had become a daily necessity.

Ninety minutes later, I arrived at work to a lobby already full of waiting visitors, chairs claimed even at that early hour. Families of all sizes, and spanning several generations, waited patiently. Like staff, all visitors were searched and walked through the metal detector to prevent contraband from coming into the prison. Walking past them, I wondered if any were related to my porters, and as my eyes quickly scanned the room, I looked for signs of familiarity. I didn't know what it was like to have a family member in prison, but if the crowded visiting room told me anything, it was that many of the men at our facility had families who loved and supported them. In this way, they were luckier than many other prisoners.

I bypassed the line and took my items up to the front counter to be searched before making my way down to the library.

The Education staff were all off today—I was the only one required to work Saturdays—so I had the entire department to myself. Even the general staff and number of correctional officers seemed smaller than it had during the week.

The library itself was far more subdued and quiet on Saturday, especially during the first shift in the morning. No one waited outside for me to unlock the door, save for my porters. The inmates, it seemed, also took advantage of the weekend to sleep in. My workers and I passed the hours in silence, and I used the downtime as an opportunity to really dig into the prison policies in my filing cabinet.

During the mid-morning break, I referenced the sheet Dr. Harald had brought back from the previous day's Seg visit, and took the requested books down to Segregation. This time, alone, I had to wait and track down one of the higher-ups with a key to be allowed in. The RIB office was closed, as Donnor was also off on the weekends, so it was up to me to distribute the books directly to the inmates through the same slot in the door that Dr. Harald had used the day before.

Because the newspapers only arrived on weekdays, there weren't newspapers to draw patrons in during the afternoon shift. That, coupled with inmates having visitors, meant the afternoon passed as quietly as the morning. At 3:30 p.m., I ushered the inmates back to their dorms for count, shut down the library, and headed home, grateful to officially have my weekend started.

After having spent the past few days waking up long before the sun, I was so happy to sleep in on Sunday and have a day of doing absolutely nothing, only sweetened by having the satisfaction that I had survived my first week.

Over the weekend, as I talked with family and shared cocktails with friends at a local bar, I was faced with a barrage of questions, all of which could be boiled down to the same single query: *What's it like?*

"Oh," I said, demurely, waving the question off. "It's really not that much different from all the other libraries I've worked in."

"Really?" they countered, fascinated and dis-believing at the same time. And they were right to detect the hint of falseness in my voice, although, to be fair, it so far really *wasn't* that much different from the other libraries. Maybe there were some more rules, or, at least, more complex rules, but the way the library functioned was the same.

The one key difference was the way I was seen. More than once over the next two years I would hear inmates joke that they *had* to be there, the staff chose to be. So who were really the crazy ones in this situation? I was an outlander. Maybe not the time-traveling kind, but someone from the outside who had *chosen* to go inside, go behind bars.

On the outside, to friends and family, I was an equally rare bird, because to them I had been *on the inside*. I had been on the other side of the bars, I had walked the halls of a prison and come out on the other side. My friends and family all had what they considered to be mundane jobs compared to mine. Nothing worthy of a game of twenty questions and exciting enough for party small talk. I was the belle of the ball. Or, of the bar as it were.

I took my new position seriously, setting myself up to regale them with all sorts of stories and to set the record straight on what it was like in prison. After all, I'd been there for a full week and had done my due diligence by checking out a book about it, so *obviously* that meant I knew everything there was to know, right?

"Well." I took a deep breath, preparing myself. "You know, there are the regulars who are always waiting outside for the library to open and stay late, and the inmates really just come in and sit and read like any library. Newspapers and magazines are super popular. They love James Patterson. *Love* him. I can't keep his books on the shelves. Really, if you can ignore the guard next door you can forget you're even inside prison."

Seven days in and I felt like some white knight coming in astride my trusty steed, Confidence. Just about the right time for hubris to kick me in the ass.

• • •

"Grunenwald," I answered, picking up the phone in the library.

"It's Kim. Did you tell Andrews he could take scissors and tape from the library?"

"Y-yes." I stumbled over the word as a cold rush passed over me.

"Right, okay, so they aren't allowed to have that back in the dorms. Finch found it during a random bunk search."

"He told me that Carol said he could." The pitch of my voice went higher at the same time I was trying to keep my voice low, not wanting to be overheard. "I thought . . ." my words faded off. My shoulders were up around my ears as I tried to make myself small.

"It's contraband," Kim said. There was a pause, then: "Finch also found the note you wrote telling Andrews he could have it."

This was bad. This was really bad. This was bad on an epic level.

Andrews had contraband in his dorm. Contraband he had gotten from the library. That would be bad enough on its own, although Andrews himself would be the one most affected. But I had taken it a step further: I'd actually given Andrews permission and had put it in writing. I realized that I didn't *have* the power to give him that permission. They were library supplies, yes, and I was the librarian and this was my library, but contraband was dictated at the state level and no amount of slips of paper with my signature was able to trump that. So not only had I basically given an inmate carte blanche to break a state law, I had given him *proof* that I had also broken state law.

Bad. Really bad. Really, really bad. Like, possible termination from the job bad.

I'd never been fired before and my anxiety spiked as my brain began firing off a million questions in every direction. What was I going to tell my parents? How was I going to explain how I got fired? Would I have to file for unemployment? How did that work? What was I going to tell my boyfriend? My getting a full-time job in Cleveland was the first step towards him moving out here and us starting our life together, but if I didn't have a job, then what? I have no idea how I managed to get lucky enough to get a job when all of my classmates were still struggling and now I'd gone and wrecked my one and only opportunity—

"Jill." Kim's snap punctuated my thoughts.

"Yes. Here."

"I said Finch already destroyed the note."

Wait. What?

"She . . . destroyed it." I repeated Kim's words back to her, feeling them in my mouth. As they passed between my teeth, the worry dissolved away like a piece of candy on my tongue.

"Yeah. She's supposed to write up an incident

report and report it to Admin, but she destroyed it and called me instead. Andrews is still getting written up, Finch just isn't going to mention the note part."

My whole body collapsed from relief. The past few minutes had been spent in a state of shock and anxiety, my bones propped up on sheer adrenaline.

"Listen," Kim said, but I was barely listening. "I gotta get back to work. Try not to worry about this. I'll see you later this afternoon."

Still in disbelief, I hung up the phone. Finch had, without a doubt, saved my ass while also risking her own. If Admin ever discovered my own misstep and then discovered what Finch had done to cover for me, we'd both be in even bigger trouble.

I turned back to the library and inmates in front of me, trying to cast the situation out of my mind. I couldn't mess up like this again.

That afternoon, Andrews hurried into the library. The line of incoming inmates made it impossible for him to reach my desk, so he positioned himself at an odd angle near the circulation desk. "Miss G.!" he said loudly, projecting his voice above the crowd.

With a deep breath, I stood up from my seat and turned to face him. "You lied to me, Andrews," I said, crossing my arms over my chest.

"No!" He furiously shook his head. "No, I didn't, Miss G., I swear."

I cocked my head to one side and narrowed my eyes. In my best stern librarian voice, I said, "Andrews."

"Miss G. I swear. She let me have that stuff—"

"But you knew you weren't supposed to."

"Miss G.—"

"I trusted you and you put me in a really difficult position." Shaking my head, I raised my hands, palms up. "I'm sorry, Andrews. I can't have you repairing books anymore."

His whole body sagged, like a balloon deflating. Andrews's head bobbed up and down a few times, eyes still on the floor. "I understand, Miss G." Without another word, he turned and shuffled back into the library, finding an open spot at a table.

From my standing vantage point, I looked down and saw my circulation staff and the line of waiting patrons all standing still, watching me. When our eyes locked, they all jolted back into the regular rhythm of library services. It was jarring; comedic, even, like a scene from a movie, when everyone goes back to pretending that everything is fine and nothing is amiss. It was also the first time I'd shown any real authority in front of my porters. Up until that moment, I'd been a fairly passive manager, mostly letting them guide the way, as I was still trying to find my place. But now they knew that I had no problem laying down the law when necessary.

Since Finch worked first shift and left the prison a couple of hours before I did, it was a few days before I happened to cross paths with her.

"Thanks," I said when I caught up with her in the yard one day. I tried to keep my voice light and casual in an attempt to play this off as just a normal, everyday conversation.

Finch looked at me. This was the first time I'd really ever spoken to her, although I could easily recognize her head of tight, blonde curls from across the yard. The female correctional officers were few and far between, making them easier to spot. She and I were roughly the same age, build, and complexion. But just standing here, taking her in, I immediately noticed there was a hardness to her, an aloof and intimidating exterior shell that seemed tough to crack. I suddenly realized how complicated it must be to be a female correctional officer in an all-male prison.

"Thanks for what?" she asked, eyes wide.

I furrowed my brow. "For the other day." Lowering my voice, I leaned in closer. "With Andrews."

She shook her head. "I don't know what you're talking about," she replied and walked away.

Before she went, I almost detected a slight

curve to her outer lip, like a fishing lure just barely pulling it up into the ghost of a smile. It was so small, so indistinct, I might have imagined it.

The yard was empty, save for a few correctional officers doing their rounds during the mid-morning count break. On a bench outside the library, I had newspapers for today stacked next to me. Instead of going inside, I had stolen a few moments of quiet outside.

Williard appeared from around the corner of the Education building and sat down next to me. I had seen him around the yard, but this was the first time we'd really spoken since the unarmed self-defense course. "Hey, Miss G.," he said with a smile. Somewhere along the line, even the staff started using my nickname, too. "How's the library?"

I shrugged. "It's fine."

"That guy Jefferson still there?"

At the mention of my evening porter, I turned my head and stared at his profile. "Yes. Why?" I asked, warily. I had about a dozen men working in the library, so why was Williard latching onto Jefferson?

Williard's eyes were also trained on the birds out in the yard. "Watch out for him."

My skin tingled, a million little pins being run all over it. "What? Why?"

He gave a small shake of his head. "Just . . . be careful." Before I could respond or press him further, Williard rose and walked down the path.

After he left me sitting there, alone, there was still plenty of time before the lunch crew started and the library opened, so I dropped the newspapers off on my desk in the library, then headed into the Education department. I made a beeline for Stephanie's desk. "Heyyyyyy," I said in a poorly conceived attempt at being casual. "I heard a weird thing from Williard." Stephanie looked up at me from her desk, waiting for me to continue. "About Jefferson," I finished.

Stephanie's eyebrows shot up. "Williard told you about that?"

"Well, he told me I should watch out for him."

"Ah." She gestured to the seat in front of her desk. I sat. "Miss Carol, the librarian before you? She and Jefferson had . . . a thing."

"What do you mean 'a thing'?"

She cocked her head to one side, giving me a "You know exactly what I mean" look.

"Seriously?"

Stephanie nodded. Her eyes gleamed, the gossip too good. "Apparently," she whispered, "they found a pair of her panties on him."

I was too stunned to speak, my mind attempting the mental gymnastics to under-stand the logistics of how that would even work. For him to end up with any of her undergarments—while also remembering I was getting all of this third, possibly fourth-hand, so ample grains of salt were required—she'd have to be naked. It's a prison, there are guards, not to mention other inmates, everywhere. Where could she and Jefferson have . . .

Ah. A lightbulb went off. The library bathroom. It was the only place. Rarely used by anyone other than me, there was little risk of being surprised or found out. Sure, it was snug, but with a little creativity it could definitely be done.

"So," I said, finally voicing my thoughts to the final conclusion, "I only have a job because the former librarian slept with an inmate?"

Stephanie raised her palms, signifying both a shrug and a question, but there was a definite smirk playing on her lips.

All through the afternoon shift, I couldn't stop thinking about it, mostly because I didn't get it. I had so many questions, the least of which was *why?* Why, in all the men in all the world, would you want to hook up with an inmate? I mean, Jefferson was fairly attractive, bearing a passing resemble to Taye Diggs and, okay, if I saw him outside the fence, just walking along the streets of Cleveland, I would probably take notice.

But this wasn't the streets of Cleveland; this was a prison. So, *why?*

The inmates' urges I understood. This is an all-male facility and even for those inmates who were gay or bisexual, sex still wasn't allowed, per statewide policy. Not that it stopped them, of course. But for those inmates who were straight and planned on staying that way while incarcerated, their only option was the female employees. It was against policy for us to have sex with them, too, and the inmates knew it. But for some of the inmates, it was a power play. A long con of sorts. Because once an employee crossed that line, that inmate had her by the proverbial balls.

I didn't yet know it, but this was not an uncommon occurrence. If anything, it was routine more than anything else: I can't speak for all prisons, but at ours, approximately every six months, like clockwork, another female at our facility was going to be caught and fired for having an inappropriate relationship with an inmate.

In the future, I'd laugh about it and gossip with Stephanie, but for now, I was too shell-shocked to even conceive of anyone entering into a relationship with an inmate, let alone more than one woman, including ones that I would eventually come to know well.

That night, Jefferson walked in and said "hello" just like last week. He took his seat at the circulation desk and picked up the stack of checkout cards that had been left by the day shift and still needed sorting. While palming them like playing cards, he slid his chair over to my desk.

"And how are you this evening?" he asked with a smile.

I looked at him for a beat, realizing that, yes, I could see how that smile had the potential to charm the panties right off a woman.

"Jefferson," I said, sitting up straight, stern librarian again. "That red line on the floor there means no inmates over here, so I need you to roll back over to the circulation desk and stay there please."

Something flashed across his gaze. He knew that I knew. He knew that I knew and he also knew that he wasn't going to be able to charm me the same way he had my predecessor.

He dropped the smile, his mouth set into a firm line, rolled the chair back to his spot at the desk, and continued counting and sorting the cards.

Jefferson never again said hello to me when he came into work Tuesday and Wednesday evenings. He spoke only when directly asked a question. He had targeted me as an easy mark, but now that I had shown I wasn't going to play that game, he had no use for me anymore. I felt triumphant: after everything that had happened with Andrews, I had been determined to not allow myself to fall victim to any attempts at playing me and, at least in this regard, I had succeeded.

In just the span of a few days I had been faced with two very different inmate interactions. I honestly still wasn't sure how I felt about the Andrews situation. Maybe he didn't lie—maybe Miss Carol *had* given him permission to keep the repair supplies in his dorm. But, like it had been for me, that wasn't something she had permission to give.

It's also possible, though, that Andrews saw me as an easy target. I've read *Primal Fear* and seen the movie adaptation. In some ways, Andrews reminded me of Edward Norton's character: shy and quiet with a nervous demeanor. A mouse, backed into a corner, twitching and scared. By the end of the film, viewers learn that this presentation is all an act, which is perhaps why I couldn't shake the feeling that Andrews's country boy politeness had been an act. If not for the saving grace of Finch, I don't know if I'd still have a job.

Then there was Jefferson, a man who absolutely saw me as an easy target and, again, if not for Williard's comments, I don't know if I would have given a thought about *why* Jefferson was being so nice to me. I just sort of took it for granted that I'm a librarian and he's a porter, and this was a routine manager/employee transaction.

His lack of communication and interest after the fact, though, proves that he was just trying to con me. Or, if nothing else, see how far he could push things with me.

I wasn't used to this. It didn't matter how many

years I had previously worked in libraries or that I had received my master's degree from a well-regarded program, nor did it matter how many books about prison librarianship I read: I was not used to or prepared for a position where every single interaction with my service population was a bomb waiting to detonate.

Chapter 6
Pomp and Circumstance

Each institution shall provide a comprehensive education program to meet the basic academic needs of the inmate population. The program shall provide eligible inmates with basic academic skills, literacy, Pre-GED, GED, career enhancement, high school credit, communication skills, and social-emotional skills.
—ODRC Policy 57-EDU-02

Slowly, I started to settle into my new job. Winter began to melt away. The roads from Cleveland to Grafton became more passable, my drive suddenly taking less time now that I no longer had to navigate snow on the roads. Inmates on grounds duty traded in their shovels for lawn mowers. The sun broke earlier and earlier each day and stayed around later each evening, crowning the day with light before dipping back below the horizon. With the change in season came a change in protocol: we had sprung ahead our clocks, gaining an hour of additional sunlight. Because the sun was still out when I left on Tuesdays and Wednesdays, the yard stayed open and I was no longer required to call in the number of inmates leaving the library each night: they were allowed to move about the yard on their own, floating freely between the library, dorms, and the rec center until the sun swapped with the moon.

Warmer weather also brought activity to the yard, inmates walking on the track or using the stationary exercise equipment set in the middle of the track. To the untrained eye, it resembled a bizarre playground set in the middle of a sandbox. Heavy steel poles poking in and out of the sand pit in all manner of directions. Parallel bars set low to the ground. Sets of bars for both pull-ups and push-ups. It was like looking at a minimalist arena meant for gymnastics. All that was missing was a balance beam.

While I'm sure the equipment could be used for gymnastics if an inmate was so inclined, that's not what it was designed for. Instead, now that the metal bars stood out against green grass, free of snow, I realized that they were meant as exercise equipment that required nothing more than body weight in order to be used properly. Other routine gym items, such a dumbbells and various free-standing weights, were a no go: those items are heavy by design, so imagine what damage could be done if someone got pissed enough to chuck a forty-pound kettlebell at an enemy. Not a pretty picture.

By using their body weight either with or against the metal poles and bars, which were standing free and out in the open, and thus within eyesight of multiple staff members and officers, inmates could bulk up in a controlled and relatively safe environment. (Because, honestly, if an inmate is determined enough, *everything* becomes a weapon.) Chin-ups, sit-ups, push-ups. There was a piece of equipment for all of them, as well as some others whose function I didn't yet know. As the weather warmed, from my vantage point at the library's only window, I saw more and more inmates taking advantage of the equipment. It was a popular way to rid themselves of pent-up energy.

The change in season extended to the porters in my library. Because the inmates at my facility in particular were in on lesser charges, they had shorter stays, so at any one time I could come in and find out I'd lost a porter because he'd been released. They could also request to be moved to a different job. It didn't happen to me very often— the library was one of the better regarded gigs and inmates were loath to lose it—but it did happen.

Over the past few months, there had been a changeover. A few old porters left the library job, while new porters came in. When it came time to request new workers, I would turn to the blue binder at my desk. Inmates were constantly asking if they could be a librarian porter, so much so that I had a wait list. Names were constantly added, with many men patiently watching for their name to reach the top.

Of course, it wasn't as simple as just picking the next name on the list. Prison has its own echelons of red tape and bureaucracy, and I was informed that I had to make sure to keep a fair balance of inmates that matched the demographics of our inmate population. Meaning, I basically had to keep an even number of black inmates and white inmates.

It seems crude, now, to put it in such, well, black-and-white terms, but that's how it was, and almost certainly still is. Granted, there were times I passed over a black inmate for the next available white inmate, and just as often the reverse happened; but no matter what, I still had to make sure that there was some sort of equilibrium.

That's how I found myself with a new crew of inmates to manage. Childers was long gone; released at the end of his sentence. One of the law porters who had been in place when I started was released so soon after my arrival that his name has been lost to time. Only a hazy memory of his brown hair and gruff appearance, like a bulldog, remains. When porters did leave—mostly because they had served their time; very few ever asked to leave the library—it was my job to fill their spot on my roster using the binder.

The day-to-day operations of the library didn't change, we still functioned the same as always, but something was different now. Before, I had inherited the inmates I managed. I didn't know them and they didn't know me. Now, though, these were my inmates, or, well, they were in the sense that I effectively hired them, even if it merely meant finding their names close to the top of the list. But somehow it was enough of a difference to make me feel more confident at my job and to take more ownership of the little library. It's like the line between renting an apartment and owning a house. I wasn't going to start painting or knocking down walls, but with this new class of inmates trained entirely by me, I had the opportunity to really cultivate the atmosphere I wanted to see and I wanted the inmates to feel every time they came to the library.

Spring was here and the desire to make positive changes was in the air.

One morning in early spring, I pulled into the parking lot and found my unofficial spot right under the lamp that rose like a skyline above the parking lot. As I tucked my cell phone into the glove compartment, I couldn't help but smile. I never really knew what I was going to be walking into once I went through those sally port doors and entered the yard, but today was different. No matter what shit went down, I knew today was going to be a good day.

Because today there would be cake. Actual cake.

Ahead of me, my coworkers moved in a pack, like a school of fish. I queued up behind them, the current pushing us forward towards the main class doors. We maneuvered around Dr. Harald, who had traded his unofficial uniform of polo and khakis for a full suit.

"Good morning, Dr. Harald," I said cheerfully as I slipped by. He gave a short wave of acknowledgment, then fell in line, shuffling along behind us.

The queue of employees lined up, first at the control booth window to drop off our badges, then at the metal detector to have our items searched. Already the lobby was starting to fill with visitors. Families sat together, mothers wrangling their children. Everyone was dressed up a bit more than usually seen on a normal Visitation Day. Because this wasn't Visitation Day, it was *Graduation* Day.

Every day, inmates sat through the multiple GED classes offered. Some were there willingly, fighting for the chance to put their time behind bars to good use. Others were there because state law required them to be. Regardless, all of them had the opportunity to come out of this experience with some sort of a win by passing the GED exam and walking across the stage in a cap and gown as part of a graduation ceremony.

Every inmate who took part in the graduation ceremony was allowed to have visitors witness the event. This was made even sweeter by the fact that this visitation was a bonus day, and so it didn't count against the number of monthly visits they were allowed.

I snuck into the library to drop my things off, then hurried next door to the Education department to get any last minute instructions before the library opened for the morning. Our daily schedule was thrown in upheaval with graduation. The library would only be open for the morning shift. While I was helping with graduation, Knapp would take the library cart around to the dorms, aided by a supervising correctional officer.

The entire Education department crowded into Dr. Harald's office. Kim was tucked into the corner behind her own desk in the office, which didn't leave much room for the rest of us. Roberta had grabbed the one empty chair, while Nancy and I stood in front of Dr. Harald's desk. Mr. Hooper, arms crossed awkwardly across his thin frame, hovered nervously behind us.

Dr. Harald sat behind his desk. Today, his suit and larger-than-life body made him look like the Godfather of graduation. "The inmates will be down at their dorms for count than are instructed to be here for lunch. The kitchen will take care of the pizzas and we'll eat in the library." He looked at me as he said this last bit.

Right. That definitely would have been good to know in advance.

"Sure!" I forced a wide smile, hoping that the surprise didn't show on my face.

He gave a short nod and continued. After lunch, Dr. Harald would lead the graduates down to the visitation area to get ready and run through the ceremony, so everyone knew where he needed to be. As Dr. Harald did that, Kim, Nancy, and I would help set up to refreshments.

"Jill. I'm putting you in charge of the music."

"Oh. Um. Okay." Music. Okay. I think I can handle that.

He scooted his chair back until it bumped up against the wall, and pulled out a drawer of his desk. He rifled through loose papers and miscellaneous office supplies until he pulled a CD out. "Pomp and Circumstance," he said, handing it to me across the desk. "Just make sure it's queued up in advance." I took the CD from his outstretched hand and flipped it over to read the track listing.

Kim flagged me and I followed her out into the outer office. "Here," she said, pointing to the small gray CD player that sat next to the computer. "We'll take this."

The CD player shared a low wooden table with our large printer. While the printer wasn't industrial-sized, like those floor models found in most contemporary offices, it was several steps above the personal printer I had at home that aided in the slaughtering of so many trees during my graduate school years.

I leaned down to inspect the CD player, my eyes following the route of the cord as it wound its way back behind the printer. The prong at the end vanished from my sight line, but the CD player was operational, so there was an outlet back there somewhere.

The outlet, it turned out, was directly behind the printer. The same heavy, large printer that was pushed almost as far back against the wall as it could go. It was a tiny, narrow room and the printer had effectively claimed most of the territory. Whatever real estate it required was backed up against the wall.

Gripping the cord, I traced it with my hand, following the plastic line back behind the printer. Eventually it stopped at the wall, the plug in my palm. I pulled.

Nothing. The printer was so far back, it had wedged the plug into place.

Next plan of attack. Bracing myself against the machine, I wrapped my arms as wide and as tight as I could around the printer, embracing it in a hug, and gave one big pull. It didn't move. Not even an inch, which is all I needed really, just enough room to narrowly remove the plug from the wall and pull it out of the dark space.

All the while, Kim stood there, silently observing.

I channeled my frustration towards attempting to pull the wooden table the printer sat on. Because if one heavy thing doesn't move on its own, then surely another heavy thing, carrying the first heavy thing, was sure to budge, right?

(Wrong.)

Finally, after watching me push and pull the printer this way and that, Kimberly stepped in. She grabbed hold of one side of the printer while I grabbed the other and together we managed to nudge it just enough to give me a gap large enough to pull the plug from the outlet. I put the now free CD player on the desk in the corner, and Kimberly and I pushed the printer back against the wall.

"The pizzas are ready," Dr. Harald called from his desk as he hung up the phone. I was so invested in the stupid CD player that I hadn't heard it ring. "You all go over. I'm going to collect our graduates."

Never having been to this part of the prison before, I let myself be led away. Breezing through the double doors, I looked around; it reminded me of the lunchroom from my school days with its long plastic tables and metal stools. Everything was attached to the floor with thick bolts and brackets.

Kimberly, our default leader, led us to the counter up front. Part of her role was handling all of the documents and files for the inmates in the GED program, so she knew these men better than anyone else on staff.

The counter also reminded me of my school days, the triple row of thick metal bars running parallel with the counter to allow trays to easily slide down. Stacked beside the trays, at the head of the counter, were dark red plastic cups, the kind of imperfect plastic that created an array of bubbles and ridges on the sides of the cup, reminding me of childhood trips to Pizza Hut.

Inmates behind the counter were starting to set out empty warming trays in preparation for lunch. A woman in a maroon chef's coat came out, her red hair held back with a hair net. Her ruddy skin was flush, presumably from the heat in the kitchen in the back.

"You here for the pizza?" she asked Kim, who nodded.

The woman returned a nod of acknowledgement, then turned and disappeared in the back.

A few minutes later the woman returned, followed by two inmates each carrying a stack of heat-and-serve pizzas from Wal-Mart. The inmates came around the counter and handed one each to Nancy and me.

"Thanks Pam," Kimberly said. Pam just nodded.

We turned to leave but Kimberly paused and looked at Pam. "Can we get a knife for the pizzas? Just in case?"

Pam waited a beat, her eyes carefully trained on Kim. Graduation Day disrupted everyone: from the Quartermaster, who had to make sure the reusable caps and gowns were clean and ready to go; to the correctional officers in the housing units who had to know which inmates were being let out right after count; to food service here. While Pam was preparing the meal for all the other inmates, we also took over some of her equipment so that the pizzas could be kept warm until we were ready to pick them up. It was an inconvenience, so I could see why she wouldn't be bending over backward for us.

Finally, though, she once again disappeared in the back. She came back wielding a knife, which she handed to Kimberly. In exchange, Kimberly removed one of the small bronze chits from her key ring and handed it to Pam as collateral.

We took the pizzas next door and dropped them onto the circulation desk. Spreading them out buffet style, we matched up duplicate flavors so one cheese, one sausage, and one veggie sat on top of three small stacks. Near the door was a large, bright-orange cooler full of fruit punch. It sat on a rolling cart, the lower shelf full of cups, plates, napkins, and a box of latex gloves.

Nancy handed me a pair of gloves from the box. I slipped them on and stationed myself behind the circulation desk while she set out the cups and plates. We took turns with the knife, cutting through the cheese and crust to make sure the slices could easily be removed without holding the line up.

After about fifteen minutes of waiting, the library door opened and Dr. Harald walked in, followed by a long line of inmates.

"Yo, Ms. G!" an inmate I didn't know but who clearly knew me called out in greeting. His eyes widened. "We got pizza?!"

I smiled indulgently. "Take a seat, first."

The tables in the library soon filled as the graduates found open spots. There were about twenty in all, nearly over the library's seating capacity. Some even had to sit behind the law library desk to make sure they had a table in front of them for their food and drink.

Dr. Harald reached into the pocket of his suit jacket and pulled out a piece of paper. "As I call your name, come up to the desk. You get *two* pieces of pizza. If there is more after everyone's gone through, we can let people come back for seconds."

Opening the piece of paper up, he began to read down the roster. "Adams. Atkins. Blake. Burke."

As instructed, the inmates came forward, giddy to the point of bouncing. Going through the line, each grabbed a plate and held it out to me, requesting two of whatever slices they wanted.

Plates loaded with pizza, they returned to their seats and dug in. After the inmates had all made their way through the line, we staff had the opportunity to get some. Dr. Harald sat at the circulation desk, and I took my usual spot behind my main desk. Everyone else was relegated to standing.

A jovial hum filtered across the room, the inmates excited for their brief respite from the rigid rules and structure of prison life. Rules were not completely suspended, however. The afternoon was still structured, there were still rules that would need to be followed, and the inmates would still be wearing their prison blues under their cap and gown. After the ceremony was over, and the cake and punch had been consumed, they'd have to say goodbye to their families and watch them leave, a razor-wire fence between them.

But in that moment, there was pizza and punch. While their peers were being ushered from dorm to chow hall, the soon-to-be-GED-graduates had an hour to relax in the library and chow down on pizza.

Dr. Harald cleared his throat. He raised his right hand and motioned towards the front of the room. "If anyone wants some more pizza, you can come up now."

Politely, inmates came up one at a time and loaded their plates up with more slices of pizza. When your slices of pizza are few and far between, any pizza is good pizza. Even take-and-bake pizza from a big box superstore. By the end of lunch, every single box was empty.

Once everyone had finished, going through seconds, thirds, and fourths in some cases, Dr. Harald stood up from his spot at the circulation desk. "We're going to go down to Quartermaster to get your cap and gowns, then head over to Visitation to practice. So if you'll all follow me."

The inmates stood up and vacated the tables and chairs, forming a single file line that followed Dr. Harald out of the library. The rest of the staff stayed behind to clean up their plates and napkins.

"The punch is coming with us," Nancy said after we were all finished and the library looked relatively clean and organized, as we had found it.

We maneuvered the cart out of the library and over the thick metal transitional piece and out onto the main walkway.

The large orange cooler bounced against the sides of the cart as I pushed it down the sidewalk. My pace was uneven, all of my attention focused on the cooler and making sure it didn't topple over. I was fairly certain Deputy Warden Francis would not approve of bright pink fruit punch staining her walkway.

Nancy walked beside me, directing me where to push the cart. We glided past the Admin building, rounding the corner to a path I had never noticed before that ran between the lobby and the far side of the Administration building.

The Gwendolyn Davis Visitor Center was named after the previous Warden, who had died only a few months before I came on board. I didn't know it at the time, but I had arrived during a time of transition. Her death threw the prison's staff leadership roles into upheaval as people suddenly bolted up the hierarchy and were placed into positions they may or may not have really been prepared to take on. It was like dominos in reverse: instead of pieces falling down, they fell forward and upright, suddenly standing in positions no one had anticipated.

"Coming through!" Nancy yelled. Spring had sprung, the sun rose high in the sky and inmates were outside in the yard taking full advantage of one of the first warm days in a while. The mob of inmates parted at her voice and I pushed the cart through the gap.

Rounding the corner of the building, I had to stop the cart from accidentally plowing into a group of soon-to-be graduates hovering near a door at the back. "Coming through!" my companion repeated. The inmates moved to form a half circle that curved along the sidewalk, forming a natural path to the door.

The cart was heavy with a wide steering range. Turning it to match the shape of the human curve required pushing against one side and slightly lifting the other to maneuver it in the new direction I wanted it to go.

"Stop!" Nancy called out, her voice higher than normal. I pulled back on the handle of the cart abruptly, my eyes watching the cooler to make sure it didn't fall off.

I looked over my shoulder. "What?"

She hurried up beside me and pointed to a door farther ahead, parallel to the one right by us. "We're going up there."

With a shrug, I pushed the rolling cart through the huddled inmates.

Once we were out of earshot, she lowered her voice. "That's where they go to get searched before going into Visitation."

"Okay?" I didn't see the relevance here.

"Strip searched."

My cheeks warmed. Well *that* would have been awkward. I looked over my shoulder to see the group of inmates joking and laughing, a few throwing glances in my direction. *Great,* I thought. *Now I'm going to be the staff member who almost walked in on the inmates naked.*

A large rectangle-shaped room, the Gwendolyn Davis Visitor's Center was bright and airy. The entire exterior wall was lined with windows that overlooked the control center and parking lot. For today's purposes it had been transformed: the bulk of chairs faced the front, classroom style.

Nancy held the door open for me as I awkwardly pushed the heavy cart over the threshold.

I had never been in here before, having had no reason until this point. The perimeter of the room was lined with vending machines. Inmates were not allowed to handle money, but their visitors could buy snacks for them. The options weren't much different than the packaged chips and candy bars that could be purchased through commissary, but food always tastes better when someone else buys it for you, especially when funds are limited.

At the front of the room stood a raised wooden platform, which served as the guard station for the correctional officers assigned to visitation days. Like the crow's nest on a ship, the higher perch gave them a vantage point to see everyone and everything.

I pushed the cart towards the table on the far wall, setting the punch at the end next to the sheet cake that sat on the table, still in the box from the bakery. Through the plastic film of the box top, I read *Congrats, Graduates!* in blue script across white icing.

"Here, let me," I heard, just as I bent down to remove the leftover plates and napkins from the second shelf of the cart. I turned to see Laura, the person in charge of payroll, hurrying over. I handed her the plates and napkins, and she set them on the table near the cake.

Free from other duties, I walked around the room. The high ceilings and tall windows brought in enough natural light that the overheads seemed almost unnecessary. Windows are hard to come by inside prison, and even those that work inside the Administration building aren't afforded much view to the outside world. It was like living permanently in a Las Vegas casino—the lack of clocks, when combined with the dearth of windows, could make people temporarily forget where they were and how long they'd been there. Without a view to the seasonal changes happening out in the yard—the growing of the grass, the piles of snow drifts, the presence or absence of birds depending on the time of year—no one inside could watch time marching on.

The buildings themselves were built in such a way that all windows that did exist pointed *away* from the closest fence. From my spot in the library, the only fence within my view was all the way on the other side of the yard. On a clear, bright day it nearly blended into the backdrop of the forest on the other side, rendering itself invisible.

On a clear, bright day, even I sometimes forgot I spent my days behind bars.

Out of the corner of my eye I spotted a flash of color, a kaleidoscope of a room that stood out against the stark white walls. Tucked below the guard post was a room full of picture books, all of varying degrees of use and wear, although most landed closer to the falling apart side of the spectrum. The children's reading room. Each institution in Ohio had one, per state policy. They may not all be a separate room like ours, but each facility had an area for visiting kids.

The children's reading room was there for fathers or grandfathers who wanted to use their visitation time for playing or reading to their children. In here, away from the other inmates and visitors, it would be easy to convince a child that everything was normal, at least for the few minutes it took to flip through a picture book. The room also offered crayons and coloring books, and tables and chairs for the children to sit at.

Most of my life, my mom had worked as a preschool teacher. I'd grown up in a house full of picture books and when I worked at the library in my hometown, I loved perusing the shelves of the children's room in search of an old favorite. When I just needed five minutes of downtime between tasks, flipping through a worn copy of *Corduroy* or any of the books by Dr. Seuss was an excellent way to give my brain a break and my spirit a boost. The titles here in the reading room were all familiar, if also a little worse for wear. I made a mental note to see if my mom had any picture books at home she could donate to refresh the small collection.

Awoken from my reverie, I was called back out into the main room to help with rehearsal. As the person in charge of music, I kept skipping the CD back to the start of the song as Dr. Harald appeared and led the inmates into the room and to their seats. After a few rounds, he took them all to the back room, and staff waited and mingled as the room began to fill up with visitors and attendees.

The program was simple and mimicked all graduation programs I myself had attended, including my own. Warden Garcia and Deputy Warden Francis made speeches, commending the inmates for completing their GED, even while incarcerated.

Each inmate grinned as he went up to receive the diploma. Even the ones who were trying to play it cool couldn't suppress the pride they felt, cheesy grins spread wide across their faces. From the audience, family members hooted and hollered as their relative accepted his diploma.

After, as we stood around eating cake and drinking punch, I thought back to my own graduations. For both high school and college, the graduation ceremony was more of an annoyance than anything else. Having to dress up and put on the scratchy polyester cap and gown. Having to sit in uncomfortable chairs for hours, while listening to adults offer life advice. For my undergraduate degree, my creative writing friends and I had stayed out late on a bar crawl the night before. In retrospect, probably not the brightest idea when we had a 9 a.m. graduation the next morning (thanks a lot, College of Arts & Sciences. Couldn't give us one of the afternoon slots, huh?), and I definitely showed up in my black cap and gown slightly hungover. And hell, I didn't even bother going to my graduation for my master's degree. The work was done, the grades turned in, and I'd already passed my final comprehensive exam. I wasn't even going to be getting my diploma that day anyway—the university would be mailing it later.

But as I stood there, a paper plate with a piece of white cake in hand, watching the inmates, I realized how much I had taken my own educational experiences for granted. I'd gone to good schools and had walked away with an advanced degree with very little debt. Graduating from high school at age eighteen was, well, just kind of a given.

What I watched that day wasn't just a graduation ceremony. It was a symbolic dedication and commitment. I went to high school because I had to, and while some of the men were young enough that they were forced into the GED program per state policy, just as many were my age or older. Their decision to get their GED was a conscious choice. They put the work in because they wanted to. They studied and took the test because they saw the value in that education, in that certificate they held in their hands.

The familiar graduation march song, "Pomp and Circumstance," takes its name from the play *Othello*, written by none other than William Shakespeare. The context and meaning of the phrase basically translates to a magnificent ceremony full of splendor and importance.

In this case, I think Shakespeare nailed it.

Chapter 7
Three Strikes, You're Out

It is the policy of the Ohio Department of Rehabilitation and Correction (DRC) that each institution establishes and maintains a recreation and leisure time program for inmates. Recreation programs shall include outdoor exercise depending on climatic conditions. The availability of interaction with the community through recreational activities and leisure time programs shall be limited based upon the security level of the facility and shall be made available in proportion to the inmate population.
—ODRC Policy 77-REC-01

The crack of the bat making contact with the baseball was so loud I could hear it from my desk in the library several yards away.

The slush of March had gone out like a lamb, making room for the fury of warm weather that was April. I had propped open the door of the library, hoping to encourage a warm breeze to blow through. The cliché of librarians wearing cardigans as uniform is not incorrect. We pretty much buy stock in them, as libraries are notoriously cold and drafty. This included my own and while it was warm outside, where the rest of the camp was out in the yard enjoying the first sunshine in months, the library was still struggling to shrug off the last remaining vestiges of winter, leaving a lasting chill.

With the warmer weather came sanctioned outdoor recreational activities and the prison, making a rare surprise move, allowed for the return of baseball.

"There was an 'incident,' " Stephanie explained one day over lunch after the memo about baseball had been sent out. I had taken to eating lunch in her office a couple of times a week, our meals spread out across her desk, while the rest of the Education department ate down the hall in Nancy's classroom. Stephanie was, it turned out, a fellow nerd and while she had not yet given *Doctor Who* a try (despite her husband's, and now my, insistence), we shared a love for *Star Wars* and the *Twilight* series, although our passions diverged at the hero of the tale. (She was head over heels for Edward, while I was a Jacob gal and could not be swayed. Having discovered *Interview with the Vampire* in middle school and shortly thereafter devoured the entire series, I was of the opinion that "Vampires don't sparkle.")

Puzzled, I asked, "What kind of incident?"

"The kind that involves a bat and another

inmate's head," Kwame quipped from the other side of the room.

Horrified, I stared at Stephanie. She nodded in agreement. "So they shut it down. No baseball. That was a few years ago; I guess they decided enough time had gone by they could bring it back."

Bats and balls were checked out from the recreation center, inmates leaving their badge behind like they did here in the library for newspapers. Today was the first game of the new season and if I managed to ignore the neon green jumpsuits on some of the inmates, and the officers in black patrolling the diamond, I could almost forget it was being played inside a prison.

Today, the library was nearly empty, most inmates outside enjoying the first true warm day in months. The baseball diamond was full, with inmates not playing filling the adjacent stands, and even a few correctional officers snatched a few minutes to join the spectators.

I did not have that luxury. I was stuck in the library. Thankfully, I had a large window right next to my desk and all of my attention for the past twenty minutes or so had been focused on the baseball diamond right out in front of my view. I was so caught up in the game—even though I wasn't close enough to be able to get any sense of the score or who was even playing—I didn't notice the inmate hovering by my desk.

161

"Almost make you wish you were outside, doesn't it?"

I turned my gaze from the window and looked at the kid standing in front of me. "Kid" is somewhat of an exaggeration, although I couldn't be sure he was even old enough to legally drink yet. He had shaggy brown hair that he didn't even attempt to control, which framed his pale face and dark brown eyes. Although not wearing glasses, he reminded me a little of Harry Potter, exuding naive innocence and trust that gave everyone the benefit of the doubt.

I vaguely remembered him from orientation just a week or so ago, but he'd been in the library every single day since. He would seek out the quietest corner he could find—not an easy feat in a room the size of a shoebox—and spend the afternoon reading and writing letters.

Slyly, I shifted my eyes quickly to his name badge then back up to his face. Inmate Connor. He really was so young. What had he done to land himself here, I wondered, although I knew statistically it was likely drug related: generally speaking the younger inmates were in on drug charges, while the older inmates were in on drunk driving charges. It wasn't a hard or fast rule, but it was a quick generalization that usually veered close enough to the truth.

When Connor asked me about being outside, I wasn't sure which one he meant, because "outside" has different meanings when you're inside. Not indoors, but *inside*.

For me, of course, it meant the opposite of indoors. Because that's where I was: indoors, in a freezing library on a bright, beautiful spring day when I would much rather be outside, sitting on the metal stands with my colleagues and the inmates watching a baseball game.

To Connor, though, outside meant more than just outside. It meant going home to his family, if he was lucky enough to still have one. (Not all inmates did—many parents, siblings, and significant others were not emotionally or mentally equipped to handle a relative behind bars.) It meant exiting through the front door of the prison rather than being brought in through the back. It meant living a life outside the razor wire.

For both of us, it meant a form of freedom. I was chained to my desk and Connor was chained to the prison, both of us yearning to be outside. The difference was, I had the option sooner rather than later. Just a few more hours and I'd be able to exit through the front door and go home and see my family. If I wanted to, I even had the luxury of going to a *real* baseball game, where there were hot dogs, and Cracker Jacks, and even beer; where I could stand and sing during the seventh inning stretch, and raise my arms during the wave, and share in the warm glow of comradery that comes with watching a beloved team. After, I could leave the ballpark slightly happier than when I had arrived and go home and fall asleep tucked into my own bed, all of my personal belongings within arm's reach.

For the men sitting in the stands outside my window, the choice to watch the baseball game was one of a limited number of options they could have made. But after this baseball game was over, they'd have to go back to their strict regimented lives, where they were told where to sleep and when to eat and where to go. Their own bed was miles away, often clear on the other side of the state, and their personal belongs were whatever state-sanctioned items could fit into a small metal locker box that sat at the foot of the metal bunk beds they slept in.

Looking at Connor, I turned up a single corner of my mouth and nodded. "Yeah," I said, "yeah, it kind of does make me wish I was outside."

He pursed his lips together into a small smile. "Have a nice afternoon, Miss G.," he said, waving goodbye as he exited. I watched him cross the grassy yard and slip into the stands, settling in to watch the baseball game. He disappeared into the crowd and I resumed my window gazing.

I'd been at the prison for a few months and by now, the bright green jumpsuits no longer fazed me, although the strictly regimented time still threw me sometimes. Bunk restriction meant

164

all of the inmates' movements were limited and heavily scheduled, even more so than the general population. The library time was also heavily regulated, with a very strict start and end time, but it was a small pocket of freedom in an otherwise structured day. The inmates on bunk restriction were known to show up before they were allowed in, in which case I would make them wait outside, but they were also known to take their time leaving. Lollygagging, as it were. Slowly folding the newspapers up, making sure all of the corners aligned and the folds were recreased.

Having a set routine while on restriction meant that some inmates I only saw when they were in trouble and in that bright green jumpsuit that designated bunk restriction. They were a deviation from the standard inmate uniform of dark blue pants and light blue shirt; a garish shade of neon green specifically meant to differentiate those on bunk restriction from those in general population.

Inmate Brown never set foot in the library when not on restriction, but he broke rules often enough that he was constantly in and out of the green suit. I honestly wouldn't have been surprised if the Quartermaster just kept a designated jumpsuit set aside specifically for Brown. As such, Brown was a regular patron of the library, although not by choice.

"Brown," I said as he breezed past me. "Sign in."

He stepped back and swiveled on his heel, signing in without a second glance at me. Still silent, he gestured to the newspaper he wanted and the porter made the exchange with his badge. One of the tables up front was open and he took a seat directly in my line of sight.

About fifteen minutes later, I looked over in that direction. Brown stared intently at me, the newspaper abandoned on the table in front of him. At the back of the room, Washington was staring at the back of Brown's head just as intently. He had an inmate in front of him who seemed to be trying to find a particular passage in a legal text, but Washington held up his index finger, indicating he needed a minute, then removed himself from his post behind the law library desk and walked down the aisle.

Washington stopped when he reached Brown and leaned down, whispering something in his right ear. They were too far away for me to hear but whatever Washington said evoked an immediate reaction.

Brown froze, his body jerking with a sudden halt. His hands appeared from under the table and laid flat on the newspaper. With Washington still standing right behind him, Brown slowly rose from his table, gathered the newspaper, and went to the circulation desk to retrieve his badge.

He left the library without a single glance in my direction. It was the first time he had ever left the library early.

When I turned my eyes to the library looking for Washington, he was back behind the law library counter, seemingly hard at work. I went back to work myself.

A few hours later, I was gathering my stuff, the shift over. Washington walked slowly behind the other inmates exiting the library. He lingered in the vicinity of my desk. Only after everyone else had left did he approach me.

"I'm sorry about earlier, Miss G.," Washington explained. "That thing with Brown." He held his familiar stack of file folders close to his body like a shield.

I put down the papers I'd been gathering and looked directly at him, eyebrow raised. "You wanna tell me what that was about?"

Washington hesitated, shifting uncomfortably on the balls of his feet. He was significantly older than most of the other inmates, a majority of whom were in their twenties and thirties. Washington, on the other hand, straddled that line between Boomer and Greatest Generation. Younger than my grandparents, but most definitely older than my parents. Whatever he was about to tell me was not something he wanted to tell a woman young enough to be his granddaughter.

"He had his hand in his pocket." Washington said this with such finality, the period a dead stop, as if it explained everything.

I continued to stare at him, uncomprehending.

He cleared his throat. His eyes shifted around the room as if to make sure nobody could overhear him even though just five minutes ago I had watched him wait until everyone left. "He cuts holes in the pockets. Inside the jumpsuit." Washington whispered this last bit.

I started to shake my head, still not understanding. "Why would he want holes in his . . ."

Then the penny dropped.

Oh.

"Oh. Oh, okay." I repeated his words back to him, walking my way through the logic. "He cuts holes in the pockets. Inside the jumpsuit. So he can . . ." I made a vague gesture with my hand and my voice dropped off as I looked to Washington for confirmation.

Washington nodded imploringly. His eyes gave way to his discomfort at having to be the one to explain the complex realities of prison life to me and the lengths some inmates would go to in order to pleasure themselves in public without getting caught.

Choking the chicken. Spanking the monkey. Shaking hands with Dr. Winky. Insert euphemism of your choice, but whatever you want to call it, masturbation was most definitely against

168

the rules. Inmates of the Ohio Department of Rehabilitation and Correction were not, under any circumstances, allowed to masturbate and, if caught doing so, could be written up and punished.

Necessity is the mother of invention and in the case of Inmate Brown, habitual masturbator, that means cutting or tearing (as it was unlikely he had frequent enough access to scissors) holes in the interior pockets of his pants and jumpsuits so as to have better access to his own bat and balls. This was the kind of game that didn't require an outdoor field—he could do it just about anytime, anywhere.

And apparently anytime, anywhere included the library during his brief time slot. While staring at me, the only woman in the entire room.

In this current age of the #MeToo movement, we have a better understanding of what sexual harassment in the workplace looks like and, make no mistake, having a man masturbate while staring at you as you are trying to go about your job is sexual harassment, regardless of the location of employment. But I didn't have the words for this at the time. I didn't even know what to *do* about this.

Public libraries have policies in place to deal with indecent exposure and inappropriate actions of patrons (and, yes, this sort of thing does happen in the public library sphere. When

I worked in the public library in my hometown, I cannot begin to tell you how many copies of *Cosmopolitan* were found tucked behind the toilet of the men's room, and we also had to keep a careful eye on the swimsuit edition of *Sports Illustrated)*. But I wasn't in a public library and I didn't know how to respond to this, or if I should respond at all. After all, *I* hadn't seen anything and was only being told about it hours after the fact. Writing conduct reports was still fairly new to me and I was still figuring out when were the appropriate moments that called for one to be written.

This was not going to be the first time I'd have a man masturbating in the library and eventually I would get so used to writing conduct reports I could whip one up within minutes. But for now, all I could do was be glad I didn't see anything and just shiver with the grossness of it all. Because as much as I appreciated Washington telling me, I *really* did not need to know.

"Right. Okay, well." I forced a smile. "Thank you for telling me, Washington." I nodded towards the door. "You better get going, don't want to be late for count."

With one final, mournful glance back in my direction, Washington left.

Well. That wasn't awkward or anything.

I had spent the past month just getting used to the security element of this job and I was finally

170

starting to maybe sort of get a handle on it. But now I had to worry about secret spankers in the library, too?

A few weeks later, I found myself standing in the parking lot of the prison, shivering in the early morning air. My eyes widened at the white behemoth parked next to my car. Compared to my Honda Civic, the white van was gargantuan.

Kimberly appeared from the other side, moving towards me away from the lobby. She held up a closed fist but she was too far away for me to be able to see what she was holding.

"Got the keys," she called out as she narrowed the gap between us. When she reached the driver's side door, she opened it and popped the locks. I pulled open the passenger side door and clambered up into the van.

Looking at the spread of a dashboard, I was so glad that a) Kimberly was coming with me, and b) she felt confident enough to drive this because there is no way I was going to manage. This was going to be like navigating a tank down an alley.

I had been forced to wake up at 4 a.m. this morning and requiring to be awake that early for work purposes definitely fell under the "other duties as assigned" portion of my job description. Kimberly and I had to drive down to Columbus together and we had to be there fairly early, which meant meeting up together at the prison earlier than that, and with my hour commute, waking up *really* early.

The van was the prison's official vehicle of choice for prison business. I would have preferred to just drive myself down in my own car: from my apartment it was a quick two hour drive, but with both of us going, Highland wouldn't allow it. Hence, the great white whale we were driving.

Twice a year, the prison librarians from across the great state of Ohio gathered together in the state capital of Columbus for an all-day in-service. While we'd be going over any policy changes that had happened in the past six months and discussing any issues anyone had dealt with, a lot of the day was really just about all of us getting together.

Up until now, I had led a very insular job existence. I was a solo librarian and while Kimberly managed the library during my Monday absences, she mostly just babysat. Any inmates with library-related questions were directed to return the next day when I was there.

I knew there were other prison librarians out there. Ohio alone had thirty institutions, which meant at least as many librarians. Some were big enough to require more than one full-time librarian. But the only ones I'd had any real contact with were Grace, the state prison librarian who oversaw all of us, and Connie, the librarian at our sister institution a couple of hours away.

Even then, though, all of our communication had been over email. Connie had introduced herself to me via email shortly after I started, and Grace mostly wrote emails strongly reminding people to send in their monthly statistics report (how many books were checked out, how many visitors came to the library, etc.) in a timely fashion.

Today, however, I'd get to meet them in person. And not just the two persons with whom I'd had somewhat regular contact, but all of the librarians and library assistants that worked within our system. I had no idea what to expect. New people make me nervous, as there's so much pressure to socialize and make a good impression. I always feel awkward and out-of-place in these types of settings. At the same time, though, while I was anxious, because mine was such an insular job, I was also excited to meet my colleagues in the field.

It was going to take us two hours to get down to Columbus and we sat quiet for most of the first hour of the drive, neither of us awake enough to make passable conversation. Somewhere around our halfway point of Mansfield—filming location for *The Shawshank Redemption*—I commented that I was looking forward to meeting all of the other prison librarians.

There was a pause. "I'm going to warn you," Kimberly finally responded, her eyes never leaving the road. "Some of the librarians are kind of . . . weird."

I peeled my eyes from the rolling hills of central Ohio and turned to look at her. "Weird how?"

"Just weird. You'll see."

Librarian stereotypes are common, especially coming from people outside of the field like Kimberly. Usually we librarians are defined in one of two ways: the flirty sex kitten who just needs some encouragement and then it's glasses off, hair down, party time; or the dowdy, matronly cat lady (under which the flirty sex kitten often is thought to be hiding). As a librarian, I of course knew this was incorrect, and took Kimberly's "weird" descriptive with a grain of salt. Then again, I was (and still am) an introvert with almost antisocial tendencies, well on her way to being one of those "crazy" cat ladies. To many people, *I* was probably weird.

The State Library of Ohio is a square building that sits snuggly in the middle of a Columbus neighborhood on the northern side of the city. It is surrounded by three major freeways, making it, if nothing else, easy to access, an important feature for a meeting that had librarians driving from all corners of the state. Nowadays, the area is one of Columbus's more trendy neighborhoods, with hip restaurants and brand new condos. At the time, though, there was abandoned construction and abandoned buildings lining the street. The juxtaposition was striking.

Kim pulled the van into the full parking lot,

opting for a space in the back to allow room to maneuver. We climbed down and I followed her into the nondescript building.

The front door led to a large, open lobby that consisted of wall-to-wall meeting rooms. I followed Kimberly down the hall, but my focus was distracted by the large room of books directly ahead of us. Before I had a chance to take a closer peek at the main section and examine the contents, Kimberly turned into the last meeting room on the left. I quickly followed.

It was like taking a time machine and entering my high-school cafeteria all over again, minus the lukewarm pizza, cold fries, and humiliation.

Long rows of tables and chairs faced the front of the room, pockets of people sandwiched throughout. Dead center were the "Popular Girls" in the room. The two slender white women—one a brunette, the other blonde—looked like they could have been cast in the *Real Housewives of Ohio*. With perfectly coiffed hair and fresh manicures, they looked like the type of women who had never gotten a papercut in their lives, let alone worked around books all day. Meanwhile, my waist-length red hair had been left to air dry on the drive down after an early morning, leaving it limp and frazzled, although I at least had managed to put on mascara. Clearly, Kimberly's reference to any weird librarians didn't include those two women.

The goddess-like pair chatted cheerfully with each other. Too cheerfully if you asked me, the one who had been awake since 4 a.m.

Like a stone thrown into a pond, the remaining librarians radiated outward from there. Huddled groups said hello, greeting each other for the first time in at least six months. At the outer rings were those librarians without any friends here. The ones who sat alone, hunched over a book. Ah. Those were the ones Kimberly probably meant by "weird."

"That's Grace," Kimberly said, pointing to a woman at the front of the room. Grace towered over us, tall and intimidating. She kept her gray hair cropped close to her skull and even just standing still managed to convey a level of intimidation that radiated across the room. If this really was my high school lunchroom all over again, she'd be the lone wolf who was too cool for school. She also threw shade as if it was as light and airy as a Frisbee, her snark well documented even in emails. It was not an easy feat, as sarcasm often gets lost in translation when it comes to written communication, but not with Grace. Her tone was always on point.

Kimberly and I stood off to the side of the room, silent. After two hours in the van on the way down, we'd officially run out of things to say to each other. At least temporarily.

A plump woman in head-to-toe black,

including, literally, the hair on her head, came over. Her fingers were weighed down with heavy rings while her neckline was decked with costume jewelry. "I'm Connie!" she said excitedly. She clasped my hand into both of hers, the metal from her rings cold against my skin. Connie was peppy and effervescent, like the school mascot hired to pump people up before the big game.

Connie was my counterpart at our sister institution, which was located on the far east side of Cleveland. We'd exchanged a few emails here and there, and she had invited me out to visit her library a couple of times, although the timing had never worked out. I shook her hand warmly, happy to finally have a face to put to a name.

As the room started to fill, I looked around and started to gather what Kimberly meant when she said some of the librarians were "weird," although a more discerning eye would call them "socially awkward." Every stereotypical high school has its set of cheerleaders, just as it has its set of highly intelligent academic whizzes who lack social tact, along with that one girl who just loved her bedazzled sweatshirts and was destined to live alone with her ten cats.

Although I didn't own a bedazzler, my love of cats had already been well-established from a young age. In high school, I was more of the artistic variety of student, involved in theater and choir. I eschewed athletics, preferring to put my energy into drama club. As a senior, I did letter . . . but in marching band. So the ones Kimberly called "weird" were the ones I would have been friends with in high school.

But even several years past high school, I was still socially awkward, and also nervous at being surrounded by strangers and colleagues, so I stayed silent and merely hovered around Kimberly. She'd been coming to these meetings long enough to know everyone. In the future I'd be attending alone but for today, I was content to let her act as my cruise director.

From her position at the front of the room, Grace called out. "Okay, everyone. Take your seats. We're going to get started soon." I followed Kimberly's lead and she took us to the far left side of the room, about two or three rows back. As soon as we sat down, there was a "Psst. Kim!" from behind us. We both turned and saw two men sitting next to each other. The older of the two, patches on his tweed jacket, raised his hand and waved. Kim waved back.

"James and Lawrence," she explained in a whisper, turning back to the front. "They work across the street."

Puzzled, I mentally reconstructed the scene outside the state library. Was there a prison across the . . . oh. Oh, right, Kimberly meant across the street from *us*. Yeah, that made way more sense.

Lawrence was the head prison librarian at Lorain Correctional, James, his assistant. Later, during lunch, James explained that Lorain is a closed camp. Unlike our prison, which had an open yard and our inmates were free to move around and go from place to place, at Lorain they were herded like sheep, with a set day and time everyone was allowed to visit the library.

"We have a new member," Grace called out to the group while looking at me. I stood and gave an awkward wave. "Jill is working with Kimberly, who has been joining us at these in the interim. Welcome, Jill."

I sat down amid the polite applause as Grace continued on with the agenda. Now, my brain was so overwhelmed with information and people that apparently my memory was unable to hold on to any of it, because I can't remember a single thing from the program of that day. The agenda of the other meetings that I attended over the duration of my time tells me that we probably talked about new policies that had been put into place for the prisons, and various issues that my colleagues had been dealing with at their facilities. I came to learn that not all of the institutions had a security staff as supportive of the library as the officers at ours. All of the guards I had come to know in my first few months of my employment found the library to be a positive space at the prison and encouraged the inmates' use of it.

At the end of the very long day, Kimberly and I climbed back into the white van and headed north back to Grafton so she could drop the van off and we could each head home. My brain was full and buzzing with information. It felt like my first day all over again.

I had been working for the prison for about three months and I admittedly still had no idea what the hell I was doing. Most days I was making it up as I went along.

But I had also been there long enough to see gaps that could be filled and solutions that I could implement. For one thing, we needed to move away from the circulation card system and introduce an OPAC or computer database. It would take some convincing—additional computers meant additional opportunities for the inmates to get online—but it was necessary and very much needed. I also needed to rework the ILL, or interlibrary loan program. As I worked my way through the pile of books that had been left behind, I realized that some of them were library books that belonged to the State Library. That is, the library I was sitting in: the previous librarian had borrowed them for the inmates to read when they requested a book we didn't have. Only somehow, in her absence, they had been forgotten, and we ended up owing some hefty fines. That said, it was a powerful program and a good way to introduce content into the prison that we just did not have the budget for. It would need some tweaking and, again, lots of convincing, but it was also something that was necessary.

Just a few months ago I had stepped onto the yard for the first time terrified and unsure of everything. While I was still unsure of most things and constantly stumbled and fell down, I was starting to really find my footing.

PART II
WE'RE ALL MAD HERE

"But I don't want to go among mad people," Alice remarked.

"Oh, you can't help that," said the Cat: "we're all mad here. I'm mad. You're mad."

"How do you know I'm mad?" said Alice.

"You must be," said the Cat, "or you wouldn't have come here."

—Lewis Carroll,
Alice's Adventures in Wonderland

Chapter 8
New Sheriff in Town

It is the policy of the Ohio Department of Rehabilitation and Correction (DRC) to require the managing officer, deputy wardens, and administrative duty officers (ADO) to make unannounced visits to the institution's living and activity areas at least weekly to encourage informal contact with staff and inmates and to informally observe living and working conditions.

—ODRC 50-PAM-02

A new season had dawned, and summer was here at last. I'd been at the prison for six months and was finally starting to feel comfortable. With the change in season, came a change in the administration of the prison: Deputy Warden Francis's job as second-in-command was being split into two.

Now, instead of there being one Deputy Warden who handled both the security and the programming side, Francis would now be known as the Deputy Warden of Operations and the facility was actively recruiting for a Deputy Warden of Special Services. This role would focus on the non-security side of things. The "softer skills" so to speak, of a prison. Recreation. Commissary. Education. And, naturally, the library.

As soon as news went out that there was a new opening, the staff began gossiping about possible internal recruits.

"I think Dr. Harald's going to apply," Kim confessed one day over lunch. Dr. Harald was off that day, an occurrence that was becoming more and more frequent, especially on either Friday or Mondays (or both). My usual lunch companion, Stephanie, was also off so I found myself eating with the other Education staff members for the first time in months.

"Really?" I asked, picking at the sloppy pile of black beans in front of me. It took a couple of months, but eventually I started getting the free lunch offered to staff members. As a vegetarian, the options were limited: if it wasn't some bland beans and rice combination, it was a small pat of peanut butter, an even smaller pat of grape jelly, and two sad, flimsy pieces of white bread. Still, my pay was low and my downtown rent high. A free meal was a free meal.

I had a hard time imagining Dr. Harald in a position so high up the prison hierarchy. He was . . . *fine* as a manager. He took a hands-off approach, which for our team here in the Education department was probably the appropriate way to manage. We all had our own tasks, did our own things, and knew we could go to him when needed.

That said, for Dr. Harald, taking a hands-off approach often meant turning a blind eye to some of Kim's more questionable absences. Eventually, though, I noticed that Kim had a tendency to take advantage of Dr. Harald's blind spot, rarely ever working a full week. It was like she had unlimited vacation and sick time, while the rest of us were constantly reminded to not go over our allotted time off hours. It was frustrating, to say the least, and did not endear her to me.

Still, her prediction was right: a few weeks later, Dr. Harald appeared at work in his suit. I'd only ever seen him wear it for graduation; after all, our dress code was business casual and Dr. Harald's standard, everyday uniform was khakis with a polo bearing the prison's logo. A suit stood out.

Even if I couldn't really imagine him in the position, he was their best bet. He already led a department within the purview of the Special Services department and had been at the prison since it had opened. He knew the facility and the inmates and he was fairly well-liked. I mean, if they wanted an internal candidate, who else were they going to hire?

"Highland?" I asked Stephanie over lunch after the announcement had been made. "Highland-Highland. Meredith Highland, Head of HR

Highland?" I shook my head in disbelief. "That seems . . ."

"Weird," Stephanie confirmed, her head bobbing in agreement. "Really weird."

"Like . . ." my voice dropped off as I parsed my thoughts. "I just don't *get* it."

Highland was head of Human Resources. She spent all of her time up in a windowless office in the Administration building, rarely stepping foot onto the yard. She had no reason to. She was the prison's Human Resources person. That is, HR for the staff. It was never necessary for her to interact with the inmates, let alone walk over the red line of delineation. If any of us needed her human resources expertise, we all knew where to find her up in the Admin building.

It was just such a *bizarre* promotion. Dr. Harald I would have understood—for him, it would have been a step straight up the ladder. But this . . . the head of HR getting the position of what was essentially co-second in command of the entire prison was kind of like that time Harry Potter tried to use Floo Powder for the first time and instead of saying "Diagon Alley" he said *diagonally* and ended up in Knockturn Alley. The trajectory was skewed.

Soon, though, I started to suspect that Highland had used her insider knowledge to her advantage. As someone who worked in Administration, she saw this prison from the inside out. Highland knew where the gaps were, both in staffing and policies. Presumably, she went into her interview with a plan of attack.

Highland was on a mission. Highland was going to whip every part of this place into shape, come hell or high water.

And, as I was soon going to come to learn, the library was one of the first objectives on her list.

"Hello, Ms. G.," Highland said politely, opening the log book. "How's the library?"

"Uh, fine," I said. Since taking over her new role as Deputy Warden of Special Services, Highland had made a commitment to keeping up with weekly rounds of the facility, something her predecessor rarely did. I had never interacted much with Deputy Francis: once in a while she'd stop by the library on her rounds. But her visits were few and far between, and even when she did stop by, it was just long enough to sign her name into the log as proof that she had visited. The library, it seemed, was so far down her list of priorities she just . . . didn't care. Granted, in a job where you had to balance an outdated copy of the Encyclopedia Britannica against homemade shivs, well, I could understand her apathy.

Not so with Highland. Because of the new job split, all of her attention could be focused on the sort of softer side of institutional living. Highland not only consistently came once a week on rounds, she always stayed for several minutes to analyze the state of the space, and chat with the inmates.

She signed her name in the log in a single flourish. "So," she said. She closed the log book and leaned forward, eyes trained on me with laser focus. "About the books."

The . . . books? I wondered. It was a library; we were literally standing in a room full of books. I needed more context.

I shook my head. "I'm not sure . . ."

"The books," she said, raising her eyebrows. "The donated books."

Right. *Those* books. The hundreds of books sitting on the metal shelf behind me. The books I had, for the most part, pretty much forgotten all about. In the beginning I had been all gung ho about cataloging the books and adding them to the collection, but as the months went on, my interest level declined and they had spent the past six months sitting in a state of neglect. There were too many books and not enough shelf space. Plus there was that spreadsheet to contend with. Every month or so a few would get added, but it was haphazard at best. A frustrating and terrible way of keeping track of the books in the collection.

Clearly, this whole "pretend the books don't exist and maybe they'll catalog themselves" tactic was no longer going to work out for me.

"Yes," I said with a nod. "Yes, the books."

Her eyes narrowed ever so slightly, just for a flash. Then she smiled. "Good!" she said, straightening. "Glad to know we are on the same page."

She turned to leave; today was a short visit apparently. As she passed through the vestibule, she pointed to the whiteboard hanging on the wall. "I like the new addition," she said on her way out the door.

The whiteboard was not new. My use of it, however, was. For months it had sat empty, since I was just never entirely sure how to fill all that white space. Then, one quiet afternoon, I was wasting time online. One of my favorite websites to visit when I had downtime was History.com, the website for the History channel. They always had a feature called *This day in History* where they compiled a list of various events that happened on that day in history and I always found it interesting to see what happened when. That, I realized, was a perfect use of the whiteboard! Every morning, I would pick a different history factoid to highlight and put it on the whiteboard. Even if the inmates never paid attention to it, I'd at least know I was doing something productive to try and draw the inmates into the library.

Another thing I had started doing to draw inmates in was to revamp the interlibrary loan program. This was something that Dr. Harald had suggested early on in my time here, and while it sounded like a very simple request, after taking a look at the situation, I knew that it was going to be far more complicated and require so much more time.

The program had required a *complete* restart, beginning with mailing back all of the State Library titles currently in our possession and long overdue. Once they were checked back into their home library, Dr. Harald signed the necessary paperwork to have the couple hundred dollar late fees paid off so we had a clean slate, financially at least, with the system.

From what limited paperwork I could find related to how Miss Christy had managed the previous ILL program, the inmates were told they would be held responsible if books were returned late, but there hadn't been any accountability or follow-through.

There also didn't appear to even be a list of any kind to keep track of the books. The State Library had an online portal I could sign into to request books, so I was able to identify which books were supposed to be in our possession, but there was no paper trail once they arrived here at the prison. I had searched through every file on my computer and dug through every drawer of the filing cabinet. It's as if the books arrived here and Miss Christy sent them out into the general population and just hoped the inmates would return them.

Granted, that's what we do with library books every day, but it's different when they are books the library is borrowing from another library. There needs to be some kind of *system* in place. Otherwise, libraries end up in the mess that I had, with overdue books and missing books and books that ended up on our own library shelves. More than once, I had one of my porters bring me a book that somebody wanted to check out but they couldn't find the card in the back. This, of course, was because there was no card, because it wasn't one of the prison's books, but an ILL book that had been mis-shelved.

Miss Christy, I was finding, had not been the most organized individual.

With Dr. Harald, and now Highland's blessing, I had reworked the system from the ground up. Now, I kept a running log of all books requested via ILL. I knew the date when the inmate requested it, when I had ordered it, when it arrived at the prison, what day the inmate returned it to me and, finally, what day I put it in the mail to be returned to the State Library.

No longer would there be books lost in the prison. At least that was the plan, and to help make sure inmates returned them, I instituted a fine policy.

Incarcerated individuals are given a sort of bank

account inside. All money they earn from their job goes there, in addition to any money family and friends add to the account. If they have a need to pay for something, like commissary or copies made in the library, they sign a cash slip that indicates how much will be removed from their account.

If I wanted the inmates to take this seriously, to understand the ramifications that came with losing a book that didn't belong to us, then I needed to hold them financially accountable. So before I would release an ILL book to an inmate, I made him pre-sign a cash slip made out for the list price on the book. The cash slip was collateral: if the book was lost or damaged, I would turn that into Administration and he'd be charged for the replacement cost of the book.

Once the ILL system was up and running, I had some inmates who would return the book and ask to watch me destroy the cash slip right there in front of them, which I was always more than happy to do. So far, all books had been returned to me on time and back to the State Library on time, too. No fines on my watch.

Even better, when developing the system, I had carefully and deliberately documented all of the steps to request books, and log books, and check out books, so that on my days off, there wasn't any disruption of the ILL service and inmates would still get their books.

At least, that's how it was supposed to work. In reality, Kim would just tell the inmates to come back on Tuesday when I returned.

Unfortunately for the inmates, after providing a steady and consistent presence for the past few months, I had my own orientation coming up and was about to be out of the library for two full weeks. I just had to hope that all of the systems I'd implemented over the past several months meant the library would still be standing when I returned.

Chapter 9
Finder's Keepers

The institution library staff shall develop a written plan for the selection of inmates to work as library aides. Institution staff shall ensure that inmate library staffing is accomplished in an equitable manner, reflecting the composition of the inmate population.
— *ODRC Policy 58-LIB-02*

Hands on hips, I cocked my head to the side, sizing up the bed in front of me. It was a narrow twin, tucked into one corner of the small concrete room. A solitary window sat high above. The frame was dark metal, the mattress slim and worn. As someone who slept on a quilted-top, queen-sized mattress, I couldn't fathom getting any sleep on such a paltry piece of bedding. Then again, I suppose if you're in prison, you shouldn't presume to be allowed a luxurious bed. After all, as the saying goes, it's "three hots and a cot." Nowhere does it promise anything of quality, in either the food or the bed choice.

I surveyed the room. Everyone else was focused on what they could see right in front of them, the taller people taking advantage of their height by extending an arm into the hard-to-reach nooks of the room.

When I was growing up, my mom had gifted me her original hardcover copies of Nancy Drew. I had devoured the series, the collection of yellow books given their own shelf on my bookcase. As a young writer myself, I entertained dreams of writing my own character that would be as iconic in the American lexicon as Nancy Drew. Only later did I learn that Carolyn Keene was a pseudonym used by multiple ghostwriters over the years. Carolyn didn't exist; she never had. She was a literary patchwork, Nancy her quilt.

Still, Nancy Drew, along with Harriet the Spy, fostered my early love of mysteries. They were a game, murder mystery novels. A race against the pages: could I solve the end before I got to the big reveal? Sometimes I did, sometimes I didn't. Either way, my love of reading mysteries had instilled in me a curious eye, an ability to read outside the box and look for clues.

That's when I realized that everyone else in the room was looking up. Nobody was looking *down*.

I smiled to myself.

Crouching, I got on my stomach and scooted forward to peer under the bed. The mattress above blocked out all light, but even as I peered into the shadows I knew there was nothing but cobwebs under there. *Damn*. I'd been so sure.

Dusting the front of my clothes off, I stood up.

I grabbed one of the metal bed posts at the head of the bed for balance, then hoisted myself up onto the mattress.

Standing on top of the thin mattress, I was able to look out the window onto the yard. From this vantage, I spotted the small square patch of land that had been roped off and utilized by the dog trainers. Everywhere else around the yard, the dogs had to be on a leash and kept close, but the prison had set up the corner of grass as a mini dog park; an area where the canines at least could get a small taste of freedom.

I looked down slightly and spotted a tube of toothpaste sitting on the concrete ledge of the window. Beside it was a crusty, used toothbrush. With its bristles going every which way, the toothbrush appeared to have woken up with a bad case of bedhead.

After putting the toothbrush back down, I picked up the tube of toothpaste. It looked full, new almost. Yet, sitting in the palm of my hand, it was too light to be full of toothpaste. It was too light to be full of anything, really. But something was definitely in there. I just had to figure out what and how it got in there to begin with.

I unscrewed the cap and peered down the mouth of the tube but was unable to see anything. Hmmm. Maybe if I felt around, like a kid on Christmas trying to guess what was underneath the wrapping paper, I'd be able to figure out what was inside. I held the tube between my middle finger and thumb and squeezed. Nothing happened.

But when I squeezed at the sides, the bottom of the tube of toothpaste flared open, like the gaping mouth of a fish. My eyes widened. I flipped the toothpaste over and stared down into the belly of the tube: snaked and coiled inside was a cluster of black wire.

Grinning, I raised my hand triumphant. "Found one!" I cried.

From his spot leaning against the door frame, Williard beamed. "Miss G found a tattoo gun," he informed the room. The others paused in their own searches to pass along their congratulations.

Huh. A tattoo gun. I knew I had found *something,* I just wasn't sure what. Staring at the pile of wires stuffed into the white plastic shell of the tube, *tattoo gun* was not what I was anticipating. As someone who already had a tattoo, I'm not entirely sure I would have trusted an ink job done using wires confiscated from around the facility.

Williard's game of hide-and-seek was part of orientation, a mandatory two-week-long program that every staff member needed to pass in order to work at the prison. And by "pass," I mean there were tests and quizzes and everything. My particular orientation class was made up of six of us. I was the only one *not* training to be a correctional officer.

I was also the only one who had already been working at the prison for six months.

State law dictated that, technically speaking, I was supposed to have gone through orientation *before* I set foot in the yard. But, desperate times and all of that. Our prison was unique in that orientation was held right at our facility. Recently hired employees at other facilities in the state would have to go down to Columbus for their training. What my prison got in terms of convenience, however, they sacrificed in the name of frequency. All training was done in-house, using current staff members and pulling them away from their positions. It took coordination of schedules and shifting of security concerns to make sure orientation didn't disrupt the ecosystem. As such, they only held it a few times a year.

Which is how I ended up with six months under my belt before getting trained. Because of the way Christy was hastily and unceremoniously fired from the job for her alleged relationship with Jefferson, the prison had been forced to quickly fill the position, training be damned. The only part of the onboarding process they could not hold off was the unarmed self-defense class I took a few days before starting.

For the past few days, my new coworkers and I had sat in a classroom in the Administration building watching training videos and listening to other employees give presentations on all areas of prison life. We learned about the different job vocations the inmates had, including the barber services where, it turns out, employees can get their hair cut for a mere $2. As we were a facility with a strong substance-abuse program, my friend Stephanie came in and spoke about the differences between drinking and binge drinking and alcoholism. We were even taught about the differences in generations: after all, the men we managed ranged in age from the Greatest Generation all the way down to boys barely out of high school.

The best lessons were the ones that dug in deep and got into the dirty side of the prison. In one of the more memorable sessions, Catalina, former Ohio State Patrolman and our in-house investigator, came in and spoke to us about Security Threat Groups.

In other words, gangs.

HH. 88. Lightning bolts. These are all signifiers of white supremacist groups. HH is a call out to "Heil Hitler." H is the eighth letter of the alphabet. The SS lightning bolts are taken from the Schutzstaffel (SS), the organization in charge of the police state in Nazi Germany. Their ranks included the Gestapo and the armed officers at the concentration camps.

Within the context of gangs, these symbols are utilized as callouts to other members of the group. They are identifiers, sort of like the Deathly Hallows or Dark Mark symbols in the Harry Potter series.

Even now, ten years after the final book was published, the Deathly Hallows symbol holds a meta status. Not only does it continue to exist the way it always has in the books, but that status as an identifier has transcended the written word. I know when I see someone with any kind of Deathly Hallows insignia that they are a fellow fan of the series. I wear my own bracelet with the Deathly Hallows charm so fellow fans can identify *me*.

Gang tattoos operate under a similar fashion, albeit a bit more permanently. That's not a coincidence, of course, as members usually don't have the option to just casually walk away from a gang as one can from a fandom.

But they are also a code because, of course, white supremacists aren't stupid: they know that tattooing the name of Adolf Hitler on their body would get them a serious side-eye outside of the prison, while inside it would be like painting a target on their back when it came to the Administration and correctional officers.

But, the security side of things isn't stupid, either. This is why my orientation classmates and I sat through slideshow after slideshow of insignias that have gang affiliations, so we can identify them when out in the yard.

It's not just white supremacists, either. Notorious rival gangs Crips and Bloods have their own symbols and tattoos as well. It goes even deeper than that, though. For certain security threat groups, it's not just some organization you are a member of. It's a community, a family. It's a way of *life*.

Part of the intake and reception process upon arrival at the prison includes having all of an inmate's identifying marks, such as tattoos, logged. This way, it's easier to know when an inmate gets a new tattoo while incarcerated.

Which is where Williard's game came in.

For his orientation section, Williard spoke about contraband. Contraband is basically anything that is not approved by Administration and Security. Both inmates and staff can be guilty of bringing in contraband. It's why staff bags were searched every day when we came in for work.

After his presentation, Williard took us out of the concrete classroom that had been our home for the past two weeks, and led us down the walkway to the medical unit. I'd never been inside before, though I had heard plenty of inmates talk about it when it came to having doctor and dentist appointments. It's not like they could book an appointment at their doctor back home, so medical treatments were done in-house. I didn't know what to expect, but it looked just like a regular doctor's office. I don't know why this surprised me so much—after all, the prison library looked just like a regular library. Why shouldn't the medical unit be the same?

One of the empty medical units had been outfitted with examples of contraband, tucked and hidden all over the room. Our job was to find it all. My history of reading mysteries served me well, because of all the contraband hidden in that room, I was the first one to find anything.

While I was up in Administration for my two weeks of orientation, the library was managed by my coworkers on a rotating shift. I wasn't too worried though: in the six months since I started, I had been afforded the opportunity to start bringing in my own porters to work the circulation desk and law library.

First there was Lincoln.

Lincoln was a gentle giant. He'd been on the wait list to work in the library since his first day. After several months of asking when it would be his turn, I finally had an opening, needed an African American to keep the ratio balanced, and Lincoln's name was next on the list. He was well-read and articulate, and would come in and work even when he wasn't on the schedule. For him, the library was a safe haven. He knew that if he was in the library, it meant he wasn't going to be in a situation where he could possibly get into trouble.

Next was Booker. Quiet and shy, Booker reminded me of myself when I first started working in my hometown library and would get panic attacks when asked to work the circulation desk. Booker would work the circulation desk if asked, but he much preferred being in the stacks, putting recently returned books away or shelf reading and making sure things were in order. Most of the other inmates disliked that part of the job—they preferred interacting with all the patrons that came in to read books or magazines. But I understand how Booker felt and as long as there was enough coverage at the desk, I was more than happy to let him be the one to voluntarily put the books away. Someone had to do it, after all.

After Booker had been on the job for a while, he recommended his friend Hoskins when there was an open position that needed to be filled. Hoskins was slightly older than Booker—in his fifties or sixties—and wore thin, wiry glasses that matched his thin, wiry frame.

Friendships in prison are fascinating to watch, especially with men who didn't know each other on the outside. It's not uncommon to have guys from the same block or even relatives end up in prison together. Those natural bonds of companionship extend into the prison, a natural friendship in an extreme situation.

But for men like Booker and Hoskins, who didn't

have friends or family inside (at least not at our prison), friendships still sprout among the garden of incarceration. Neither Booker nor Hoskins had loved ones in the immediate area, so they were always willing to work on the weekends—with visitation every Saturday, it was sometimes difficult to find men to work that day when they knew they had a standing visiting appointment.

Watching them together, they reminded me of Red and Andy in Stephen King's *Rita Hayworth and the Shawshank Redemption*. Minus, y'know, the contraband and escape and all of that.

Although Red was played by Morgan Freeman in the film version, in the original story, he and Andy were both white, just like Booker and Hoskins. Like Red, Hoskins was far more extroverted. He loved the people-to-people interaction that came with working the circulation desk, and while he would put the books back on the shelf when asked, it wasn't his favorite thing to do. He much preferred the conversations that came with the desk, and was naturally loud when he spoke.

Booker, as previously mentioned, was quiet and introverted, just like Andy Dufresne.

They were two peas in a pod and yet complete opposites. Then again, isn't that how so many friendships are? They complemented each other well and their shared energy served the library and its patrons tremendously.

I also had hired a new employee for the law library. Jackson was still there, but Koch had been released, so now I had McDougal. He was loud and brash, and some of the other inmates found him abrasive, but when it came to the law library and the information inside of it, McDougal knew his shit. With the law library in particular it was important to have someone who knew how the system worked. Who knew which forms to provide, which court cases to look up to help solidify an inmate's case.

That said, not all of my hiring choices were successful.

Hoskins once told me that the library was the most popular place to work. *Everyone* wanted a job in the library. It was indoors, with heating in the winter, and while we didn't have air-conditioning, there were big box fans that I kept circulating through all of the warmer months. But there were also chairs for the porters behind both the circulation desk and the law library desk. I didn't think much of this until I realized that there were very few job assignments where the inmates could just *sit*. Hell, there were very few places in the prison in general where the inmates could just sit and be. They were herded, like cattle, around the camp, always told to keep moving, no loitering.

Plus, Hoskins told me, I had a good reputation as a manager. I was firm with the rules, both for my workers and the men who used the library, but I was also fair. I was consistent in my firmness: I wouldn't allow one inmate to get away with something, only to draw the line with another.

Because of this, the waiting list to get a job at the library increased with each month, but as established inmates were released and gaps were created that needed to be filled, my choice in which inmate to choose always came down to the race of the inmate that had left, since I was required to keep a racially balanced group.

Morton had been on the wait list for months and after Jefferson—the inmate that had allegedly had an inappropriate relationship with my predecessor—had been released, I was finally able to bring Morton on board.

Unfortunately, Morton was one of those inmates who only wanted to work in the library because he thought it was an easy gig, what with the whole indoor seating part of the position. He was combative and resistant to instruction. Even training him was a struggle, as he didn't like being told what to do, even within the context of his job. Maybe his distaste was because the instructions were coming from me, a woman, or from one of the other inmates who had been at the job longer that I had tasked to show Morton the ropes.

But removing an inmate from a job assignment was a bureaucratic nightmare of paperwork, so

I admittedly chose the path of least resistance and assigned Morton to the minimum required amount of hours. It was the easiest solution.

There were others, of course: Webb, the diminutive man with the raspy voice of a smoker who looked like Denis Leary; Conway, all gangly limbs and red hair, his white skin giving away his Irish heritage; Carlton, with a pick in his afro and wearing thick retro glasses long before hipsters; and Peck, quiet and attentive to details, the circulation cards quickly alphabetized with the speed of a card shark in his dark hands.

After six months, I honestly wasn't sure I *liked* being a manager, but if Morton's attitude was my only issue, I think I was fairly okay at it.

Chapter 10
Bat out of Hell

Program/work supervisors may make referrals to the Program/Work Assignment Committee for non-routine program/work assignments for inmates. The committee shall review all requests and complete the assignment unless sufficient reasons exist to make an exception.
—ODRC Policy 54-WRK-02

"Yo, Ms. G. I thought you quit."

I turned from my spot at the newspaper station to look at Doyle. He stood in front of the circulation desk, badge in hand, ready to hand it over. His blonde hair had been washed by the sun, lighter even than normal. "Nah," I said, grabbing the latest edition of the *Cincinnati Enquirer* for him. "You aren't going to get rid of me that easy."

Doyle guffawed. He flapped his hand in the international sign of "oh, you" and took a seat in the back.

Orientation was officially over. At least for this year—every year going forward I'd have to sit through a brief refresher course going over the most important talking points. On the final orientation exam, I—the only one not on the security side—was also the only one to get a 100 percent on the test, which delighted Highland to no end.

I also managed to earn us a few bonus points right before the exam when Lieutenant Hall asked us a trivia question: What was the name of the first music video to air on MTV? While my colleagues offered up Michael Jackson's "Thriller" and A-HA's "Take On Me," I loudly and vehemently proclaimed the correct answer was "Video Killed the Radio Star." There was one holdout, who was convinced it was Michael Jackson, but he was outvoted by the rest and we went with my answer, which, of course was correct.

Pro tip: if you're building your own trivia team, consider adding a librarian to the mix. Our heads are filled with the most random pieces of information. In fact, in grad school, my classmates and I spent every Wednesday at a bar near campus for Trivia Night. Our team was called the Do Me Decimals (as in Dewey Decimal. We were so clever) and we consistently drank our share of free beer for winning.

Pro tip: If *I* am the librarian on your trivia team, listen to me when I am adamant about an answer. Like, obnoxiously, insistently adamant. Because I only get obstinate about things I know are right. So even if everyone else on the team is pretty sure *Dead Man Walking* was directed by Sean Penn and I'm in my little corner insisting it was Tim Robbins, please listen to me. (What? No, I am not still salty about that point we lost. Why do you ask?)

Whatever. The cheese stands alone.

Because staff orientation ran Monday through Friday, by the end of the two week break, I had earned a three-day weekend. But, it was now Tuesday and I was back in the library. During my absence, the library had been covered by my coworkers. Kimberly continued her usual Monday coverage but the rest of the days saw a rotating door of coworkers sitting at my desk, many of them from Administration. It had probably been years since several of them had crossed the bright red "no inmates beyond this point" line and entered the yard.

The subs' only role was to maintain order. They were overpaid babysitters, even more so than Kimberly on her regular day. Kimberly at least had a vague, general idea of how the library functioned and she'd been doing it for years. For everyone else, this was way outside both their comfort zone and job description.

One coworker in particular, Ms. Driver, worked in Administration and while she only had to sacrifice a few hours total to covering the library, she had decided to use that time to reorganize and rearrange my work space. Whatever setup

I had wasn't working for her, so she just took it upon herself to change it. "You're welcome!" she indicated on the note left on my desk. The hand drawn smiley face did not alleviate my annoyance.

But, after two weeks away, I needed to jump back into the job. The work space would have to be dealt with later.

Ten minutes after we opened for the afternoon, Lincoln hustled in. He pushed his way past the standing line of inmates waiting for newspapers and joined me behind the desk. "I'm sorry I'm late, Ms. G. They were giving me trouble back at the house." He began taking badges from inmates and exchanging them for newspapers.

"It's fine," I said, taking a step back from the newspapers and letting him take over. "Did I miss anything?"

Lincoln shook his head. "I'm just glad you're back. That Driver, man." He raised a hand and gestured to the new arrangement.

I grimaced. "I noticed."

"We couldn't really stop her—"

"No, no, it's okay."

He opened his mouth but before he could say anything more, he was interrupted by another inmate calling my name.

"Ms. G.! You're back!"

I turned from Lincoln to see Woodson standing at my desk, a tremendous grin spreading across his face like a rising sun.

"I am indeed," I said, rolling my chair back towards the counter.

"Man, Ms. G. Don't ever leave again, okay? Those people who were in here had no fucking clue what they were doing."

I suppressed a smile. "I will try my best."

Woodson hovered, not leaving. I waited. Woodson was one of those inmates who had made the library his first stop when he arrived at the prison a few months ago. Oh, eventually everyone wanders into this room full of books at some point, but only a select few make this their *destination*. Just a few weeks ago, in fact, I had an older gentleman come in, fresh off the bus, looking for *The Brothers Karamazov*. He was absolutely delighted to discover, 1) I knew how to pronounce Dostoevsky; and 2) the library had a copy available for him to check out.

Let this be a lesson in the little things in life.

The silence stretched. "Is there something I can help you with?" I asked Woodson, raising an eyebrow.

"I need a job, Ms. G.," he finally confessed. It rushed out in one breath: *IneedajobMizzG*, as if he had been holding onto it in his mouth all this time. "I'm on grounds crew and . . ." His voice faltered.

Grounds crew was an extremely labor-intensive job. The yard was huge and needed to be maintained: mowing the lawn during the spring and summer, and shoveling the walking paths during the winter. Thankfully, all trees were outside of the fence (lest, of course, someone climbs one and attempts to jump over) so there were no leaves to rake during the autumn, but still. Grounds crew was physically demanding and while some of the inmates were more than happy to take on a job of manual labor, not all were. Woodson, it seemed, fell into the latter category.

Along with coming to the library on his first day at the prison, Woodson also put his name down on the porter wait list during the original visit, too. I pulled the blue binder from its spot on the bookshelf behind my desk and opened it.

My eyes scanned down the page, looking for Woodson's name and found it at the top

I couldn't make any promises. Even when I put in a request for a specific inmate, it was no guarantee. Administration still had to approve the transfer to the library. But, none of my previous requests had been denied.

Spencer—the inmate who had helped me survive on my own very first day six months ago—was getting released soon, which meant I would have an opening and Woodson was next on the list. But, because I couldn't make any promises, I had to be vague.

I closed the blue binder and replaced it on the shelf. I looked at Woodson. "I'll see what I can do."

Woodson left, temporarily placated.

The next few days passed without incident or

issue. For the most part, the majority of inmates seemed happy to have me back. If nothing else, the "On This Day" whiteboard started getting consistently updated again. Despite having left my binder of historical dates, only one of the subs had bothered to update the board.

Not *all* of the inmates were pleased to see me back behind the library desk. Unsurprisingly, these were the ones who always viewed the rules more as, shall we say, suggestions than actual rules. Who knows what they had been allowed to get away with in my absence.

On Thursday, almost as soon as I had entered the Education department after the morning shift, Kimberly cornered me. She had news. "Did you hear?" she asked.

I shook my head. I'd been out of the gossip loop for so long, I was still catching up on all the old news. There was no way I was ahead of the curve on the new news.

Kimberly smiled smugly. "Pam got walked out."

I froze, water bottle inches from my mouth. I finished my intended sip and forced a swallow.

"They found letters," she continued. "Routine bunk search—they were in the box of one of her kitchen workers."

"Love letters?"

Kimberly nodded. "He kept them. Who knows what else she was doing with him besides writing letters," she added with an eye roll.

I barely knew Pam and hadn't interacted with her since graduation day. I guess I couldn't say, one way or the other, if she was the type that seemed like she would have an inappropriate relationship with an inmate. Then again, I didn't really know what I imagined that "type" to be.

I also couldn't help but be reminded of my own incident with Andrews and Finch. It seemed so long ago now and I was, once again, grateful that Finch had covered for me.

I was so lost in my thoughts, I didn't hear Kimberly as she continued speaking.

"—married."

"What?" I asked, shaking the thoughts from my head.

"She's *married*," Kimberly repeated, enunciating the last word. She let out a puff of air, shaking her head. "Imagine having to go home and tell your husband not only were you fired today, you were fired for gettin' it on with an inmate."

Kim's frankness startled me, and yet I have to admit I had wondered the same thing. People get fired for all kinds of reasons, sure, but getting fired for writing love letters to a man who is incarcerated at the prison where you work is all kinds of awkward.

Since Highland's one visit, I had been slowly, but actively, making a dent in the donated books. Most of my time was really spent just sorting them into two piles: appropriate books and inappropriate books.

Part of my education in becoming a librarian involved many a classroom discussion about why librarians shouldn't judge the reading choices of their patrons. A professor told us a story about how she was working the reference desk one day and a patron came in requesting literature that was pro-white supremacist. Personally, the professor took issue with that viewpoint. But professionally, she had to put all of that aside: she had a patron standing in front of her and he wanted a book and, as it happened, the library did carry materials that met that patron's information needs. So, as much as it personally pained her, she got up and took him to where the books were.

Also in grad school, I learned about the Five Laws of Library Science, as outlined by S. R. Ranganathan in 1931. One of these laws—number two, as it were—is "Every Reader His Book." Every member of a community, Ranganathan argued, should be able to walk into a library and find the material they want. Libraries should exist for all patrons and provide a collection that meets the needs of everyone in that community, not just certain demographics. It's a great standard for most libraries.

Yeah, so, that's not a thing behind bars.

Prison libraries have an entirely different set of rules when it comes to access of materials.

Freedom of information doesn't exist in prison. Patron privacy doesn't exist in prison. Outside, if a patron came to me and asked for, say, a book on bomb making, I would never in a million years dream of reporting that to anyone. Librarians on the outside, when faced with a demand to break confidentiality from law enforcement, have fought back and they have fought back hard by pushing against requests for private information about patrons.

But those real-world freedoms don't hold in prisons. All books that were deemed unacceptable were identified as such because they posed a security risk to the institution. Like, say, books on bomb making. Anything too sexually or violently graphic was an automatic no-go, the belief being the materials would encourage sexual or violent thoughts and actions in the inmates. So, included in all of my documentation was a list of books that were not allowed inside. The process of books being deemed inappropriate often started in the mail room, when copies would be sent to the men inside, whether from family or an approved vendor. Like all incoming mail, packages were searched. Potentially problematic titles were sent to a committee, which determined whether or not they were allowed inside. If a book was not allowed at one prison in Ohio, it wasn't allowed at any prison in Ohio. Books stayed on the list for four years and then dropped off; after that, they were allowed inside unless challenged again.

Every day, when an inmate requested a book we didn't have, I had to check it against the list. Every day, as part of my job, I practiced censorship.

I hated it. I didn't become a librarian in order to keep books away from willing readers. I became a librarian because I believe, with my whole heart, in the freedom of information and access to information. But, as a matter of security, I had to follow the rules, and I had to follow the list and keep out books that weren't allowed.

But while some of the banned titles made sense, there were some books that were bizarrely deemed acceptable.

Shortly after the ILL program was up and running, two white inmates came into the library and hovered at my desk. Their eyes kept darting around, as if they were afraid they would be seen or heard.

"Hey," one of them whispered, waving me over. "Hey, Ms. G."

I rolled my chair over to my desk. "What can I do for you?"

They looked at each other, daring the other to ask whatever it was that needed to be asked. "We have a question," said the one on the right side. I stole a quick glance at his name badge. Hardy.

"Okayyyy," I said, drawing it out, intrigued.

Another beat. Another minute of them passing glances back and forth. Finally, Hardy gave a resigned sigh. He leaned in close, lowering his voice. "So, um, what would happen if we were to request *Mein Kampf* from the outside library?"

I knew these inmates. I knew this was merely a philosophical exercise, not something they were seriously considering, nor was it a book they wanted to read. They were testing the boundaries. That said, *Mein Kampf* was an interesting title to select because while it *was* allowed in the prison and, therefore, I wouldn't have to practice any kind of censorship, I *would* have to break patron confidentially and report it to the security team. And I *really* didn't want to do that. There'd be red tape and paperwork and incident reports, plus that whole nonexistent patron privacy thing, all for men I knew didn't really want to read this book.

"Well," I started. "If you were to request *Mein Kampf*, I would put in a request and you would be allowed to read it. However, I would have to report you to Catalina."

Catalina was our resident Investigator. A former Ohio State Patrolman, Catalina handled all internal investigations and information related to security threat groups. Technically speaking, just having this conversation was enough to report to Catalina but, again, I *really* didn't want to have to do that.

"So," I continued, "did you want to put in an ILL request?"

They smiled and shook their heads. With a wave, they left the library. The interaction left me conflicted. On the one hand, I knew these men well enough to know the request for *Mein Kampf* wasn't a security threat and that, more likely, the question was about satisfying their own curiosity. On the other hand, what would happen if an inmate, who I felt posed a risk, requested the book? Would I get it for him? Outside, at a public library, I would have had no problem providing a book a patron asked for. Inside, I was still against censorship, but also realized that the rules existed and I had agreed to hold them up when I accepted the job.

To be honest, I'm still not entirely sure what I would have done if a different inmate had asked for that book. But I liked to believe that I'd follow the protocol: I'd have to tell Catalina, but *Mein Kampf* was allowed inside. It was not banned, so if an inmate asked for it—regardless of what I knew about him—I would hope I'd get it for him. Sometimes, when your professional passion feels challenged, you have to figure out how to circumvent the rules when you can. And as I'd learn, even I like to test boundaries sometimes, too.

One sunny summer day, I was sitting at my desk, updating the Excel spreadsheet with some of the donated books. I couldn't guarantee how accurate it was when it came to the titles that were on there, but I *could* maintain accuracy going forward as I added new titles.

I picked up the title on top of the pile. It was a V. C. Andrews title, *Crystal*, from the Orphans series. Albeit a slightly older title, but V. C. was impossible to keep on the shelves, her books always checked out and reserved, so I was excited the donation pile included several of her books. Holding the paperback in my hands, I held it up close to my face to look for the miniscule encircled R that came after her name indicating V. C. Andrews was a registered trademark.

The real V. C. Andrews died in December of 1986. She had written the original four books in the Dollanganger series, starting with the notorious *Flowers in the Attic*, and a small collection of series starters including *My Sweet Audrina* and *Heaven*. But everything else attributed to her name had been created at the hands of a ghostwriter. One ghostwriter, in fact: Andrew Neiderman, who is a bestselling thriller writer under his own name. But along with writing his books, Neiderman has kept the V. C. Andrews legacy alive for over thirty years and is still publishing books to this day (many of which I have read. Sorry not sorry.).

I opened the paper to the copyright page so I could start inputting some of the necessary information into the Excel spreadsheet. After just two keystrokes, I noticed something fluttering in my peripheral vision.

I leaned forward in my seat, squinting. What *was* that thing?

In the far back corner of the room, up near the ceiling, there was movement. *Fantastic.* I thought. *Had a bird gotten in again?* A few months before, a sparrow had flown in one day, piggybacking through the open door when an inmate entered. She perched on one of the ceiling rafters, happy as could be. She was too high for any of us to reach, but the last thing I wanted was for her to get too comfortable and start nest building. When Officer Chester came by on his hourly round soon after, I pointed up to the bird and asked how to get her out.

Chester laughed at me. Actually *laughed.*

"Eh. She's not bothering anyone," he said.

Well, okay, well that wasn't entirely true, as she was bothering me. The last thing I wanted to do was deal with bird poop on my entire collection. That was way above the normal repair procedures and if we had to throw out the books, I didn't have the budget to buy new copies.

Sure, she was a little sparrow and how much damage could she really do? But to quote Shakespeare, "Though she be but little she is fierce."

But my opinion on the matter didn't count it seemed.

In the end, it didn't matter: the bird stayed for a couple of days before sneaking out, presumably the same way she came in. One day I came to work and she was just gone.

Still squinting, I tilted my head, hoping to gain a better vantage point without having to physically go into the stacks. Whatever was back there, I didn't think it was a bird. But what else had wings—

My eyes widened.

I was about to find out whatever was back there, because the damn thing was flying towards me. No, not towards me: *at* me.

I hurled myself against my chair and kicked off with my feet, rolling into my porters like a bowling ball just as a reddish blur brushed past my cheek. Behind me, there were two thumps in quick succession: the first, when whatever it was hit the window by my desk, and the second when it fell on top of the pile of books right beneath said window.

For several seconds, nobody breathed, let alone moved. The only sound in the room was a rustling of wings and paper. My swift reaction and roll got the attention of every inmate in the library, and they all fell silent.

My office chair had rolled in such a way that I was facing my inmates and the stacks of the library. I pushed myself up off the chair, using the back of it to steady myself, then took a deep breath and turned around.

I gingerly took a step forward, slow and patient as if I thought the floor might fall beneath my feet. Like a giraffe, I craned my neck in the direction of the rustling sound.

A bat laid on its back, wings frantic against the books beneath it. Caught in a moment of flight or fight, the bat had chosen flight, only it was unable to right itself up. That nice little crash into the window probably hadn't helped. I was honestly surprised the run-in with the glass hadn't knocked the thing unconscious.

As it twitched a little, I jumped back.

By now, several of the inmates who had been seated were standing, trying to get a better view of whatever was going on by the window. Because of the circulation desk and my desk, they couldn't see anything. Some of my porters from the law library had come forward and gathered around the circulation desk.

"So," I started. I glanced over my shoulder once more at the furiously flapping wings then faced the room. "There's a bat."

"You better get away from him, Ms. G.!" McDougal yelled from his spot back in the law library. "Bat's gotta be sick if he's out in the daylight."

That had not occurred to me, *so well now that's just great.* There's not only a bat by my desk but now I was at risk for rabies? I'd rather have the sparrow back. Bird poop, while annoying, was a much better option than rabies. I've read *Cujo*. Sure, Stephen King himself has admitted he was blitzed out of his mind on cocaine while writing the book and, sure, this was a bat not a dog, but that somehow made it worse, not better.

This was, surprisingly, not the first time I'd ever dealt with a bat in a library setting. When I was still working in my hometown, the staff came in one morning to discover that a bat had gotten in overnight and decided to stay. There he was, hanging from the ceiling in the reference section, right above the phone books, his black wings wrapped tightly around his body like a Vampire's cloak.

The managers cornered off that small section of the library temporarily, patrons encouraged to stay away until a professional could come in and take care of the bat.

That bat at least knew the rules of the library: be quiet and don't disturb the other patrons. This bat, however, did not.

After the incident with Chester laughing at me, I had no idea what to do. Surely a bat flapping his wings on a pile of books was a bigger problem than a bird cheerfully hanging out in the rafters, right?

While internally panicking, out of the crowd came Draper, an inmate who was an exact mimicry of Jon Hamm in *Mad Men*, down to the perfectly polished black hair. He didn't say a word, just walked past me removing his state-issued lightweight blue jacket in one fluid motion.

I was so confused as to his intentions that I didn't even notice, let alone chastise him, when he stepped across the faded red line on the floor and came behind my desk. I merely took a few steps back and moved out of his way.

Arms outstretched, hands draped by his jacket, he leaned down and enveloped the flapping bat in the folds of his open jacket. Draper hugged the ball of fabric and flight close to his chest and quickly exited the library.

I pressed my head against the window, angling to watch him release the bat into the wild. He shook his coat out and walked back in and resumed his seat at the table right in front.

"Thank you," I said. Draper merely nodded, resuming his reading of the *Canton Repository* as if nothing had happened. "Uh," I continued, "you probably want to take that jacket to Quartermaster and get another one." He made some vague gesture with his hand and went back to reading, the newspaper in front of him far more important to him than whether or not the jacket he received from the prison was infected by whatever that bat may or may not have been carrying.

Priorities.

Later, while we were closing up, Washington was near to bursting with laughter as he came

228

towards the door. "Man, Ms. G.," he said, shaking his head. "I ain't never seen anybody move as fast you did in that chair." He clapped his hands and dragged his right palm across his left. "Woosh."

I nodded. "Yeah, yeah," I deadpanned. "So hilarious."

Washington was released a few months later, free to return to his wife and kids and grandkids on the outside. Without fail, at least once a week right up until the day he left, he would remind me of that bat and how quickly I moved out of the way, his retelling punctuated by his laughter.

It's been ten years and I still think about that bat all the time. I hear the rapid flapping of his wings, imagine how terrified he must have been to realize he had no way of righting himself up and escaping. And that's all he wanted to do, really: escape. He probably snuck in through the vents and ended up in our little library. To him, that window looked like freedom. He didn't know, of course, that it was a window. All he saw was the vast green field of the yard and the cool blue sky of summer. And so, when he had what he thought was a moment, his one moment, he made a mad dash for that great green expanse, only to dive headfirst into plate glass.

In some ways, we're all the bat. All of us—me, the inmates, the staff. We all have goals and aspirations and sometimes, more often than not, there are invisible obstacles that get in the way of our achieving our goals. Obstacles that we don't see until we literally run into them. We get knocked on our backs, staring up at the ceiling, wondering how the hell we're going to get out of this predicament.

Like Blanche DuBois in *A Streetcar Named Desire*, sometimes we all depend on the kindness of strangers.

And if we are really, really lucky, our rescuer will look a little bit like Don Draper.

Chapter 11
Heartbreaker

Investigation: A process that attempts to draw conclusions of fact in a complex or disputed matter, or when known facts are ambiguous. An Investigation is distinguished from problem-solving processes designed to evaluate and improve administrative procedures after collecting undisputed facts. An Investigation is an undertaking that seeks to clarify or discover factual information. A problem-solving process is an undertaking that collects undisputed information in order to seek improvements in the efficiency of programs. An Investigation should not be substituted or blended with a problem-solving process in most cases, particularly if the incident itself is controversial or complex, unless this blend is specifically desired.

—ODRC Policy 09-INV-03

There's a saying in prison. An attitude and approach to working inside that is shared among all staff. A mantra, if you will:

Keep your shit at the gate.

It doesn't matter which direction you're moving, whether you are just starting your shift, or on your way out the door. Either way, you leave it all at the gate.

Highland used a pair of shoes as a reference. "I have a pair that I only wear here," she explained. "When I get home at night, I take them off right away and leave them right at the door. Here, we walk all around the grass and the dirt—who knows what my shoes are picking up. I don't want to track that into my house, so the shoes stay by the door."

To be fair, she was literally talking about a pair of shoes she wore, but the concept remains the same. Working inside requires a level of defense beyond the razor-wire fence. I was lucky: my job in the library meant that the vast majority of the time, the inmates I saw were polite and well-behaved. But still, even polite and well-behaved inmates had bad days.

It was not even just dealing with bad days, though. It was about dealing with bad situations and dealing with being unable to do anything because they were incarcerated. Sometimes it was emotionally exhausting.

For example, there was an earnest, quiet kid who had a baby mama in California trying to force him to sign away his parental rights while he was in a prison in Ohio. Whenever her attorneys sent him another packet of papers, he would bring them to me in a desperate hope

I'd be able to help him navigate the legalese.

There was the older man suffering from a long-standing hernia, who kept getting the runaround from the infirmary because the doctors didn't consider it bad enough to act on. Every time I politely asked him how he was doing that day, I braced myself for his usual complaint. He knew I couldn't do anything, he just wanted someone to listen.

In the law library, we saw inmates dealing with all sorts of legal difficulties, from housing foreclosures to divorce. I often had to notarize and sign my Jill Hancock on papers dealing with the marital relationships of the inmates, the life they had outside gone with a single signature.

The absolute worst, though, was the young twenty-year-old whose three-year-old son was murdered at the hands of his mother. The incident was so horrific, it made the front page of the local newspaper, his story and loss on display for all of us to see and read about.

He was given a single day leave to attend the funeral but then had to immediately return to the prison to deal with his grief from inside.

These are things you don't want to track into your house. These are the shoes you want to leave at the door.

The reverse was also true as well, though: no matter what was happening at home, we as staff members could not bring that inside with us.

Letting our personal problems in distracted us, made us less effective at our jobs. When staff members got lazy and stopped paying attention, they put the safety of the entire prison at risk.

However, in the summer of 2009, I did not do so well at leaving my shit at the gate.

It started when my boyfriend called me up one day and said something to the effect of, "I don't think I want to be in a relationship anymore. Also, I cheated on you back in December."

We were long-distance, as he lived two hours away. Just a few days prior he had spent Fourth of July weekend in Cleveland, and we had celebrated our two-year anniversary. Now he wanted some space to figure out his feelings. I wanted to jump in my car and drive to see him, desperate to talk this out, to salvage this in some way. We'd been friends for years prior to dating, surely there was a way to fix this.

He talked me out of it.

I called off work the next day and spent it in bed. I returned on Saturday, specifically knowing the staff would be limited, and I wouldn't have to do too much explaining. During the morning break, I locked myself into the Education building and took a nap on the worn blue mat in the middle of the room.

I was so stressed I gave myself a nosebleed.

After work was done for the day, I went home, grabbed my cat Chloe, and spent the night at my parents'. All told, I didn't eat for three days, and by the end of the weekend, we had officially broken up.

I never saw him again.

In the weeks after, I struggled to keep my shit at the gate when I came to work every day. Like dirt on the bottom of my shoe, I tracked it everywhere I went. Every day was a fight. A fight to wake up. A fight to get out of bed. A fight to take a shower and put on clothes and get in my car and drive to work. Once I arrived at work, I was just fighting to make it to the end of the day so I could go home and crawl back beneath the comfort of my bed and fall into a restless, dreamless sleep.

I was Alice. I'd fallen down the rabbit hole and was now drowning in a pool of my own tears. I was Esther Greenwood, suffocating under the weight of the bell jar that covered me like a dome. It wasn't lost on me that Sylvia Plath had given the fictional version of herself the Anglicized version of my own last name.

I am. I am. I am.

Was I?

The correctional officers rotated posts every few months, their position and tasks changing with them. This meant that every officer was essentially cross-trained on every position within the prison, but it also meant nobody got too comfortable or complacent.

The Education department and, by extension, the library, now had CO Dutch on duty. Dutch always seemed out of place in prison. Too earnest, eager to please. He was like a big giant puppy dog. Granted, I never saw him in action when there was a situation between inmates, but he always just seemed far too . . . nice.

On that particular morning, I was having a bad day. Like, a really bad day. A terrible, horrible, no good, very bad day. The kind of day where I knew five minutes after arriving that I should have just stayed home. I could have cashed in some sick time, taken a mental health day, and slept. Of course, by then, it was too late: I'd already made the hour commute and was signed in and had had my bags checked. I was just going to have to go to the library and sit and wait until the end of the day.

And wait I did, my eyes constantly counting down the minutes until I could go home for the evening. I was just so *tired*. I was tired of work and tired of working. I was tired of the entire concept of work. *Why did we have to work at all? Why couldn't I just stay at home all day and sleep? Why wasn't that an option?*

Really, I was just tired of everything. I was tired of the inmates and the staff and having to come to work every single day and deal with people. So many people. I was surrounded by people. As an introvert, I was already always drained by the end of the workday, but my depression only compounded the issue. It was as if the marrow deep in my bones had crystallized into heavy pieces of stone the length of my limbs. I had to drag and pull my extremities behind me, their weight felt in every step, every movement of fingers and tilt of the head.

I just wanted to sleep. But I couldn't because of this whole work thing so it was, on this terrible, horrible, no good, very bad day, that Dutch walked in on his normal hourly rounds.

"Heyyyy, Ms. G.," he said. Dutch always spoke softly; slowly. "How ya doing?"

Dutch, unknowingly, had walked right into my crossfire.

I snapped. I snapped from exhaustion, from grief. I just snapped, like a sheet of ice that breaks, shards cutting every which way. "How do you *think* I'm doing?" I scoffed, half exhausted, half exasperated. "I'm stuck here with these stupid inmates!"

It was only after the words were out of my mouth that I realized, a) what I had said and b) how quiet the library had suddenly become.

Fuck.

I stared at Dutch. Really stared at him. My eyes bored into him, drilled down. I had to channel all of my energy and focus on the correctional officer standing in front of me, because I was too terrified and too embarrassed to shift my gaze to the inmates who had witnessed, and overheard, the exchange that had happened.

Directly to my right, I knew, was Lincoln, who was quietly counting that morning's circulation cards. Out of my peripheral vision, I could see the table in the front row. Both inmates had lowered their newspapers, watching. Waiting.

Dutch narrowed his eyes at me. Suddenly, he looked mean. Hard. This was not a guy I wanted to fuck with. Suddenly, I realized why he made such a good correctional officer.

"Ms. G.," he said, voice cold. "You just went through Orientation, right?"

"Yes," I answered meekly. My voice was so small, I could barely hear it as it came out of my mouth. I wanted to crawl into a hole and hide.

"And in Orientation, did they talk to you about how you are supposed to treat the inmates here with respect?"

In that moment, my cheeks hot with embarrassment, I hated him with every fiber of my being. How dare he dress me down in front of the inmates—in front of my *employees*. Weren't we, as coworkers, supposed to show a united front when it came to the inmates? If he wanted to take me to task in private, that was fine. Because he was right—just a few weeks ago, I *had* sat through a lecture, at least one lecture, on the appropriate way to communicate with the inmates.

Spoiler alert: calling them stupid was not okay.

I knew it wasn't okay and I also knew my personal issues happening outside the prison weren't an excuse. I hadn't left my shit at the gate, and look at what had happened.

But, even then, I thought, *did Dutch really have to talk to me like that in front of all of them?*

Now, though, a decade later, I get it. I had crossed a line. I'd crossed a big line in regards to how I was supposed to treat and speak about the men in our care. Their being in prison, regardless of the crimes they had been convicted of, did not mean I was now entitled to treat them as lesser than me.

Dutch *had* to call me out on it, right then and there. He had to both let me know that my behavior in that moment was completely inappropriate and he had to let the inmates know that my behavior would not be tolerated.

Satisfied he had gotten the message across, Dutch left.

I kept my head down the rest of the day, if not physically—as I still had to keep an eye on the library—but mentally. I barely spoke to anyone and was grateful for the high desk that I could effectively hide behind.

Not leaving my shit at the gate had other consequences as well. It also left me distracted to the point that, over the course of several weeks, an inmate was allowed to walk out of the library with books he hadn't checked out.

Inmates were allowed two books at any one time, but during a bunk search, COs discovered that Jameson had about twenty in his bunk. None of them had been checked out. He just walked out with them, paperbacks stuffed into the oversized pockets of his oversized coat. I was too up in my own head to notice.

Why anyone would steal library books, which are already free, I'll never understand, but Jameson did. Frequently. All right out from under my nose.

I was struggling. I didn't just need a mental health day, I needed a mental health life.

But, as Jane Eyre once said, "Even for me, life had its gleams of sunshine."

One afternoon, a few days after my breakup, I came into the Education building and was cornered by Stephanie. Looping her arm through mine, she took the paperwork in my other hand and put it on top of the copy machine. "Those can wait," she said, leading me towards the door.

"But—" Like a salmon moving against the stream, I turned away from her in an attempt to go back towards the copy machine.

"We're going to lunch," she said, pulling me closer to her. "All of us." Stephanie stopped short and looked at me, eyes questioning. "How do you feel about Mexican?"

Over the past week, I felt like a leaky faucet.

Everything set me off. It was as if a lifetime worth of tears had been stored in my ducts and the dam had broken and the tears had nowhere else to go except out my eyeballs. "Thank you," I whispered, my eyes prickling, the dam waiting to break once again.

With a smile, Stephanie squeezed my shoulder.

Leaving the prison for lunch just wasn't done. Not that it wasn't allowed or anything, but it was such a production that staff members rarely left during their free time. We would had to have bags searched on our way out, and then searched again on our return. Plus, the prison was out in the middle of nowhere. There wasn't really anywhere to even *go.*

But Stephanie was not deterred. The group of us, including Kwame, Kim, and Nancy, piled into two cars and headed into town. Turns out, much to my admittedly privileged surprise, the village that I had pegged as nothing more than remote and dusty six months ago, had a cute downtown section. It was small to be sure, but cute all the same, with a Main Street lined by storefronts and mom-and-pop shops.

One of the stops along Main Street was a Mexican restaurant. Stephanie pulled her car into an open spot in the parking lot and we all headed inside.

It was a hole in the wall, the lamination peeling at the corners of the tables and the wall

241

decorations faded from too much sun exposure. But the food was cheap and tasty. We ate our fill of chips and salsa until our entrees arrived, all orders served with a side of hearty laughter that, at least momentarily, made the rest of the shit in my life not matter.

I knew that this was just a small respite. That after lunch was over, we'd have to go back to the prison and back to work. Life would resume for all of us, the good and the bad.

Still, desperate times called for desperate measures, and this lunch helped to make things a little less desperate. Too bad drinking margaritas at a lunch in the middle of the day was frowned upon.

A few days later, I received a call from Catalina. A former state patrolman, Catalina took a position as a correctional investigator after retiring from that gig. Any issues that arose that seemed to need a deeper level of inquiry were handed off to him. This included possible gang affiliations or inappropriate relationships between staff and inmates.

So what the hell was he calling me in for?

Catalina's office was in a part of Administration I'd never been to before, way back in the far corner. The rest of Administration was painted standard, industrial beige (save for Hall, head of IT, who had an office in scarlet and gray, indicating his The Ohio State University affiliation), while Catalina had the walls of his office painted a dark brown that almost looked wood paneled. Throw a moose head or two up there, and I could momentarily pretend it was a hunting lodge.

Instead, what he did have hanging on the wall, behind glass, was his former state trooper uniform, alongside medals earned while in the service of his duty.

"Grunenwald," he said, welcoming me. "Come on in."

I was so used to being called Ms. G. by both staff and inmates that it was a bit bizarre to hear myself referred to by just my surname. It also added an intense air of formality to this meeting, and put me on the defensive.

Catalina's desk was large and ornate, made of heavy wood. It reminded me of the Resolute desk in the Oval Office, and all I could do was stare at it, wondering how he'd managed to get it into the room. The room itself was also large, far larger than any of the other rooms or offices I'd seen around the prison Administration building. Filing cabinets lined the walls, full, no doubt, of information from all his previous investigations and findings.

I took a seat in one of the chairs seated in front of his desk. Nervous, I sat on the very edge, not wanting to make myself too comfortable.

Catalina settled himself in his own chair behind the desk. He made a steeple with his index fingers and placed them under his chin. He stared at me for a minute or two, gray eyes steady. I forced myself to maintain eye contact, not wanting to be the one to break it. My only previous experiences with law enforcement had involved speeding tickets and fender benders. Catalina's beady gaze felt like being in a noir mystery, the tough detective playing Bad Cop in order to get information out of the unsuspecting suspect.

Finally, Catalina leaned forward and picked up a pen. "How often do you visit Segregation?"

I momentarily stumbled. "Oh, um. Twice a week? Fridays I go down to see if inmates want books and then I go back on Saturday if needed to deliver them."

Catalina scribbled something on the legal pad in front of him. The jagged scratch of pen against paper was the only sound in the room.

"And when you were there last Friday, did you hear or see anything out of the ordinary?"

I thought back to my visit last week. Davis and Bolton were both on duty, just as they had been for months now. I'd come to enjoy the company of both of them, enough that even after I'd spoken to all of the inmates and written down their book requests, I'd stay down in Segregation for another ten or fifteen minutes to chat with

Bolton and Davis. Both were parents, so our conversations centered upon their kids. On that day in particular, I remembered that Davis was feeling frustrated with her son.

Many of the inmates were still asleep when I went around on my rounds, just as they were most Fridays. Nothing really stood out as being out of the ordinary, and certainly not at the level to require any kind of internal investigation.

"Um, I don't think so," I finally answered. "It was just like any other visit."

"And the officers," Catalina pressed. "How were they acting?"

I shrugged. "No different than usual."

"There wasn't a disagreement between them at some point?"

Disagreement? "No," I answered. "Not a disagreement exactly. I guess there was one point when one of the inmates needed to speak to one of the COs, and it was sort of a holdout. Neither Bolton or Davis wanted to have to get up, but Bolton finally did."

That sound of pen scratching on paper again as Catalina jotted down notes.

"Davis didn't say anything that struck you as odd?"

I furrowed my brow. Davis? "No," I said, shaking my head. "No, the only thing she said . . ." I paused, reflecting back on the entire visit. I sighed. "Her son was having trouble in school with his grades, and she said she was going to beat him over his report card."

Catalina scribbled down some more notes, then put his pen down. He looked up and smiled. "That's all I need, thanks."

Startled, I pushed the chair back and stood up. "So . . . that's it? I'm all done?"

"All done," he confirmed. "But, please be discreet about this visit." I left, still as confused as I was when I walked in.

I returned to the Education department in the middle of lunch. Nancy had picked up a lunch for me from the chow hall, which I grabbed and took down to Stephanie's office to eat.

"What was that all about?" she asked. They'd known I'd been called down to Catalina's office.

I shrugged, flipping open the white Styrofoam lid of my lunch. "Oh, he just had some questions about an incident from Seg."

Stephanie nodded, satisfied with my answer. I was grateful she didn't press the issue, as I wasn't sure what I would have told her. Mentally, I'd been prepared to talk about some incident involving inmates. I wasn't prepared to talk about a fellow colleague. Especially a colleague I really liked. I was still sorting through my feelings on the matter.

I never found out what had happened with the information provided to Catalina or even what sort of information he'd been fishing for. But by the following Friday, Davis had been rotated out of Segregation and placed in a post in one of the housing units.

Apparently, Catalina had found whatever he'd been looking for.

Chapter 12
Because I Could Not Stop for Death

Constant Watch: A more intense level of suicide precaution that requires contin-uous, uninterrupted observation, with documentation at irregular, staggered intervals not to exceed fifteen (15) minutes on the Crisis Precautions and/or Immobilizing Restraints Log (DRC2534).
—ODRC Policy 67-MNH-09

The memo was directed to all staff. Those of us who had dedicated computers received it through our email while the security staff got to read it on the bulletin board outside of the Major's office.

Deputy Warden Francis was leaving, transferring to a prison down south. An opportunity had presented itself and she was trading in the snowy winters of Northeast Ohio for the balmy summers of Florida. Can't say I really blamed her.

She had also planned her exit well: the heat of summer was starting its descent into autumn, meaning she had missed the height of the steamy heat in Florida, but was going to also leave before winter began its annual crescendo, the snow piling high around the prison. After Francis left, summer continued its languid pace, slowly shuffling along into fall.

Autumn has always been my favorite season. Long before the stereotype of the Basic White Girl emerged, I spent all year longing for the crunch of leaves beneath my boots, the crisp snap of air that sends a shiver down my spine. I live for the time of dressing in sweaters and boots, my hands wrapped around steaming cups of pumpkin spice lattes, the sweetly spicy smell of cinnamon filling my nose. I love that in autumn, stores start stocking up their back to school supplies, of which I still buy far too many despite not being a) a child or b) going back to school. (Ah, to be a kid again, armed and prepped with my new backpack and My Little Pony lunchbox, toting a bouquet of freshly sharpened pencils and a collection of notebooks to guide my way.)

I love that during fall, there is a sacred sense of renewal. Like a snake shedding its skin, trees are given new life, new opportunities for growth. It's like opening the cover of a brand new notebook and staring at a blank white page. This isn't a test, there is no wrong answer, just a chance to take a deep breath and reset.

But—despite all its benefits and blessings—with autumn also comes a deepening of my depression. During this season, the grooves of malaise and melancholy etch themselves, like carvings on my bones. *Sometimes in September, often in October, never in November* was always my mantra for the autumn months, a way to track my slide down. I could usually get through September without much trouble and was usually starting to come out of it by the time my birthday rolled around in mid-November, but October always presented a challenge even when everything else in life was fine.

This year looked to be a challenge: on top of my usual seasonal depression, I was also fighting against the post-breakup wave of depression inflicted on me by the end of my relationship. So as eager as I was for autumn's renewal, I entered the season with hesitation and trepidation.

Prior to taking the job at the prison, I considered myself a fast reader. I averaged about fifty books a year, helped, in part, by listening to audiobooks during my commute.

I had first discovered the magic of audiobooks a few years prior, when I first graduated college and moved back home. I was working two jobs at the time, but my main job was forty-five minutes away from my parents' house. This was before Spotify, and while Pandora and iPods were both on the market, I wasn't aware of either. I wasn't really a radio person, so CDs or silence were the only options for me on those rides.

When I wasn't working my Monday through Friday office job, I spent Saturdays working at the library in my hometown. There, I was able to scan the collection of audiobooks available on compact discs and check them out. Depending on the length of the audiobook, I could reasonably get through one a week while driving.

I devoured the entire *Shopaholic* series of Sophie Kinsella, a "chick lit" series about a London woman with a spending problem. It was light fare, the kind of title often classified as beach reading, but it was fun and kept me entertained. Often to the point that I would take the long way just to give myself additional listening time.

Through audiobooks I also discovered travel writer Bill Bryson. He is best known for *A Walk in the Woods*, his memoir about hiking the Appalachian Trail, but through his often hilarious books I also learned about his adventures in Australia and England, along with learning facts about cities in my own country here in the United States.

Audiobooks also introduced me to David Sedaris. To this day, while I have read almost all of Sedaris's books, I've never, technically speaking, "read" any of them. Instead, I've always opted for the audiobook version, which Sedaris usually narrates himself. Something about having the author of the memoir narrate the audiobook adds such a nuanced layer to the experience of reading the book. Reading words on the stagnant page required relying on my own background and voice. With memoirs, that reading experience is elevated when the author presents the inflections and tone just the way they wrote it.

The prison owned a copy of *Me Talk Pretty One Day*, which I was delighted to discover when I perused the shelves one quiet afternoon shortly after starting at the prison. I pulled the title from the shelf and went back to my desk. Opening the familiar chalkboard green cover, I started to read the words on the page, but it all fell flat. Even when I tried to mimic Sedaris's voice in my head, it wasn't the same experience as *hearing* Sedaris narrate it.

Audiobooks are a bit controversial in the literary community. My stance: whoever says they aren't the same as reading a physical book is full of shit. It's also ableist to suggest that it doesn't "count" as reading. Audiobooks are certainly a *different* way of reading, but it's still reading. For some individuals, audiobooks are the only way they *can* read and ingest books. It's like arguing Braille books don't count because the person uses their hands instead of their eyes.

My current commute from my apartment in downtown Cleveland to Grafton meant that audiobooks were a must. There was no way I was going to get through such a long drive without them.

That said, even with all of my reading, both physical books and audiobooks, I had nothing on the inmates at the prison. With little else to do but sit around and read, the library had a regular rotating group of inmates who visited on a daily basis, often in need of new books each day because they had already plowed through the ones they had checked out the day before.

Other than their assigned job, which took up three or four hours a day, the inmates didn't have much else to do. The rest of their day was essentially made up of free time. For the inmates, their idea of free time consisted of visiting the recreation room or the library or hanging out in the yard, weather permitting.

But even as far as prisons go, that's a privileged position. Because this was a minimum security camp, the inmates were free to roam during open hours. At other, higher-security facilities, every minute of the day is planned and organized. The inmates are herded from building to building, no choice given as to where or when they go. At maximum security prisons and super-max, inmates stay locked up for twenty-three hours a day.

More than once, I had an inmate tell me he consistently came to the library because it kept him out of trouble. Back in the main house, there were too many opportunities for trouble. Being bored left a door open for situations to arise or conflicts to combust. But the library was only open for a few hours every day, so during those times when we weren't open—often at night, when their only option was to hang out in the bunks—they needed something to occupy their time.

So they read.

They read James Patterson and John Grisham and V. C. Andrews. They read Tolstoy and Dostoevsky. They read Nora Roberts for the romance and J. D. Robb for the suspense, not always realizing they were the same author. They read fantasy and science fiction and historical fiction and romance. They read to remember and to forget.

Through the ILL service they requested *The Help* and *The Lost Symbol*, because they had seen the titles on the *New York Times* Bestseller list. One inmate, an older white gentleman with a close clipped mustache, was determined to get *The Shack* because his family had recommended it to him. I also had multiple requests for *The Secret*, despite it being a few years old by that point. However, when your options are limited, you try to change what you can however you can.

Men found religion among the pages of The Left Behind series. The pages were torn, spines cracked from so many times being read. The series was so popular, the individual titles impossible to keep on the shelf, that the prison chaplain kept the last book in the series under lock and key lest it be swiped by stealing hands.

Like all readers, men in prison read to escape. My love for George R.R. Martin's sweeping fantasy series *A Song of Ice and Fire* (the inspiration behind HBO's *Game of Thrones)* isn't just because of the dragons and magic involved. No, it's because for the duration of my reading—which, given the length of each book, is a long while—I am temporarily transported to the world of Westeros.

In prison, outsiders tend to think there is only one means of escape: up and over the razor-wire fence, or digging holes underground (or, if you're Andy Dufresne, through holes in the walls hidden by posters of Rita Hayworth). But, in fact, like on the outside, if the situation is so dire, there are other means of escaping.

I continued my weekly visit every Friday to the Segregation unit to see if anyone wanted any books, with a potential return visit on Saturday to fulfill any requests. The unit had a small black metal bookcase tucked into the corner near the recreation area that I kept stocked with paperbacks, rotating them out every month or so to make sure there was always fresh books for the inmates to read.

On a particular September Saturday, as I was walking down the long hallway, a shiver ran down my spine. It was an austere hallway, empty of all staff because it was the weekend. Something about the silence unnerved me. Something was wrong.

When Bolton opened the door for me, my eyes zeroed in on an unfamiliar correctional officer sitting in a chair in front of the closed door of a cell, a notebook balanced on his lap. The meal tray, usually closed, was open, the gap in the door at eye level with the officer.

Bolton silently waved me in.

I stepped into the space, shifting my basket of books to my other arm. I leaned down towards Lopez. "What's going on?" I whispered.

Lopez used his chin to gesture in the direction of the unknown correctional officer. "Connor is in there," Lopez said, 'in there' being the cell. "Suicide attempt."

I gripped the basket to make sure I didn't drop it and disrupt the silence. My own mental health was razor thin these days, although I hid it as best I could. It took all of my mental and emotional energy to keep my shit at the gate, to not bring it here to the library. But in doing so, I had no mental or emotional energy to spare. So when intrusive thoughts began to gather in my mind, climbing into the corners like cobwebs, I didn't have any brooms left to sweep them away.

"He was in the medical unit," Bolton continued, not noticing the white-knuckle grip I had on my basket of books. "Used his bedsheets. One end tied around the bedpost, the other end around his neck."

Jesus. I didn't know Connor well, but I knew who he was. He wasn't an everyday visitor to the library, but he came by frequently enough. Just a few months ago, in fact, we had that conversation about the baseball game and now . . .

"So the officer. . ." I asked.

"Douglas," Lopez said with a nod towards him. "Suicide watch."

Suicide watch in prison takes multiple forms, depending on the severity of the risk. *Close watch* requires a staff member to check in on the inmate at "irregular, staggered intervals not to exceed fifteen minutes." Five minutes this time, eight minutes the next time; two minutes here, one minute there. The officer can't allow a pattern to happen, otherwise pockets of free time can be found and a plan can be executed.

But I wasn't witnessing close watch. I'd been standing there for two or three minutes and Correctional Officer Douglas hadn't moved. His gaze hadn't shifted, either: all of his energy was focused on Connor inside that cell. I was witnessing *constant* watch.

Constant watch is just what it sounded like: for a period of time, as defined by the prison, Connor would be constantly watched. Whereas with close watch the correctional officer on staff could come and go for small intervals, the officer assigned to Connor had to sit close by. And watch. Constantly. The notebook he had balanced in his lap was there so he could write notes about anything Connor said or did while Douglas was monitoring him.

"What happened?" I finally asked, my voice barely above a whisper.

Somehow, Bolton knew what I *wasn't* asking. "We had to strip his cell," he said.

Lopez and Bolton went on to tell me that Connor had been in the medical unit. The medical unit at the prison worked a little bit like a hospital, where there are staff members who come and go, and check on the patients. But unless there is any indication that the inmate is at risk for harming himself, he isn't watched more closely than any other inmate in there.

While in his cell, Connor tied the bedsheet into a noose and attempted to strangle himself. He was found and rescued before any real injury could occur, but because of the suicide attempt he was moved from the medical unit to the Segregation unit where Bolton and Lopez could keep close watch on him.

But, that apparently wasn't enough to deter Connor. Whatever was going on with him was severe enough that he once again attempted to kill himself while in jail, this time from his Segregation cell. Segregation cells are quite bare, containing nothing but the most basic of necessities, like a bed and a toilet. In an effort to minimize the potential for more incidents, Lopez and Bolton had stripped everything but the absolute bare minimum of items required in the cell. Nothing else was allowed and now Connor was on constant watch: twenty-four hours a day, someone would be watching him and writing down everything. Every little thing was monitored and put on the record. As someone who already leans towards jittery, thanks to both anxiety and copious amounts of caffeine, just the idea of being constantly watched set my teeth on edge, while the thought of having every action, no matter how minor, recorded set off my fight-or-flight response. I was struggling with my own internal issues and this hit a bit too close to home.

Not to put too fine a point on it, but figuring out a way to shuffle off this mortal coil had passed across the hazy dark fog of my brain more than once over the past few months. I had a support system of friends and family, but I was embarrassed to ask for help. To admit how bad things were. I didn't know how to tell people I spent evenings crying over some asshole who cheated on me. It felt, well, pathetic. It had been several months since our breakup, so why was I still this upset? Why was I still struggling every morning just to get out of bed?

I had thought about suicide, more than once.

Connor, it seemed, had made an attempt to do so. And the prison, while perhaps not a person's first choice of support system, wasn't going to let him succeed.

People's feelings regarding suicide in prison can be complicated. In September 2013, Ariel Castro, the man guilty of holding three Cleveland women hostage in the basement of his home, was found hanging from a bedsheet. He wasn't on suicide watch, but due to his notoriety, Castro was subject to frequent checks. Or he was supposed to be; later, it was discovered that two of the corrections officers had falsified their log documents. ODRC pushed back, suggesting his death had been accidental, the result of auto-erotic asphyxiation. But the coroner held firm to her suicide ruling.

After the news of Castro's death broke, reactions were mixed. Some people were happy he had killed himself. Happy that he was dead. On the other side, I remember discussing it with some of my now-former colleagues at the prison, and we entertained the idea that he had done it because he knew his life in prison was going to be hell, and he was looking for an out. I still think it was an easy out, that he had somehow cheated the long prison sentence he deserved for what he had done to Michelle Knight, Amanda Berry, and Gina DeJesus. More than once we called him a coward in regard to his death.

For the prison, suicides—especially high-profile suicides—are a lot of red tape, a lot of paperwork, and a hell of a lot of bad press for the facility, so it would make sense that the Ohio Department of Rehabilitation and Correction would suggest an alternative explanation for Castro's death. It also would explain why our prison worked hard to keep a man alive who clearly did not want to be.

Was it just an effort to cover their own ass and avoid any negative publicity? Probably? Maybe? I honestly don't know. I also don't know how I would have felt myself in that moment, if I had made an honest attempt and ended up being saved and revived. Sure, now, a decade later I'm thrilled to be here and to have a thriving life. But I wasn't in prison. I wasn't struggling to make it day by day by day, minute by minute by minute behind bars.

I also don't know what happened, ultimately, to Connor. After his time in Segregation, he was moved back to general population and, eventually, was released. But I don't know where he is now or if he is even alive. If he is, I at least hope he's living a life that makes him happy that the staff and officers at our prison refused to let him die, even if it was just so they didn't have to deal with a mountain of paperwork.

Chapter 13
Something Wicked This Way Comes

Inmate library aides shall be utilized to assist in providing services to the inmate population. Inmate library aides shall be utilized to provide support services to the library including, but not limited to, book processing, shelving, and maintenance of the library itself.
—ODRC Policy 58-LIB-02

October had arrived. The prison was surrounded by a forest of trees, leaves ablaze with the colors of late fall. Every drive to and from work was a rising spectrum of sunsets and sunrises, the language of late autumn translated through a blend of reds and oranges.

As Lucy Maud Montgomery once wrote, "I'm so glad I live in a world where there are Octobers."

Halloween fell on a Saturday that year, the perfect culmination of the celestial calendar. Halloween is my favorite holiday and my favorite part of autumn, which is saying something as I was born in November. My friends and I had plans to go out that evening, and our costumes had been planned months in advance. First, though, I had to get through my shift at work.

Unfortunately, dressing up was not an option. In grad school I was able to at least get away with a pair of devil horns and a red shirt (although I would often get double takes from colleagues. I can still envision the looks on their faces when it suddenly dawned on them why the quiet librarian was sporting red horns). The prison, however, had a strict dress code: business casual, and no denim (not even skirts or jackets). Even our shoes had to be professional. No open-toed shoes allowed.

However, about once a quarter, the prison did hold a staff dress-down day for charity. If we wanted to dress down, we had to pay $1 upon arrival, which would go towards that quarter's charity. The charities were always personal, usually benefiting the school of one of the staff members' kids, or helping with a family member's medical expenses. Correctional officers were exempt from being allowed to dress down, although they could still always donate to the charity.

Unfortunately, Halloween was not one of those days, and while the skeleton crew of staff members meant I could probably get away with a slightly more casual look, I didn't want to risk it and opted to maintain the standard business casual dress code.

When I arrived that morning, I noticed an eerie silence lay thick and heavy like a fog. In this weather, the fitness equipment looked like the skeleton of some yet unidentified creature of a science fiction movie, the bleak clouds rolling in behind it a dire warning. Blackbirds perched and bounced along its metallic bones, their sharp *caws* cutting through the still air. A storm was minutes from breaking, the clouds opening up and flooding the yard. I knew rain was in the forecast for the evening, which would be a serious damper on my Halloween festivities.

As I unlocked the door of the library, I kept peeking over my shoulder to watch the fitness equipment, wary. I knew my Hitchcock films. The last thing I wanted to deal with was a flock of blackbirds attacking me outside the library.

"Good morning, Ms. G.," Booker said as he walked into the library for his morning shift. I stood in the foyer, erasing the whiteboard and putting a new historical fact up. Shortly after deciding to start utilizing the whiteboard in this way, I had taken the extra step of coming up with an interesting "On This Day in History" selection for every single day of the coming year. That included February 29, for those leap years. From now on, I no longer had to scramble to pick a fact every morning and, in my absence, even my coverage could update the board, too.

"Morning Booker," I responded. I uncapped

the black dry-erase marker and held the tip to the board. The open binder was balanced in my left hand as I began writing with my right: *October 31, 1926: Magician Harry Houdini died.*

I put the cap back on the marker and closed the binder. Stepping back into the main part of the library, I settled myself back behind my desk. I glanced at the schedule on my desk and frowned. Carlton was running late, although I knew the prison's administration had switched the order of the housing units for meals, so it's possible he got stuck back at the house and the officers wouldn't let him leave to come to work.

It was a balancing act, managing the schedule, while still adhering to the rules of the prison. It didn't help that the hours of the library provided an overlap that made it easy for the inmates to exploit and bypass the rules themselves. The housing units went down to meals one house at a time: if they were on the first shift, they would have to go back to the housing unit before the library was opened and while some would walk very, very, veeeeeeeery slowly to wait the time out, most of the time they were ushered along by correctional officers. Loitering was not allowed, and if an officer was feeling particularly ungenerous, the inmate could be written up for it.

Even if the officers knew an inmate needed to be at the library for work, they didn't have to let them out of the house. Not if the yard wasn't open yet, which it usually wasn't until the end of the entire meal service.

On my way in that morning, I had stopped at Administration to pick up my mail. I didn't get interoffice mail that often, but I still made a point of checking a few times a week.

This day, I only had one official looking document: a notice from Job Coordinator Sarah Becker, the woman in charge of classifying inmates for their jobs around the prison. The corner of my mouth turned up in a small smile as I glanced over the name of the inmate who was being classed to the library.

"Booker," I said, reading down the page for more information. "We have a new inmate being assigned to the library on Monday." I lifted my head and looked at him. "Would you be interested in training him?"

He looked at me, wary. "Who is it?"

I suppressed a grin. It was a fair question. Like any small group of individuals, bringing another person into the mix changed the energy and group dynamics.

"Woodson," I said. My request for him to be classed to the library had been approved. Booker nodded, satisfied. Apparently, at least according to Booker, Woodson's addition to the team of library porters wasn't going to disrupt the energy.

"Sure, Ms. G."

My decision to allow the current porters to

train the incoming ones was something I'd been contemplating for a few weeks; it was just a matter of waiting for the right inmates to test it out. Not only did I have to pick the right inmate joining our crew, but I also had to identify a current inmate who had the right temperament to instruct a peer, without being overbearing or taking advantage. Being good at the job and knowing the ropes wasn't enough: Hoskins was good at his job, but he was too easily frustrated, too easily flustered to properly guide another inmate. Booker, on the other hand, was far more mellow and patient. I knew he was a good candidate for this first try.

The door opened and a cold crosswind blew in from the yard. I suddenly noticed how dark it was outside, the impending storm even closer than it was an hour before. Carlton walked in. He stuck his pick into the halo of his afro. "Happy Halloween, Ms. G.!" I smiled in response, grateful that this Halloween was turning out to be more treat than trick.

A few hours later, the library closed for the morning shift. I picked up the basket near my desk and headed into the shelves. Yesterday, when I had visited Segregation, several of the inmates had requested "scary" books and I was determined to find books for them to read.

Granted, I don't know what they had in mind when they asked for scary books, but for me, the answer was easy: Mary Shelley's *Frankenstein.* Bram Stoker's *Dracula.* And, of course, the collected works of Edgar Allan Poe.

Along with the chilling weather that comes with the season, I also love the macabre books that feel as if they can only be read this time of year. One of my favorites is *The Historian* by Elizabeth Kostova. A book that expands on the mythology of Vlad the Impaler and Dracula, *The Historian* is an atmospheric novel that only fits in this time of year. Oh, I've certainly tried reading it during other seasons, but the magic is lost when the sun is shining and flowers are blooming. Something about the mystique of the book, of the legend of vampires, is tied to autumn.

I pulled the books from the shelf, examining each one before dropping them into the basket. The books were old, the pages yellowed with age. But when I flipped open to the back covers and pulled out the checkout cards, I realized they were blank.

Really? *Nobody* had ever checked out *Frankenstein*? Or *Dracula*? I mean, I realized that the classics of English literature canon maybe aren't exciting and, okay, a little dry, but how had nobody checked these out before?

I pulled the checkout cards out of the books and put them on my desk: my way of knowing which books were down in Segregation. If the inmates down in Seg wanted scary books, I was more than happy to oblige, and I was going to take advantage of the situation to expose them to the classics. Besides, who doesn't love vampires and monsters and haunting hearts beating beneath the floorboards?

The books selected, I piled them into the former grocery store basket that now acted as my book basket and carried them down to Segregation. The metal bookcase in the far corner looked the same as it had yesterday. And the last time I had visited. And the time before that, worn paperback books growing dusty with neglect. With CO Bolton trailing behind, heavy key ring in hand, I began passing out the books to the men who had requested scary titles, handselling them as I went along in an effort to encourage them to at least try the English canon: Poe's *The Cask of Amontillado* is about a man who enacts revenge on his enemy while *Frankenstein* is about a doctor who creates a monster. *Dracula* introduced readers to vampires long before *Twilight* (an immensely popular book in the library) and Shirley Jackson's *The Haunting of Hill House* was one of the more terrifying books if there ever was one.

I knew the men in Seg were probably expecting more mainstream and popular horror novels, like Stephen King, but because hardback books were forbidden in the unit, I was limited in what I was allowed to offer. Old school horror books were a dime store paperback a dozen, and literally paperbacks, making them easy to recommend as they were the only books I was able to bring in to the unit. Unfortunately, when I returned a week later, none of the men had read the books I brought but by then, the holiday was over and the desire for scary books had passed.

Happy Halloween indeed.

Chapter 14
Gangsta's Paradise

It is the policy of the Ohio Department of Rehabilitation and Correction (DRC) to give two-step tuberculosis skin tests to all new direct care staff prior to job assignment. Tuberculosis (TB) symptom screening conducted by DRC nursing staff shall be completed annually thereafter as an integral component of the Department's TB surveillance and control program.

—ODRC Policy 31-SEM-09

Out of the corner of my eye, the nurse leaned down close to my arm. The tip of the needle brushed against my skin and I squeezed my eyes shut.

My body stiffened, bracing for impact as the needle went into my arm.

"All done!" the nurse said cheerfully.

I opened my eyes and examined the small bruise already starting to form on the inside of my arm.

"Two days," she instructed. "We'll be here checking."

"Thanks," I said, standing up. I glanced up at

the clock hanging on the wall of the entry room and frowned. This detour had thrown off my entire morning and now I was running behind schedule.

Along with the mandatory tuberculosis testing that came before being hired, staff also need to be retested annually. It was a big production, the nurses from the medical unit administering the tests. They set up shop in the entryway during the 11 a.m. count and lunchtime. I got lucky, arriving for the day while they were already set up, so I was able to get it done and out of the way as I made my way into work for the day. Others would have to find time in the afternoon to come up to the entryway to have their test done.

I gathered my belongings that had been sitting on the floor beside my chair and headed towards the security desk, dumping my items onto the counter to be searched.

Just another day in paradise.

A few days later, I was sitting at my desk reading when Toth walked up. I was so fully engrossed in my book—John Grisham's *An Innocent Man*—that I didn't see him right away. Just that morning I'd been reshelving some of the books that I had picked up from the Segregation unit on Saturday, and hadn't gotten a chance to check back in yet, when I came across the John Grisham title on the shelf.

I'd read a couple of Grisham novels in the past: he is one of my dad's favorite authors and while my parents are readers, they don't own that many books, choosing instead to take advantage of the local public library. That said, Grisham was one of those authors whose books had made the cut, and were in the house. As I grew older, when I was at home and in need of something to read I always knew I could count on finding a John Grisham novel on the bookcase.

The Innocent Man was different, though. This was non-fiction, the story of a man who had been falsely incarcerated for a crime he didn't commit. Long before the podcast *Serial* exploded onto the public conscious, Grisham explored the criminal justice system and the exoneration of a free man.

I found the narrative so compelling, helped by the same writing style that made John Grisham a runaway bestselling thriller author, that I didn't realize Toth had been standing there, patiently waiting, until he cleared his throat.

"Oh!" I looked up and quickly shut the book. "I'm so sorry, Toth. How can I help you?"

Toth pushed the shaggy blonde hair out of his eyes as he leaned across the desk that separated us. "Hey, Ms. G.," Toth said, voice bright as the Tuesday afternoon outside. "I need a book."

I glanced up from the paperwork at my desk to meet his blue eyes. They perfectly matched the heathered blue of his state-issued uniform. and in any other situation I would have believed he dressed that way on purpose, carefully curating his closet to best suit his own features.

Smiling, I nodded. "What book are you looking for?"

"Well," he said, ducking his head slightly, "that's the thing. I don't know. I'm hoping you can find me one."

I was intrigued. Most of the time when an inmate asked for help with a book, they knew what they wanted—they just didn't know where to find it in the library. Or, perhaps more to the point, they *thought* they knew what they wanted, but some information had gotten lost in translation. Like the inmate who came in looking for a copy of *The Silence of the Lambs*, but he wanted the version written by the other author. He and I went in circles for ten minutes: I was trying to determine if he wanted a book that was like *The Silence of the Lambs* while he was quite sure he wanted *The Silence of the Lambs*, even breaking down the plot for me, but he was utterly convinced that some other author had written their own version of the book. Even when I patiently explained that's just not how books work, he was not entirely convinced, and also rebuffed my offer to give him the book as written by Thomas Harris.

Then there was the inmate who specifically wanted the Oprah Winfrey edition of *The Sound and the Fury* by William Faulkner. We didn't have the special edition with the updated cover image and Oprah Book Club seal, but we had an older version of the book. No, the inmate insisted. It had to be the Oprah edition.

"Why?" I asked, curious at his refusal of reading the exact same book with a different cover.

He stared at me. His intense gaze indicated a belief that I was highly overpaid for my position here and had no business calling myself a librarian.

"Because," he said speaking slowly so as to make sure I was able to comprehend, "Oprah rewrites the books and makes them easier to read."

I bit back a smile. I'll admit that to a casual viewer it does seem like Oprah has some pretty amazing superpowers, but that isn't one of them.

Even John Grisham got caught in the mix when an inmate came in asking for a book but he was unsure of the author's name. "Quisham?" the inmate offered. "Or Shisham?" It wasn't until he explained that the book was *The Testament* that it clicked.

With Toth, though, this was a new opportunity. I hadn't been able to flex my librarian muscles in this way in, well, in the entire time I'd been working at the prison.

I pushed my copy of *The Innocent Man* to the far side of my desk, giving Toth my undivided attention. "Okay then. What *kind* of book are you looking for?"

Toth bounced back and forth on the balls of his feet, his face lit with excitement. "So, I'm in the GED program, right?"

I nodded.

"Okay, so, I dropped out of high school, right? And I'm realizing there are all of these, like, books that I never read. But now that I'm back in school I want to, like, do better and make better choices for me and my kids outside. I've wasted too many months here just getting in trouble and I don't want to do that anymore, so I was hoping you could help me find the books that I should have read in high school, but didn't."

My eyes widened, delighted at the prospect of Toth's request. He had, unknowingly, opened a Pandora's box of literature. Before me was the entire English literature canon, available for the picking and recommending.

Granted, I knew that schools offered more than just classic literature. My own high school English classes introduced me to *Ender's Game* by Orson Scott Card, a science fiction book about an elite school in space that trained young children to become soldiers against an impending war with aliens. Certainly not your traditional, standard fare of assigned reading.

But I could also tell from the way Toth framed his request, that he really *was* looking for the traditional standard fare of assigned reading. While a few weeks ago I had to force the classics like *Dracula* and *Frankenstein* onto the guys in Seg (none of whom read them), Toth wanted and was willing to try his hand at all of the dry, boring books he had shrugged off back in school.

I had to be careful, though. Pick the wrong book as a starter and I was going to turn him off completely. Because as much as he said he was willing to read them, once he started, he may decide it was an error. I had to be thoughtful in my choice and recommendation.

I leaned back in my chair, analyzing Toth. Here was a man in prison. He was close to my age, in his late twenties, maybe even early thirties. He didn't have to participate in the GED program: he was well over the required age that would automatically place him there. This was a *choice* he was making. Wanting to use his time here productively was a choice. Seeing this as an opportunity to make himself better was a choice. Wanting to better himself was also a choice. Not all of the inmates I saw pass through here viewed prison through the lens of opportunity, but for Toth it absolutely was.

I then thought about all of the books I had read in high school and even college. All of the assigned texts I read (or, admittedly, in some cases, didn't read), and studied, and analyzed, and took tests on, and wrote reports on.

My smile broke wide. "I have the *perfect* book for you."

Eager, Toth followed me into the stacks.

Work in a library long enough and any librarian or library employee can read the shelves like a map. We are cartographers of our own making, the books touchstones that guide us on our path. Standing at the end of the shelf, staring down the corridor of books, I knew that the Left Behind series was to my left on the very top shelf, filed under LaHaye, Tim. The book I was looking for would be under the Fs, so I turned to my right and took a few steps down the row, my index finger skimming the row.

Ah, Fitzgerald. There he was.

I pulled the copy of *The Great Gatsby* off the shelf and held it in my palm for just a moment. This edition was the same as the one I had read in high school, with the iconic blue cover and forlorn eyes staring up. The small rosebud of a mouth hovering above the fiery delights of a fair.

In school, I was always one to read ahead, never satisfied with the slow pace of studies set forth by the class syllabus. One chapter a night was never enough for me, especially not with a book as short at F. Scott Fitzgerald's 1925 novel. I was hardly an industrious student, often ignoring homework altogether, or doing the bare minimum required for a passing grade. But English class . . . English class was always the exception. In

English, I was always ahead, finishing the books days or even weeks before required. I was the student who had to carefully guard her tongue to avoid spoiling the end of the book for any of my classmates.

I remember reading *The Great Gatsby* in particular because a week or two into the section on the book, my English teacher had the class watch a short video on F. Scott Fitzgerald from an A&E Biography series. A true teenager, I was always game for a movie in class, especially when it is interjected with clips from the film adaptation starring Robert Redford.

What my teacher *didn't* realize, most likely because she hadn't screened the video in advance of class, falling under the assumption that because the school board had already pre-approved it and several other English teachers had shown it in their classes, was that the episode covered the plot of *The Great Gatsby*. The *entire* plot of *The Great Gatsby*.

There I was, sitting in my English literature classroom, neck craned awkwardly to be able to view the television screen. On the big black television anchored near the corner of the ceiling, there was Robert Redford as Jay Gatsby . . . getting shot. And dying.

My eyes darted frantically around the room. Did anyone else notice? Was anyone else even paying attention? The teacher certainly wasn't, her focus on the computer in front of her as she read through some of her emails. Holy hell, we'd barely started the book and A&E had just given away the ending. Was I—possibly the only student who had already finished the book—the only one aware of what we had just watched? WHY WAS NOBODY ELSE FREAKING OUT ABOUT THIS? It was one of the ultimate shockers in classic literature.

I shook my head, erasing the memories of high school from my mind. Raising my eyes from the cover, I handed the book to Toth. He held it in front of his face. *"The Great Gatsby?"* He lowered the book and met my gaze.

I nodded. "It's about gangsters in the 1920s. There was a girl Gatsby, the main character, loved, but he felt he needed to better himself before trying to win her. There's Prohibition and bootleggers. It was one of my favorite books in high school."

It was a simplified version of the plot, sure. But all I needed to do was give him a hook, something to make him at least want to give it a try. As a man trying to also better himself, I figured that part of Jay's motivation would appeal to him. Plus, well, if I had learned anything over the past nine months, it's that criminals loved reading about other criminals.

Apparently it was enough, though, because Toth beamed. "This is perfect. Thanks, Ms. G.!"

Quickly spinning on his heel, he went over to the circulation desk and immediately checked it out. He was still smiling when he exited the library.

I turned back to the bookshelf and arranged the books to minimize the gap left by the absence of Jay and Daisy.

Out of my peripheral vision, I noticed an inmate standing down near the Cs. In his hand was a copy of Michael Crichton's *Jurassic Park*. He looked at me, single eyebrow raised. "What do *you* know about gangsters?" he challenged.

I smiled. "What do you think the G in Miss G stands for?"

With a wide grin, I turned and headed back to my desk. Whatever he had been expecting, it wasn't that.

Chapter 15
Deck the Halls
with Boughs of Folly

Meal variations from the cycle menu may be allowed during major holidays and emergency operations provided that basic nutritional goals are satisfied.
ODRC Policy 60-FSM-02

I ran my finger down the clipboard on my desk, comparing the daily worker schedule to the handful of inmates currently sorting that day's newspapers. "Where's Willis?"

Woodson and Lincoln shared a glance. Their hands busy with the newspapers, neither said anything. While they looked at each other, both strategically avoided my gaze.

I narrowed my eyes and put my hands on my hips. "Where. Is. Willis?" I repeated, enunciating each word.

Willis was new to working at the library. He had been classed here a few weeks ago and so far had shown himself to be a steady and predictable employee, and he got along well with the other porters. Lincoln had trained him and Willis caught on quickly. So him not showing up for work was, at least as far as I could tell with what little information I had about him, out of character.

In front of me, Lincoln and Woodson held an entire silent conversation with their eyes. *You. No, you.* My own gaze flickered back and forth between them, a veritable tennis match. Their eyes widened and narrowed, each imploring the other to break the bad news. And make no mistake, whatever was about to come out of one of their mouths was most definitely bad news.

Finally, Lincoln gave a sharp sigh and looked at me. "Willis is in Seg, Ms. G."

Seg?

In my mind, I had predicted maybe Willis was sick, or had gotten a midnight transfer to another facility, or something like that. But Segregation? He had a clean record inside, what could he have done to land himself in Seg?

"Yeahhh," Lincoln continued, extending the last syllable out. "They made hooch back at the house."

I raised an eyebrow.

Drugs and alcohol were forbidden in prison. Not, of course, that it stopped anyone from attempting to bypass the rules. Drugs could be smuggled in via visitors, but alcohol was a bit trickier. Okay, alcohol was a *lot* trickier. A bottle of beer wasn't something that could easily be tucked into the bottom of a shoe.

But, necessity is the mother of invention and

given that this was a prison with a substance abuse program, we had men incarcerated who liked drugs and drinking. Not that drinking on its own was an issue: like many independent adults, I was known to imbibe on the weekends (and, sometimes after a particularly bad day, during the week as well. I live in Cleveland, after all: home of Great Lakes Brewery. My fridge could always be counted on to have a bottle of Eliot Ness red ale waiting for me after a grueling day). No, the inmates who were at our prison weren't there because of their drinking problem. After all, alcoholism isn't illegal. Instead, the inmates at our prison were there because of their drinking and *driving* problem.

As the entrepreneurs of the Prohibition era learned, alcoholic beverages are fairly easy to make with a simple ingredient list: fruit, water, sugar, ketchup packets, and bread. (The ketchup adds acidity, while the bread introduces the yeast that is necessary for turning the rest of the ingredients into a refreshing alcoholic beverage.) These items all get dumped in a bag and are left to sit and ferment somewhere warm and well-hidden. A few days later, *voila*. A noxious bag of fermented fruit and sugar that most likely tastes terrible but will, if nothing else, get you drunk. It wasn't exactly moonshine or bathtub gin, but more of a cousin to the illicit spirits of the 1920s.

Almost all of the items required could be

collected from the chow hall. It took planning and coordination, but if a couple fellas were determined enough and used the pockets on their coats to their advantage, they could easily smuggle out the necessary ingredients.

Fruit on the other hand . . .

Fruit was not allowed out of the chow hall under any circumstances. It was frequently *served* with meals—an orange with breakfast or an apple with lunch—but if an inmate wasn't hungry, saving it for later wasn't an option. Fruit was use it or lose it, and if an inmate was seen walking out with a piece of fruit—even if he had absentmindedly tucked it into his pocket—he could be written up if the officer on duty wasn't feeling particularly charitable that day.

A couple weeks before the hooch incident, a local church came by the prison with some donations. They had very generously put together care packages for the inmates, consisting of toiletries and some snacks, including oranges. As generous as the donation was, Highland had to inform the church that all oranges would need to be removed from the care packages. The toiletries could say, but the citrus was out.

Maybe some of the oranges had been missed. Or maybe some had made it off the breakfast trays and into the cargo pockets on the heavy winter coats that were back in circulation for the season. Either way, the inmates had been creative enough to not only smuggle fruit of some variety back into the house, they had collected all of the other ingredients, and managed to let that shit sit and ferment in its dark happy place, all without any of the correctional officers finding out until after the fact.

And my porter had gotten drunk off of it and thrown into Segregation. Well, former porter, I should say. He was going to be in Seg for a while for this one. He was only a few months away from being released as it was, so chances were he wasn't going to be making it back to the library anytime soon.

House-made hooch wasn't the only home-brewing that happened in prison. The other drink of choice was a Foxy. This brightly-colored drink, usually pink based on preferred Kool-Aid flavors, was non-alcoholic but still packed a punch: it was basically pure sugar and caffeine. The prisoner's version of Red Bull.

Inmates threw anything and everything in there: sugar, coffee, soda, coffee grounds, candy of any and all varieties. Anything that would give them a sugar and/or caffeine rush. No two Foxy drinks were the same, although the men had their preferences and recipes down cold. They knew how many scoops of Kool-Aid to add to how many cups of coffee. The flavor profiles changed depending on who was making it, some liking this flavor over that one or preferring more sugar and less caffeine.

After throwing everything into a water bottle, they would add some ice cubes, then screw on the lid and shake it to make sure everything dissolved. Throughout the day, they would keep shaking it to make sure the ingredients didn't separate or settle. *Shake shake shake.* It was like listening to bartenders with cocktail shakers.

Trust me, it sounds utterly disgusting to me, too, but desperate times, man. It was desperate times and, at least for Willis, desperate times called for risking time in Seg in order to have some prison-made hooch.

With gentle fingers, I peeled open the layers of paper, holding my breath. For the past few minutes, I had been making careful cuts into the precisely folded paper. Sharp angles and discarded triangles covered my desk.

I gingerly pulled the layers apart, holding them out in front of me. The paper was still all attached, so that was a good sign. Once the whole thing was unrolled, I held it up and looked closely. *Damn.* I had cut a bit too much and instead of having snowflakes, I had butterflies. Given it was the middle of December and there was three feet of snow outside, not exactly what I had been hoping for. But, then again, I'd never been good at making paper garland.

It was Tuesday night and I was bored, hence

the attempt at holiday decorations. The library was nearly empty, the frozen tundra that had previously been the green yard, keeping everyone back in the housing units.

Jackson swaggered past my desk, two friends trailing behind him. Swagger was the only way to describe the way he walked, that characteristic dip in the hip, the swing in his shoulders. He was a scrawny kid, like a baby bird. The state-issued coats didn't come that small and he disappeared into it, the hood falling over his face.

"Where you going, Jackson?" I called out, not looking up.

He paused, looking over his shoulder. "Rec." His eyebrows came together, confused at my confusion, like it was the most obvious thing in the world, of *course* he was going to Rec! How could I think anything different?

"Yard's closed, Jackson." I looked up with a smile. "Have to stay here for . . ." I looked towards the clock high on the wall in the law library then back at him. "Another fifteen minutes."

Jackson tilted his head up towards his followers in a simple nod. A flash of understanding passed between all three of them and Jackson swaggered up to my desk. His arms rested on top and he stretched his neck to peer down over the counter top.

"This is my last night, Ms. G."

"That's great, Jackson." I gave him another

smile. "Don't do anything stupid while you're out there, I don't want to have to deal with you again."

He snorted his amusement. On the outside, Jackson was a drug dealer, who ran the local streets on the east side of Cleveland. This was not his first time behind bars, and it certainly wasn't going to be his last. For Jackson, dealing was the ideal profession: he was an entrepreneur, ran his own business, made his own hours. He had a steady stream of clients probably already waiting for him out there. Sure, every once in a while, if he made a misstep, he'd be caught and sent to prison, but here there was the "three hots and a cot." There was also, inevitably, a few inmates he knew. Inmates that would follow his lead, like the two trailing him this evening. For the most part, he put his nose down, did his time, and waited until it was time to get out so he could get back to his regular, and preferred, routine.

Jackson wasn't a troublemaker, although he did have an attitude and bravado that belied his small stature. Think of it as the Napoleon Complex.

"What time you get off work, Ms. G.?"

Oh. So it was going to be like that. I made a joke about Jackson doing something dumb after he got out, apparently I needed to be worried about him doing something dumb twelve hours before he was released.

I forced a neutral expression on my face. My

lips formed a hard line, my eyes a steady stare. To be fair, my version of a neutral expression is Resting Bitch Face, although it has served me well while working behind bars. "Why are you asking?"

He grinned. " 'Cause I'm going to be outside waiting by your car when you get off tomorrow night."

I internally face-palmed myself. Not just at the comment, but at the fact that he even considered it safe to say. Maybe some of the prison employees were willing to overlook minor transgressions when an inmate only had hours left, but I was not one of them.

But, okay, if Jackson wanted to play, I'd go ahead and play along. "Really?" I asked. "And how do you know which car is mine?"

"Oh," he said with a knowing smile. "I *know*."

The conduct report was practically writing itself.

This was not the first time an inmate had made reference to the type of car I drive. A few months prior, I was gathering my personal items at the end of the evening and had taken my key ring out of my purse to put into my coat pocket. Later, an inmate who had been in the library at that time made reference to my Honda Civic. I was startled, but logic told me that if I can identify inmates out in the yard from the employee parking lot, the reverse would also be true.

I looked at the inmate standing in front of me.

"Jackson," I repeated, "the yard is closed. You cannot leave the library for another fifteen minutes."

Grinning, Jackson just gave me a wave and exited.

I immediately picked up the phone and called the officer next door. "Hey," I said when he answered. "I'm just letting you know I'm writing Jackson up for establishing." This was short-hand code for violating rule #24 from the Ohio Inmate rules of conduct: *Establishing or attempting to establish a personal relationship with an employee.* When I repeated the story, the officer sighed.

"I'll be over in a few minutes."

After hanging up the phone, I rolled my chair over to my computer and pulled up the conduct report template I kept saved on my desktop. I typed quickly, fingers flying over the keyboard. Facts. Just the facts.

Just as I hit print, Officer Warwick walked in. I handed him the conduct report.

He read it over, standing there. As his eyes traveled down the page, he kept shaking his head.

"I suspect you'll find him at Rec," I said.

Warwick nodded. He gave me a wave and left. Ten minutes later, I took count of the inmates, called up front with the numbers, and closed the library down for the night.

"Yo," Greene said, leaning over the circulation desk. "You hear what happened to Jackson?" It was the next morning. This early in the day, there was only a small scattering of inmates seated at tables, deep into reading the newspapers from yesterday they couldn't get to.

Lincoln's fingers flew as he organized the recently returned checkout cards. His hands moved so quickly, it was like watching a Vegas dealer at work. He shook his head, but didn't look up, not wanting to break his concentration.

"Spent his last night in Segregation."

Huh. News travels fast in a place with limited communication.

With the limited number of inmates in the library, Greene didn't bother keeping his voice low and quite a few of the seated inmates had heard. His statement caught their attention, a few heads raised in response.

The hum of cards paused. Lincoln looked up. "What?"

A small crowd had formed around Greene, hoping for more information. Because of the limited communication, the men lapped up whatever bits of gossip they could. "Grabbed him in the evening," Greene continued, "and took him down. He was released right from Seg."

"Who wrote him up?" Lincoln asked.

Nobody answered. Glances were passed as everyone hoped someone else knew. I smiled to myself. Turns out, the gossip mill only provided so much detail.

After a few seconds of silence, I finally spoke up. "I did." Other than those two words, I didn't acknowledge their conversation at all, the book in my hand by far the most interesting thing in the room and the recipient of my full and undivided attention.

Greene scoffed. "*You*, Ms. G.?" He peered at me through his Buddy Holly glasses, tilting his head, as if the angle would provide him a different view, a different perspective. Dissatisfied with what he saw, he turned back to the others and lowered his voice. "Yeah, right."

I frowned. What did *that* mean? Was there something about me that said I wasn't the type to send a guy to Segregation? Never mind the fact that I didn't send Jackson to Seg; he sent himself. I just wrote the conduct report that got him there.

"No, really," I said. I turned in my chair to face them. "I wrote Jackson up and sent him to Segregation on his last night."

Greene's eyes went wide. He turned to Lincoln. As my porter, he was the one among the group who was apparently able to read me best and, therefore, the only one who could administer the lie-detector test.

"What did you write him up for?" Lincoln asked.

"Establishing."

The clot of men all looked at each other. Raised eyebrows moved between them, silent words spoken. The takeaway was a group of genuinely puzzled men, the unspoken message being "Her?"

Okay, well, *now* I was feeling offended. I realized that, to most people, I would perhaps not be considered traditionally attractive: on the prison librarian spectrum ranging from The Real Housewives of Cleveland, to the weirdo loner who hangs out at a table by himself without any friends, I would like to think I'm somewhere in the middle. I try to dress at least reasonably fashionable, while still maintaining the professionalism dictated by the prison. If nothing else, the inmates were probably mentally imagining Jackson and me together. Not, like, together-together, but just picturing us standing side by side and found the image absurd. I couldn't blame them. Jackson was a petite man, the Kermit to my Miss Piggy.

The night of the incident, Jackson was just hours from his release, where he probably had a woman waiting back home for him.

"Establishing, Ms. G." Lincoln repeated. He put the circulation cards down on the counter. His gaze was steady but there was a slight glint of amusement hovering at the corners.

"Yes," I emphasized. "Establishing. He came in last night and started asking about what time I get off work tomorrow, and that he'd be out by my car waiting. So, I wrote him up."

Now the men couldn't hold it in anymore and started chuckling.

Lincoln's smile was patronizing as best. "Ms. G." I got the sense that if he could pat me on top of the head and call me adorable, he would. "He didn't mean it. He was just kidding."

I refrained from rolling my eyes. "Yes, Lincoln. I am aware of that. I didn't really think he was going to be out waiting by my car. But when you are still incarcerated here, you have to follow the rules. It doesn't matter if it's the night before your release. If you break the rules, I will write you up, even if that means sending you to Segregation on your last night."

My words just hung in the air, the inmates stunned silent. In that moment, whatever impressions they had of me had been stripped away. The quiet, meek librarian they had come to know was merely a costume. The real librarian was hiding underneath. Up until then, I had apparently looked like an easy target to them, but not anymore.

In the words of William Shakespeare, *"Look like th' innocent flower, but be the serpent under 't."*

Greene was the first to break the silence. "Damn, Ms. G. That's *cold.*"

I grinned. "No, boys, that's gangsta. And don't forget it."

And with that episode, I had finally made it to year's end. Incredibly, 2010 was just around the corner. I had been working for close to a full year.

A year ago, I was a recently graduated librarian with no idea what the future held. I certainly didn't predict I'd find myself working in a prison of all places. But here I was: almost a year into the gig and liking it far more than I thought I would when I first started. It wasn't easy and it was still surreal knowing that there was a constant threat level I always had to be aware of, but overall I enjoyed working with the men.

Now all I could do was wonder what 2010 was going to bring.

But, if nothing else, I could celebrate the fact that I had made it to 2010.

For the entire second half of 2009, I was battling a daily fight. It was particularly bad in the final weeks of the year, winter and snow driving me inside to an empty and lonely apartment. The tide threatened to pull me under every single morning and every single morning I had to force myself to get out of bed. Because of my cat.

Chloe needed fresh water and food every day and if I wasn't going to do it, there was no one else who could. I couldn't let my feelings, my choices, cause her to starve. Whatever shit I was dealing with, that wasn't fair to her.

So every morning, even on those when I couldn't move for fear something catastrophic was going to happen if I moved a single muscle, I dragged myself out of bed and into the kitchen so I could get her food and water. And then I decided since I was already out of bed, I might as well take a shower. And after showering, I might as well eat breakfast. And then go downstairs. And get in my car. And drive to work.

This was my pattern every morning for the last few weeks and months of 2009.

Perhaps it sounds overdramatic to say I owe my life to my cat. But now, ten years later, I can all but guarantee that without Chloe this story, this year, would have had a very different ending.

PART III
THE SAME LITTLE CORNER OF SKY

" . . . and then you would think that whole years would go by, and you would still come to look through the cracks in the fence and would see the same ramparts, the same sentries and the same little corner of sky, not the sky that stood above the prison, but another, distant and free."

—Fyodor Dostovesky,
The House of the Dead

Chapter 16
Ghost in the Machine

No prisoner in a private correctional facility, county correctional facility, municipal correctional facility, or correctional institution under the control of the department of rehabilitation and correction shall access the internet through the use of a computer, computer network, computer system, computer services, or information service, unless the prisoner is under direct supervision and is participating in an approved educational program that requires the use of the internet for training or research purposes, and in accordance with this rule.
—Ohio Admin. Code 5120-9-51

Born in 1981, I straddle that fine line between Generation X and Millennial. These days there is more and more literature and research about the particular microgeneration that I fall into. This "microgeneration" is not yet widely accepted and so for those that support the concept (myself included) there are multiple names that are given to us, including Xennial and Generation Catalano.

My personal favorite is the Oregon Trail Generation.

That old pixelated computer game where you choose oxen and manage supplies and hope your best friend doesn't die of dysentery? Yes, *that* Oregon Trail.

The necessity for needing to learn computer skills cannot be understated. When I was in graduate school in 2007 and 2008, so many of our classroom discussions centered upon the concept of the digital divide: the very real gap that exists between those people who have easy access to computers and technology, and those who don't. Often based on gender, education, race, and/or income inequality, the digital divide means those people who have ready access to a computer and use it on a daily basis have an advantage over those who don't. In a rapidly growing technological world, this gap grows larger and larger with every passing day.

For me, this was never more apparent than when I worked at the prison.

Back on my first day, now almost a year ago, I came across typewriter ribbons and wondered who would use a typewriter. Turns out: lots of people. At least lots of inmates at my prison.

The typewriter was familiar and safe, and inmates—especially the older ones—understood the technology involved. It didn't require mouse skills or knowing how to manipulate screens in order to type something up. While the idea of searching on the LexisNexis software was intimidating, searching through the law library books was not.

That said, there were inmates incredibly fluent on the desktop computers kept back in the law library. One of those inmates was Monroe.

Monroe was one of those inmates that had set himself up as a jailhouse lawyer. He wasn't a lawyer- I'm still not entirely sure what his background was prior to getting behind the wheel of the car while inebriated one too many times—but he fancied himself educated enough on all manners of the law that he could aid inmates who weren't as educated or familiar with the legal texts. Every day, Monroe would be waiting outside the library door, anxious for me to unlock it. Waiting, loitering, hovering, whatever you wanted to call it, he was there. Didn't matter what time of day, he had the library schedule memorized cold. Morning shift, afternoon shift, evening shift. There was always Monroe.

In many ways, Monroe reminded me of King Henry VIII. Just a few years prior, I had read Philippa Gregory's historical-fiction bestseller *The Other Boleyn Girl*, about ill-fated second wife Anne Boleyn and her sister Mary. While I later learned that Gregory played fast and loose with the facts, the portrayal of Henry as this young, arrogant, brash king anointed to the throne by God himself, wasn't too far off.

Every day, Monroe would arrive at the library and set up court at one of the back tables. Not just any back table: always the same back table, right by the law library counter, much to the annoyance and frustration of the law porters. The porters couldn't offer legal advice—they weren't, after all, lawyers—but they were instead forced to watch Monroe attempt to poach inmates that headed their way.

He walked around with a Walkman, a single earbud tucked into one ear. In his hands were stacks and stacks of papers, his own legal narrative stuffed into as many file folders as he could carry. Generally speaking, he was the first one to arrive and the last one to leave.

Once, Monroe was running late, as he got stuck in the daily rotation of the lunchtime lineup, and by the time he arrived someone else had already claimed his table. He appealed to me, asking me to make them move so he could have "his" table back. I had to politely, but incredulously, inform him that it was not "his" table but the library's table. It was, for all intents and purposes, *my* table, and my tables were first come, first served and he had to go sit somewhere else.

When he wasn't sitting at his table, Monroe could be found on one of the computers.

The rules of the law library computers were

simple: legal documents and legal research only. The computers were also first come, first served, and could only be used for thirty-minute increments. Monroe, more of a "letter-of-the-law" kind of guy, would come in first thing and sign himself up over multiple time slots. Frequently, other inmates would come to me complaining because they couldn't get on a computer: Monroe had signed himself into all of the spots. When I would tell him he needed to give someone else an opportunity, he'd push back, angry. He'd followed the rules, he said. He'd signed-up in thirty minute increments, not understanding why I was focused more on the part where he had been sitting at the computer for four hours.

The law library computers were connected via an internal network to a computer in Dr. Harald's office. If an inmate had something he wanted printed, he would save it on the law library computer and fill out a cash slip to cover the cost of the printed pages. During the breaks, I would go to the office computer and print out all of the documents that had been requested. Then, at the next shift, inmates could come and pick up their printouts. I viewed each document prior to printing, and had the discretion to not print if I felt it wasn't a legal document.

Legal document was a somewhat flexible term, although, in that instance, most inmates followed the spirit of the law and only used the computers to type up letters to their judges or attorneys. Other inmates, well, not so much.

Along with Monroe, another inmate frequently seen hovering around the law library was Gardner. When Monroe wasn't signed up for the computer, Gardner usually was.

One day, my law library porter, McDougal, came up to me, complaining that Gardner was using the computers to type up a personal document. The inmates saved all of their documents onto the network, which was how I was able to access them to print, so during a break I went and looked at what Gardner was working on, which appeared to be a novel of some kind. Definitely not a legal document.

I went to Dr. Harald, who called Gardner into his office and explained that he was no longer allowed to continue working on his book.

Gardner, furious, complained all the way up the chain to Warden Garcia, who told both Dr. Harald and myself that Gardner had his personal permission to work on whatever he wanted. It was infuriating, watching Gardner manage to sweet-talk his way into having special permission directly from the Warden himself. But my hands were tied. Gardner was allowed to type up whatever the hell he wanted, while all of the other inmates were forced to comply with the rules.

One afternoon, when I was going through that day's computer printouts and came across a rather large file that belonged to Monroe, I assumed he, too, had decided to write his Great American Novel while incarcerated. He and Gardner would hardly be the first: Oscar Wilde and Nelson Mandela had both published books taken from the writings they made while in prison.

But the more I kept reading, the more I realized this wasn't a novel. It wasn't even anything coherent. This read like the ramblings of a madman; enough to make the character of John Doe from the movie *Se7en* seem sane.

It was a letter to, presumably, Monroe's judge. The one who had sent him here to our prison. Letters to judges are not uncommon, the inmates often attempting to appeal to a judge for a lighter sentence. Most inmates, when writing someone in a position of power like that, choose to take the polite, tactful approach.

Not Monroe.

Monroe had . . . well, Monroe had gone off the rails. He was wishing upon his judge the most vile, grotesque acts I could imagine. No, wait, they were so vile and grotesque that even I, with my infinite imagination, couldn't have imagined the things Monroe wrote about. It was like wishing he could send his judge into a Stephen King novel as punishment.

When I showed Dr. Harald the document,

he sighed and shook his head, disappointed in Monroe. He instructed me to not print it off, and if Monroe had any questions about his document, I could send him to Dr. Harald.

That evening, when Monroe came to pick up his document I explained that I hadn't printed it out because the library computers were for legal documents only. "You know that," I said.

Monroe frowned, confusion dancing across his pink face. "That was a legal document. I'm sending it to my judge." His tone was flat, sincere.

"You—" I started, but stopped, completely thrown off. "You were *actually* going to send that document to your judge? The one where you said you hope he gets raped in prison. That one. That's the document you are going to send to your judge."

The tips of Monroe's ears prickled pink. "I admit, it's a little risqué . . ."

"Yeah, that's not quite the word I would use. Regardless, I don't have it. You'll have to go talk to Dr. Harald if you want a copy."

Monroe turned and exited the library, looking over his shoulder at me, as if he still wasn't entirely sure why I wouldn't have printed it out for him.

He did, however, convince Dr. Harald to print it out. If Monroe followed through on his plan to mail it to his judge, I never did find out. Although

I seriously would have loved to be a fly on the wall in the judge's chambers when *that* document arrived.

Almost a year into my job, and I was still tediously working my way through the donated books, adding them to my collection when I could. It was insufferable work, mostly because of that Excel spreadsheet. That stupid, ineffective, inefficient spreadsheet.

The Excel spreadsheet provided multiple challenges, the least of which is that I wasn't entirely sure how accurate it was, or the last time it had been updated. Because of that, if an inmate came in asking if we had a book, I had no way of knowing if we owned it or not. Even if I knew it was a title that was in our collection, all I could do was check the shelf. With our checkout system, the cards were filed by due date. I had no way of working backwards to see if a title was checked out.

Like I said: ineffective and inefficient.

The spreadsheet was only one half of the problem, however. There were also the cards. The library cards and the pockets in the back of the books. It was an antiquated system, but I knew there was a better way.

Highland was in on her weekly visit to the library when I decided to first present my suggestion. At this point, I thought I had earned myself enough clout to make a proposition so as she was finishing up her visit and leaving, I called out her name.

"Um, I've been thinking," I said.

Highland turned back to face me. "Mmm?"

"Well," I said, extending the *ell* sound. "Would it be possible to get an ILS—I mean, a computer catalog—in here to keep track of the books? The current system is an Excel spreadsheet, which is not the most efficient."

Highland's eyebrows shot up at the word *computer*. I may as well have just suggested smuggling drugs in.

"It's just . . . I'm trying to catalog these donated books," I gestured behind me to the tall metal bookcase, "and add them to the current collection. Some are duplicates of books we already own and there's no good system of knowing which books we have, which copy is checked out. A computer catalog would be the best way." When she didn't stop me, I took it as a sign that she was at least considering the idea and plowed ahead. "The porters could check out inmates based on their ID number and we'd always know who had what out."

I was venturing into delicate territory here. The library had four computers: the three computers in the law library and the one at my desk. The inmates were not, under any circumstances, allowed to touch my computer. My computer had full internet access and while the prison's filters blocked all social media sites on my computer, there were other ways to communicate with the outside world, such as email. We worked on a closed network, so I didn't even know if what I was asking was technically possible. But if the word processing software on the law library computers spoke to each other, why not a cataloging and circulation software?

Introducing a new computer into the mix posed security risks and it was just one more thing on top of a million other things that would have to be monitored and carefully watched.

What I *didn't* tell her was that, down the road I hoped there would even be a computer dedicated for searching books. Ideally, an inmate would be able to go to the computer, look up a title, and know if we owned it, or if it was checked out.

Highland gazed at me for several minutes. I stood still, waiting. Waiting and more waiting. It was a battle of wills, neither of us wanting to be the first to flinch.

"Do some research on software," she finally said. "Send me a proposal to look over."

She was gone before I could say thank you.

Chapter 17
I, Too, Sing America

Whenever an inmate is being considered for a program/work assignment in a sensitive area the Program/Work Assignment Committee shall complete the Sensitive Work Area/Job Assignment Screening Review (DRC2087)
—ODRC Policy 54-WRK-02

I stood in the dark library, staring at the small collection of encyclopedias that lined the bottom shelf. This bookcase, isolated from the others, made up the library's paltry reference section. Alongside the encyclopedias were dictionaries and a thesaurus, a few World Almanacs going back at least five years and a *Guinness Book of World Records* that was even older.

Somewhere in here was the making of my new project.

Hanging on the wall to the side of the reference bookcase was a bulletin board that I had passively used over the past year to highlight various monthly events. Due to our puppy program, back in October I had a bulletin board highlighting Adopt a Shelter Dog Month. Prior to that, I built an entire bulletin board around the theme

"Go Anywhere with a Book." On the American Library Association's website I had found a set of bookmarks with either a retro looking airplane or cruise ship with that slogan. I purchased a set to keep on hand at the circulation desk for inmates as they were checking out their books, but with the bulletin board, I wanted to highlight all of the books within our collection that were set in places other than Ohio. Or even just the United States.

All of my previous bulletin boards had been passive. The inmates would come into the library and hopefully look at the board and maybe it would encourage them to check out a book or two on the subject presented on the bulletin board. But this month, I wanted something more engaging. I didn't want them to just look at the bulletin board, I wanted them to *look*. I wanted them to see and engage.

It was February and given that about 50 percent of the inmates contained at our prison were people of color, it was important to me that I celebrated Black History Month by calling attention to the accomplishments of Ohioan African Americans.

My plan was a scavenger hunt of sorts: on the bulletin board were different bits of information related to African Americans who had lived in Ohio for some period of time. Like Harlem Renaissance poet Langston Hughes, who graduated from high school in Cleveland. Or Nobel and Pulitzer Prize winning novelist Toni Morrison, who had been born just a few miles away in Lorain, Ohio. It wasn't just writers, though. I also included inventors and activists. The only rule was they had to have some connection to the Buckeye State.

In conjunction with the bulletin board was a stack of printouts sitting on my desk that had fill-in-the-blank questions the inmates needed to fill in, with all of the corresponding answers found either on the bulletin board or in one of the reference books nearby. I also had a plan to utilize the whiteboard and whenever possible, putting up "This Day in History" facts that answered questions on the scavenger hunt sheet. If an inmate wanted to get all of the answers, he'd have to come to the library every single day to see if the daily history fact was an answer to one of the empty blank spaces.

I was truly evil.

All of the inmates that filled in all of the correct answers by the end of the month would be entered into a random drawing. I had already cleared it with Dr. Harald that the winner of the random drawing would get a king-sized candy bar of his choice.

It wasn't much. But inside, a free candy bar—and a king-sized one at that—was like a gold brick.

I was awkwardly standing on my tiptoes, trying to staple a factoid to the upper right corner of the bulletin board when I felt a presence standing next to me. Turning my head just slightly to the left, I saw Monroe standing there, his eyes washing over the information presented on the bulletin board.

After a few seconds, he looked me straight in the eyes. "When's White History Month?"

I lowered my heels to the ground and straightened my spine. Watching him, I kept waiting—or, well, hoping—for him to break character. For him to give me some indication, a smile or a wink, to let me know he was just kidding.

"That's *every* month, Monroe."

Warily, he put his single earbud back into his ear and walked away, shaking his head.

With a sigh, I grabbed the next piece of paper with a data fact on it and scanned the available spaces on the bulletin board to find the best fit. It was a little like taking a step back from your lit Christmas tree and squinting your eyes to find gaps where the next ornament should be.

I couldn't wait for March and Women's History Month.

The river of blue that poured into the library parted as Lincoln cut his way to my desk.

Cocking an eyebrow, I gestured to the clock

hanging on the wall above the law library. "You're late."

Lincoln shook his head. "I've been reclassed."

I stared at him. "What do you mean you've been reclassed?" I asked, giving a short shake of my head.

He shoved a piece of paper in my direction. I took it, my gaze not breaking eye contact.

Opening it up, I immediately recognized the standard inmate classification sheet. I scanned it quickly. "The lobby?" I lifted my head, stunned. "You got assigned to the *lobby?*" Most inmate classifications were done at random, with little to no prerequisites required. (One exception was the library, where all porters needed to have at least a high school diploma or GED.) But getting a job up front, such as the inmates who cleaned Admin, required a higher level of trust than most. But the job that required the most trust were inmates who cleaned the lobby. The same lobby we employees used day in and day out. The same lobby with a door that led directly to the outside world.

"Gerry requested me."

Of course he did.

Gerry was a Captain, the highest ranking officer below Major. He was in charge of overseeing and selecting the porter who cleaned the lobby. He was mostly well-liked by the inmates, and had a habit of working up a rapport that usually got him what he wanted, which, more than anything, was

316

information. During our in-service, he bragged about his snitch: a young man who would relay information to Gerry in exchange for special favors or some of those king-sized candy bars.

I handed the form back. "Well." I shrugged, resigned.

Lincoln's eyes widened. "Ms. G."

I held up my hands, a sign of helplessness. "I can't do anything. If Gerry requested you, there's nothing to be done." And there wasn't, as much as I hated it. I had little say in porters being reclassified, and I definitely didn't have a say in it when it came to Gerry requesting them.

Staff weren't supposed to have favorites, or play favorites, or show favoritism in any way when it came to inmates. One of the rules of success that was drilled into us was consistency. Always be consistent with your interactions with the men at our facility. It was the main reason the situation with Gardner pissed me off so much— the Warden had shown Gardner favoritism. He'd marked him as someone outside of the rules and now Gardner could type up whatever he wanted on the computers. If any other inmate came in wanting to type a non-legal document up, I'd have to tell him no.

All of that said, it was easy to find favorites among the men who were porters in the library, and Lincoln always stood out among the rest as a hard worker, dedicated to the library, and a voracious bookworm. I would have fought for him if I could, but my putting up a fight about his reclassification to the lobby would have raised suspicion among the security staff.

Lincoln looked like I had broken his heart, his jaw dropped, slack.

I sighed. I didn't know what to tell him, there was literally nothing I could do. Except . . .

"Look," I said, "the best I can offer is allowing you to, I don't know, volunteer in here when you have free time." His face broke into a grin, teeth bright against his dark skin. *"But,"* I continued, lowering my voice, "you cannot let Highland find out. Volunteers aren't supposed to be a thing, and we'll both get into trouble."

"Sure, sure," Lincoln said, head bouncing like a toy. "Not a problem, Ms. G. Thanks, Ms. G." He said this last bit slowly, sincerely.

"Yeah, yeah," I said. I waved him off. "Don't keep Gerry waiting." I watched Lincoln leave, wondering how, if ever, I was going to manage to replace him and his strong work ethic here in the library.

A few days later, on Saturday, I woke up to snow. Lots of snow.

Snow in Northeast Ohio in February is fairly common. We get snow throughout December and January, but February is when it always seems to hit the hardest. Aside from the two years or so I lived in Kentucky, I've been up here my entire life. I'm used to snow.

But this? This was something else entirely.

This was Snowmaggedon.

The snow had started the day before, on Friday. I spent the afternoon at my computer, constantly refreshing the weather website for any and all updates on the trajectory of the impending storm. The rest of the Education department was lucky: they could go home and make their hot chocolate and curl up in bed, layers of blankets piled high. In the morning, they could sleep in, snuggled deep into their cozy beds like hibernating bears.

But not me. Because I had to work.

When I woke up the morning of February 6, 2010, the first thing I did was look outside. My downtown apartment overlooked the city skyline, the buildings' shadows against the 5 a.m. dark cloaked the still-sleeping city.

This particular area of the city was often neglected by the snow plows. On the one hand, that meant getting out of the neighborhood could be a challenge on particularly snowy days. This was not helped by the fact that Cleveland is situated in a valley, down by the river. There were two roads to get out, both of which required a hill of some variety. More than once I was convinced I'd have to essentially call in "sick" because my cute little Honda Civic just could not and would not get up that hill. *I think I can, I think I can, I think I . . .*

On the other hand, because the roads were usually not plowed, they were always a good litmus test for my morning drive.

This morning, it didn't look that bad. There was a couple inches on the ground, but nothing like the storm that had been predicted across all of the news stations the day before. So, none the wiser, I made my coffee, finished getting ready, and got in my little Honda Civic, and while I struggled a bit to get her up the hill, she eventually made it and then I made my way towards the prison.

And that's where things got interesting.

Turns out, in all of my weather website stalking the day before, I had missed one key fact: I was so focused on what the weather was going to be like in downtown Cleveland when I woke up, I sort of forgot to pay attention to what it was going to be like when I got in my car and started driving to the prison.

More specifically, I missed the part where the snow was going to be worse the farther west. Which was the direction I was headed.

Because of course it was.

The prison was just over thirty miles from my apartment and I always had the benefit of driving against rush-hour traffic, so on a good day— the kind of good, clean spring day that inspires Shakespearean sonnets—I could get there in about forty-five minutes.

This morning, it took me over an hour to drive fifteen miles.

I made it as far as North Olmsted, a west-side suburb located halfway between my apartment and the prison. The snow was horrendous out here, the drivers acting like complete assholes who had apparently forgotten how to drive in snow.

Even just getting as far as North Olmsted was treacherous, the inches of snow on the roads increasing with every mile I drove west. I was already late, and since I was only halfway there, I knew there was no way I was going to make it anytime soon.

As slowly and as carefully as I could, I merged right and took the next exit. The ramp curved up and I had another panicked moment that my car wasn't going to make it. That I was going to have gone through all of this, only to get stuck on the side of the road on the exit ramp in North Olmsted in the middle of a fucking snowstorm. But luckily, with a little pressure and a lot of praying to a deity I don't believe in, the car made it up the final hurdle and I was able to turn around and head back into the city.

On the drive back, with the snow calming down as I made my way east, I pulled out my cell phone and called the prison. "This is Ms. G.," I said. "The librarian. Yeah, I'm not going to make it in today. The snow is just too much."

The caller on the other end, a correctional officer I'd never spoken to before, gave a heavy sigh as he wrote down my name. Turns out, I was the next in a long, *long* line of similar calls: it sounded like most of first shift had run into the same issues and also hadn't made it in. Third shift (who were on duty currently) was going to be getting a lot of mandatory overtime this weekend.

The rest of the weekend flew by, as I had essentially earned myself a bonus three-day weekend. I got home, made some hot chocolate, and curled up on the couch with my cat and some books.

By the time Tuesday rolled around, the snow had melted enough to make the roads passable. Still, I gave myself a big buffer of extra time just in case there were any more issues on the road.

When I made it to work for my normal shift, I told Dr. Harald that I didn't make it in on Saturday and he told me it wouldn't have mattered: the snow was so bad inside, the prison closed the yard for the day. Inmates weren't allowed to leave the housing units, so even if I had made it in, I would have spent the entire Saturday sitting in an empty library.

The end result would have been the same, I would have spent the day reading, but at least I was able to spend it in my pajamas.

Chapter 18
Erin Go Bragh

Section 5120.035 of the Revised Code requires the department of rehabilitation and correction to establish and operate a community-based substance use disorder treatment program for eligible prisoners. The purpose of this program is to provide substance use disorder assessment and treatment through community treatment providers to help reduce substance use relapses and recidivism for eligible prisoners while preparing them for reentry into the community.
—Ohio Admin. Code 5120-17-01

My porters were running late from lunch, so I was handling the checking in and out of the newspapers until they arrived. Out of the corner of my eye, I saw an arm reach over the barrier that divided the far corner of the circulation desk and the stacks. At the apex was the edge of the newspaper shelf.

I quickly snapped around. "Gardner."

His outstretched arm froze midair, inches above the newspaper he was trying to pilfer. Clutched in his hand was his ID badge. "I'm just going to—"

"No," I said sharply. "You're not. You know the rules."

He withdrew his hand and stalked over to the line, getting in position at the back. By the time he got up to the front, the only issue of that particular newspaper was one he had already read. Had he just gotten in line when he first arrived, chances are he would have gotten the edition he wanted, but I didn't feel it necessary to point that out to him.

Gardner had a problem with not *caring* about the rules. Gardner only cared about what he wanted and getting what he wanted. Much of the time that included getting an edition of his hometown newspaper, the *Canton Repository*, and if he didn't feel like he should have to wait in line, well, then he'd just reach over and get it himself. It was often a daily battle.

This had been an ongoing problem with Gardner. Sometimes I caught him in the act, other times he was fast and stealthy enough to get it before any of us noticed. To his credit, he did leave his badge in exchange for the paper, but I had had enough. The following day, I had a sign printed above that corner of the circulation desk: *Newspapers are to be handled by library porters only*. I had a feeling it wouldn't be enough to deter Gardner, but at least I had something to point to.

Sure enough, Gardner came in and completely

bypassed the waiting line. He maneuvered around the crowd and angled his body over the barrier.

"Gardner," I said firmly, walking over. "What does the sign say?"

Confused, he looked to where I was pointing. "I—"

"What does it say?" I repeated.

"But—"

"No." I raised my eyebrows and shook my head. "Get in line. I will write you up for this."

He held my gaze for several seconds, as if attempting to employ some Jedi mind trick to get me to back down. But I wasn't going to. This was a hill I was going to die on. The Warden might play favorites and let Gardner get away with shit, but I wasn't going to. After a minute, he huffed and got in line. Once again, to his credit, he never attempted to reach over the barrier again but, suffice it to say, I was not his favorite person, and this was not going to be my last time going toe-to-toe with him over library services.

Other men had seen the exchange and clearly remembered it, because a few days later two inmates came in mid-conversation. I missed the first half of the conversation, but didn't miss the part where my name got mentioned.

"Ms. G is tough," the first inmate said, his face solemn and serious. "She'll fight."

His companion screwed up his face. "No, she's a nice, lovely lady."

The first inmate vehemently shook his head. "Nah, man. 'G' stands for 'gangster.' "

I raised an eyebrow in surprise. Apparently the whole "Ms. G as in Gangsta" was catching on.

I was back in the law library when Lieutenant Hall arrived. Previously in the day, McDougal had informed me that we were out of the Power of Attorney forms, so I would need to make new copies. I usually relied on the law library porters to inform me when we were low on forms, and then would only make copies after they had just used the last one, so while I was back there, I decided to go through and make a list of all of the forms that needed copies.

There were certain forms, like assigning someone your power of attorney, which we were always low on. Others that were popular were motions to change filing deadlines or hearing dates. Many of the inmates didn't have the option of a support system outside, including having an attorney who could do the work for them, so they were left navigating the legal system entirely on their own. It was overwhelming, and also why an inmate like Monroe was able to set himself up with an in-house side hustle helping his peers.

It was only as I was walking back to my desk, list in hand, that I saw Hall standing by my desk. A Lieutenant, and our resident IT technician, Hall was rarely seen down in the yard. His appearance here in the library could only mean one thing.

"It was approved?" I asked, hurrying over.

Grinning, he held up a box of software. "It was approved!"

After Highland had given me permission to research cataloging software systems, I had started immediately. I knew it was a big ask, and if I was only going to get one shot at this, I wanted to make sure that whatever software I chose did everything I needed it to do—both right now and in the future—but also wasn't going to break my library's non-existent budget.

While the main focus was the cataloging software, there were other functions I needed as well: I wanted to be able to check out inmates by their ID numbers, which meant along with keeping a database of books, the system also needed to keep a database of patrons; beyond just knowing what books we owned, I needed to know where they were at any given time: on the shelf? Checked out? Being repaired? Eventually, I also wanted to have access to patron records. I didn't care what they were checking out—this wasn't *1984* and I wasn't Big Brother—but I did want to know if anyone was over the two-book limit. I also hoped to be able to set up a system that gave inmates the ability to look up that same information about the book from a separate computer in the library.

What I needed was an ILS, or an integrated library system.

A big behemoth of a database, an ILS is what allows libraries to function and perform basic tasks, including managing the collection. From all of my years working in libraries, I knew there were some big-name ILS out there, but there was no way I needed, or could afford, the Cadillac of ILS available. Thankfully, there were smaller technology companies who realized that equally smaller libraries needed a different service when it came to their own information management system. After researching all of the options that would have met both my needs and my budget, I put together a proposal for Highland that outlined why it was necessary and how it would help automate the library.

After not hearing back, I had assumed the proposal was still sitting in a pile on her desk somewhere, but apparently I had so successfully outlined the need for an ILS that she had gone ahead and ordered it. Hall was here to install it on my computer.

"That one?" he asked, pointing at the desktop tucked into the corner behind my area of the circulation desk. I nodded. "You're the only one with access to this, right?"

I nodded again. "Just me."

Hall sat at my computer and opened the book, pulling out the CD-Rom. I lingered by as he went through the set-up process, watching over his shoulder. After a few minutes, everything was installed and he stood up. "All yours," Hall said, gesturing that I should sit in the chair.

"Thanks!" I said.

"I know this requires a second computer," he told me, "for your porters. But I don't want to bring it down here quite yet. We still have to figure out the network side of things."

"Okay," I replied. "It's going to take me a while to catalog everything anyway."

After he left, I logged into the new ILS, not entirely sure where to start. There was just so much I could do and so much that needed to be done, but I also wanted to be efficient. Work smarter, not harder, and all of that.

Despite having spent a couple weeks researching and writing up the proposal, I had still forgotten just all of the functionality the software I had chosen offered.

Make no mistake, there was a ridiculous amount of work ahead of me. Once the system was up and running, the library would be automated and the inmates would be able to check books out with just a few clicks of a mouse. But before that, though, I had to input everything into the system. All seven hundred inmates needed to be in there, along with all eight thousand books that made up our collection. Plus, I still had several hundred more donated books to go through. There was no efficient or easy way to do this. I'd just have to start at the As and work my way down the list. And then just keep repeating that over and over again until everything was captured. There were no barcodes, scanning wasn't an option so I needed another system for tagging books and it was going to take months.

None of that mattered, though, because my library was finally out of the dark ages.

Despite the sheer amount of work ahead of me, I couldn't stop grinning.

"You Irish, Ms. G.?"

I looked to my left, where Woodson stood, a pile of books in his hands. "What?"

He nodded towards the new bulletin board I was putting together. Despite originally considering putting up a Women's History bulletin board, I opted instead to introduce the inmates to all of the authors in the world who can claim an Irish heritage: James Joyce. Oscar Wilde. Maeve Binchy. My research into the subject surprised even me, not realizing that Bram Stoker was Irish (or that Bram was short for Abraham. Totally made sense after discovering it, but I hadn't known that was a nickname).

"Oh!" I said. "No, no I'm not. I'm German."

Woodson nodded thoughtfully, chewing this over. "You going to go out for St. Patrick's Day?"

I mentally checked myself, trying to remember if I knew what Woodson had done to get incarcerated at our facility. Last year, both St.

Patrick's Day and 4/20 happened just a couple of months after I arrived, but I still distinctly remembered all of the inmates who made casual comments about both days, often in a self-referential way.

I was pretty sure this was just Woodson making conversation. "No," I responded. "I'm not. I don't really get into the whole St. Patrick's Day thing."

Woodson nodded. "Me either," he responded before turning away and heading towards the shelves.

On the other hand, my other porter, Conway *was* in on drunk driving charges. He was also getting out on St. Patrick's Day, a Wednesday this year.

A few days before his release, on Saturday, I had one goal for the day: do *not* lock my keys in the library staff bathroom as I had done the previous two Saturdays. Doing so always meant, embarrassingly, having the call the officer next door in the Education department—overseeing the AA and NA meetings that happened throughout the day—and asking them to come over just to unlock the door for me so I could retrieve my keys. It was always just absentmindedness. A matter of unclipping my ring of keys from the belt loop on my pants and, after unlocking the door, putting them aside momentarily on the sink, or on the shelf that held the cleaning supplies or miscellaneous office supplies. I'd finish my business and step outside, back into the library, and shut the door behind me. As it was closing shut, just as the lock clicked, I realized I'd left the keys inside.

The first time? Okay, a reasonable mistake. It happens. But a second time? Two weeks in a row? It was mortifying, having to call the officer back. I really did not want to have to make that phone call again so I had to be extra careful with my keys this morning.

Conway was working that morning, his last Saturday before being released.

Inmates, for the most part, get a little bit of the prison version of senioritis in the days leading up to their release. They know the end is in sight, and, unless they were like Jackson back in December, they weren't going to do anything dumb to risk their last few days before freedom.

"Just four more sleeps," Conway said. The inmates counted down their time not by days, but by nights. How many sleeps they have left in the uncomfortable metal bunk beds back in the dorm rooms. "I can't wait to go out and get a nice big green beer."

I sighed. "Conway."

He turned to me, grinning. His smile had missing teeth, his joy shining through the gaps. "Don't worry, Ms. G.! I have a designated driver."

"Just don't do anything dumb, okay? I don't want to see you back here."

Conway's face turned solemn. "I don't want to see me back here either."

The following Tuesday evening, the night of Conway's last sleep, I had just opened the library for the evening shift. It was still quiet, the men working their way through the dinner line when the door of the library opened and a tall, imposing figure walked in. I did a double take, not entirely trusting my eyes. Then again, how many men out there pass a striking resemblance to Taye Diggs?

As he made his way back behind the circulation desk acting as though not a day had gone by since he was last there, I knew my eyes weren't deceiving me:

Jefferson was back.

Chapter 19
Last Dance with Mary Jane

Rule Violation: (40) Procuring or attempting to procure, unauthorized drugs; aiding, soliciting, or collaborating with another to procure unauthorized drugs or to introduce unauthorized drugs into a correctional facility.
—Ohio Admin. Code 5120-9-06

When it came down to it, the thing of it is, only one thing really separated me from the men at the prison: they got caught for their crimes. It was like that for all of us staff members. We weren't any better than or superior to the inmates—we just got lucky. I may not have done or sold drugs like some of them, but I certainly had driven slightly inebriated. I just had managed to get home in one piece and without hurting anyone else or myself. In other words, I got lucky.

Prison can become part of a cycle. The guy gets out, goes back to his habits, gets caught again, comes back to prison again, and then eventually gets out again. The cycle continues. For some, doing time is just a necessary evil. Something they have to do sometimes to maintain their lifestyle outside. They see no need nor have a desire to break the pattern, so they continue to behave in the same manner, to engage in the same activities that got them in the first time around—or the second or the tenth—and they keep catching cases.

The facility did what we could to keep the recidivism rates down, but we could only do so much. Part of my role was maintaining a Reentry Resource Center in the library. This tiny collection of reference books had titles related to writing resumes and cover letters, specifically tailored towards inmates. I had a list of halfway houses in the area for those inmates who didn't feel confident enough to go straight out into the big world, and wanted a period of transition first (some were also mandated per their sentence). There was information about Ohio University's college-degree-by-mail program for inmates in Ohio, meant for those that wanted to extend their education while incarcerated.

We did what we could, but it wasn't always enough to reduce recidivism, which is how Jefferson ended up back at our facility. Because he'd been at the library before, the Job Coordinator just reassigned him to that same position.

For me, it wasn't enough of an issue to fight or try to have him classed somewhere else. He only came in twice a week, a maximum of about six hours a week. Besides, it was hard to get porters to want to work the evening shifts on Tuesday and Wednesday nights, so if I had someone who did want to work then, I might as well take advantage of it.

Jefferson maintained the status quo that had been enacted the last time he'd been here by not talking to me or addressing me in any way. Once he knew he couldn't charm or flatter me into giving him favors, I was considered *persona non grata*, which was fine by me. As long as he did the work, he could think whatever he wanted about me.

"Hey boys." The door into Seg slammed heavily behind me.

Bolton and Lopez lit up. "We've been wondering when you were going to come see us."

I grinned and scanned the whiteboard above their desks, taking in the names. I stopped short halfway down the list, my smile fading. "Why is Lincoln here?" In all the time I'd known him, his record had been spotless. No incident reports, let alone anything severe enough to book a room in the Segregation motel. Then again, if I had learned anything from Willis's surprise stay back in December, it's that I can't discount the possibility of any of my porters, or in this case former porter, landing in Seg.

Lopez raised an eyebrow. "Oh, his baby mama left him some drugs. In the lockers up front."

"Seriously?"

"Oh yeah," Bolton said with a nod. "There's no way he's getting that job back up front."

There were only so many ways to get drugs in and out of the prison, and while it didn't happen very often, it did happen. Routine and random drug tests were given several times a year, and inmates often had a test come back hot for some drug or another.

Lincoln and his baby mama had apparently figured out one of those methods: when she came for visitation she'd use one of the brown lockers in the back to keep her personal items in while she was visiting him. Included in that collection of personal items were drugs that she'd leave behind. As the foyer cleaning porter, part of his job included going back to those lockers, where he could just grab the drugs and slip them into the pocket of his uniform and go about his day.

That idiot. I was going to kill him. I was not thrilled to lose Lincoln as a porter, but I came to terms with it knowing that, if nothing else, Captain Gerry had seen something in him that showed promise and trust. But now that idiot had gone and thrown it all away for a fix.

When I got to Lincoln's cell I stood there, one eyebrow raised. "Lincoln."

I didn't bother hiding my anger, mixed with a dash of disappointment. And I was angry. Despite the whole "not playing favorites" thing, Lincoln was one of my favorites, since he was someone who was motivated enough to make changes once he got outside. He had kids, he didn't want to continue the cycle of selling drugs and spending time in prison. And he'd just wasted it.

It went beyond just Seg. Oh, sure, he'd spend a few days in there and get out and get reclassed to another position and hopefully not make the same dumb mistake ever again. But by bringing drugs into the prison, he'd risked his sentence, too: if the prison administration was feeling uncharitable towards him, they very easily could extend his time for this.

He lowered his head to one side. "I fucked up, Ms. G."

A short burst of laughter escaped my lips. "Uh, yeah ya did."

Lincoln shook his head. "I don't know what I was thinking, Ms. G." After another pause, "I have a favor to ask."

I hesitated. I know he probably didn't really mean favors in any kind of exchange way. Like I would do something for him and he'd owe me. Inmates traded favors inside as means of payment, but when staff got involved, things got tricky. Still, Lincoln didn't seem like the type to risk asking staff for favors. Even if he was, doing it right here in Segregation with officers just a few yards away was about the dumbest thing I could think of.

Then again, I wouldn't have pegged Lincoln to be the type to try and smuggle drugs into the prison, so what the hell did I know?

"Okay," I finally said, wary. "What is it?"

He lowered his head, shy. "After I get out, can I come back to the library?"

Like with everything else, I couldn't make any promises. But good library workers were hard to come by, so I promised I'd do what I could.

That weekend, I found myself doing something I hadn't done since childhood: roller skating.

I never learned how to properly roller skate. Not officially. My form of roller skating is a variation on skateboarding: I plant one foot and use the other for movement and momentum. But here I was, a late twentysomething, pretending she knew what she was doing on a rink. Because I love my friends and sometimes I put myself in really awkward, uncomfortable situations when it's their thirtieth birthday and all they want to do is go roller skating.

Despite spending most of the night people watching—or, perhaps, because of that—I decided I wanted to finally learn how to properly skate. To be fair, what I *really* wanted to do was learn how to roller skate so I could live out my dream of being a roller derby girl. In true cart-before-the-horse fashion, I already had several Roller Derby Names selected, even though I had no idea what I was doing when it came to rolling around on shoes that had wheels attached. (These included Kink Floyd, in an ode to one of my favorite bands; Quiver Strong, a play on River Song from *Doctor Who*; and Hatelyn Snark, in honor of one of my favorite characters from *Game of Thrones*. Of course, after the HBO adaptation came out I learned that Catelyn Stark's first name is pronounced Cat-lyn, not Cate-lyn, but whatever.)

I was at my local thrift store the next day and wandering around when I came upon a pair of Rollerblades in my size. Rollerblades aren't exactly the same as roller skates and this pair had a missing brake on one of the skates but it was a good start, especially at thrift store prices.

My apartment had hardwood floors, so for the first few days I just skated around my dining room, bracing myself against the wall or table or counter when necessary, which, admittedly, was often. After several days of this, though, I was confident enough in my non-abilities to take it outside.

Don't try this at home, kids.

In all my excitement to go skating and buying Rollerblades, I forgot one thing: pads. As I was soon to find out, roller blading on uneven city sidewalks in an industrial part of a city, where there is gravel everywhere, is a much different experience than roller blading around the safety and comfort of the hardwood floor of my downtown apartment.

I fell a grand total of three times in my brief jaunt: as soon as I stepped out the main door of the building (who knew thresholds could be so treacherous?), half a block down, and then at the end of the block. That last one, where my arm slammed into the concrete, was the one that convinced me to take the Rollerblades off and walk back upstairs in just my socks, gravel be damned.

That night, my arm ached. My wrist in particular had limited movement and felt like it was sprained. As a child I had broken my wrist ice skating while attempting to live out my dreams of being a figure skater (I'm starting to sense a theme), but I didn't think the wrist was broken this time around. I've had few broken bones, but multiple sprained ankles, and this felt like a sprain, so I propped it up and iced it overnight.

The next morning, however, I couldn't extend my arm back far enough to clasp my bra, and I realized the situation may be a little direr than I had originally thought. I could get the arm itself back there, the shoulder rotated just fine, but when I tried to lift my hand up towards the line of my bra strap, pain shot down the length of my arm.

I am not a woman who can function in the

world outside my apartment sans support system, so this was a bit of an awkward problem.

"This is Jill," I said as soon as Dr. Harald's voicemail picked up. "I'm not going to be in today. I had a fall last night and I'm going to go to the ER to make sure my arm isn't broken."

I had no intention of going to the emergency room, but "I can't put my bra on" wasn't the most eloquent way of describing my situation, accurate as it was.

A few minutes and no progress later, however, I thought maybe I *should* go to the emergency room. Just in case. Mostly, though, to cover my ass, knowing that Highland would without a doubt be asking for a note from my doctor regarding this. Especially since I said that's where I was going.

There was a hospital less than a mile away from my apartment, so I gingerly carried my arm out and drove myself to the hospital, much to the combined horror and amusement of the receptionist: since moving back to Ohio, I hadn't yet updated my driver's license, which still showed me living an hour away in my hometown.

"Did you really drive here all the way from Hudson?" the intake nurse asked, staring at my driver's license. With a smile, I said no and explained I lived just a couple of blocks away.

The emergency room was empty—I seemed to be the only patient this Friday morning.

The nurse walked me back to the spiderweb of rooms, turning on the light in one as she went through the intake process. Handing me a cup, she gestured to the sad sterile bathroom with the harsh yellow light, requesting a pregnancy test before conducting the necessary x-rays. I sat on the toilet several minutes before, yet again, offering to sign any and all papers that would let them off the hook for liability if I ended up being pregnant (although, with my relationship having ended almost a year ago and no bedroom shenanigans since, I knew I was fine).

After gingerly twisting my arm this way and that so x-rays could be taken, I was taken back to the room. I cradled my arm gently, waiting. My legs swung beneath me as I sat on the edge of the hospital bed.

The door opened and a slightly older woman with short copper hair walked in. I hadn't seen her before but she was the only one not wearing a lab coat or scrubs, which, oddly enough, seemed to lend her an air of authority in a hospital. "I'm Dr. Hornby," she said, shaking my good hand.

I smiled brightly, prepared to be told it was sprained, here's a prescription for mild painkillers, give it a rest for a day or two, and be on your way.

Dr. Hornby rolled a stool over. On closer inspection, she looked like a vintage French movie star, with her auburn hair pinned back, and her ivory limbs, lithe and delicate, stark against her all-black clothes. Perched on the stool, she clasped her hands between her knees and leaned forward. All that was missing was a jaunty beret and a slender cigarette perched delicately between her dark red lips.

"Your elbow is broken," she said. Stated, really. So precise and finite. Just a simple statement, like it was no big deal.

Still smiling, I nodded. My elbow is . . . wait. What did she say? Did she say *broken?* My elbow couldn't be broken. First, it didn't *feel* broken. But even if it did, the pain wasn't in my elbow, it was in my wrist. My *wrist* was the issue. How could my *elbow* be broken?

But, more to the point, nothing was supposed to be broken at all. I had only come here so I could get a stupid doctor's note to excuse me from my job for a day or two. It wasn't supposed to require any medical attention beyond resting, ice, compression, and elevation.

Oh gosh, if it was broken, how long was I going to be dealing with this? When I was a kid and broke my wrist I was in that ridiculous bright green hard plaster cast for months. I couldn't be in a cast for months! HOW would I work?

Female correctional officers who were pregnant or injured could be rotated to the security booth upfront, away from inmates. As the librarian, I didn't have that option.

There, in the emergency room of Lutheran Hospital, with my anxiety-prone mind moving into worst case scenario mode, I promptly burst into tears.

Chapter 20
Them's the Breaks, Kid

It is the policy of the Department of Rehabilitation and Correction to provide medical services and continuity of care to incarcerated offenders. Continuity of care is provided from admission to transfer or discharge from the facility, and shall include referral to community-based providers when indicated. These services are to be accessible to all offenders, include an emphasis on disease prevention, and reflect a holistic approach in accordance with approved levels of care.
—ODRC Policy 68-MED-01

CO Price's narrowed eyes followed me as soon as I pulled open the heavy glass doors into the prison lobby. It was a Wednesday, my late-start day, which meant I thankfully didn't have to wait in a long line of coworkers to go through the metal detector and have my bags searched. Of course, this also meant that Price didn't have anywhere else to focus her attention as I slowly made my way across the faded yellow linoleum.

After my impromptu visit to the hospital, I hadn't been to the prison in nearly a week.

Armed with a doctor's note and a prescription for Tylenol with codeine, I went home and spent the week nursing my wounded arm.

I went over to the control center and dropped my name-tag into the drawer, then went back over to where Price stood. Using only my right arm, I slung my purse over the side of the lobby desk and waited for her to start going through it.

"Does *she* know about that?" Price asked, overly emphasizing the second word. Her gaze focused on my left arm, which was fixed into a ninety-degree angle, wrapped in ACE bandages, and supported by a blue sling.

'She,' of course, was Highland.

The anxiety from my coworker was justified: while I'd like to think it was care and concern about my broken elbow, I know it was really about how my broken elbow was going to affect my ability to manage within the four walls of my little library.

"Yes," I said, "Highland knows."

"Uh-huh," Price retorted, eyes still narrowed behind her glasses. "I need to see the sling."

Right. Because if diapers have to be checked in case baby mamas are using their infants as mules to sneak shit in, then I very easily could also be sneaking shit in with the lovely, cheap blue vinyl fabric supporting my arm.

I removed the sling and handed it over to her, using my other hand to support my splint. My elbow was broken, but the break was miniscule

347

enough that I didn't require months in a plaster cast. Instead, a half-cast—plaster molded to the bottom of my forearm—kept my arm braced in place and the whole thing was wrapped up tight, making the arm immobile.

I *could* say that this was all my fault, because I was the one who bought the Rollerblades from the thrift store, and I was the one who decided to use them without elbow or knee pads even though I had never, ever properly learned how to skate. I was also the one who decided to take them outside onto my very uneven city sidewalk and attempt to skate without said pads, knowing full well that my balance was not where it needed to be. I, of course, was the one who fell right on her ass, slamming her elbow down onto the concrete.

Satisfied I wasn't attempting to smuggle in any contraband, Price handed back my sling and allowed me to go through the metal detector, which stayed silent. Once on the other side, I grabbed my purse.

The phone rang. Price picked up then gestured for me to stop. "Yeah, she's here." Her eyes cut to mine. "Yup. Bye." Placing the handset in the receiver, she said: "Highland wants to see you."

Of course she did.

Highland's office was located in Administration. I found her seated behind her desk, waiting for me. Outside her window, the summer sun coated the green grass and empty yard. Soon, the inmates would be filing out of their housing units for lunch, and I was impatient to get down to the Education building because there were always copies to make and books to file before the afternoon shift. Plus, y'know, there was that whole being gone for a week thing, and wanting to find out what, if anything, I had missed in my absence. Prisons run on order and routine and this meeting, however necessary, was a kink in my carefully planned schedule.

"Take a seat," she offered when I walked through the door.

I sat down across from her, anxious and nervous. I hadn't been in her office since she made the move to Deputy Warden, and as a means of distracting myself, I let my eyes wander. Family photos were displayed on the bookshelf in the corner. On the wall behind her was a cheesy motivational poster lauding the value of teamwork.

"How are you feeling?" she asked, clasping her hands together and leaning across her desk towards me.

"I'm okay," I said with a shrug. "It's a small fracture, should only be for two weeks."

She nodded. "I'm not really sure what to do about this."

Not sure what to say, seeing as how I wasn't entirely sure what "this" was, I simply sat and waited.

"Well," she continued, gesturing towards my sling, "you're down an arm. If something were to happen in the library, you'd have no way to defend yourself. How important is the sling?"

I furrowed my brow. Did she think I was wearing this as a fashion statement? "Um, very?" I tried to keep the annoyance out of my voice, though I wasn't entirely successful. "I mean, y'know, I need it. For my elbow."

Highland sighed. "Right, of course, it's just . . . it's not a breakaway sling."

Ah. Now I understood.

When an inmate broke a bone, or injured his arm in some other capacity that required a sling, they were given one that had a breakaway Velcro strap, so if another inmate pulled down on the sling, the strap would break apart.

Mine didn't do that. Mine was your standard hospital-issued, non-breakaway sling. If someone decided to pull down on *my* sling . . . well, basically Highland was trying to save me from possible strangulation at the hands of an inmate.

I knew I worked in a prison. I knew I worked with men who had been convicted of crimes. I knew I wore a panic button for a reason. But I didn't really understand what that truly meant until that exact moment in time.

"My elbow is in a fixed ninety-degree angle," I told her. "When I'm sitting down at my desk it won't be a problem, but walking around the yard, I need the sling."

Highland's head bobbed in understanding. She studied me, eyes intense. I could practically see the cogs working in her brain, trying to figure out how to accommodate my injury while also reducing the risk of ending up with a dead librarian. "Okay. Okay, here's what we'll do. When the yard is closed during count and meals, you can wear the sling. But anytime you are around inmates, including in the library, no sling. Got it?"

I nodded. Because, really, what choice did I have? If nothing else, at least when I was sitting in the library I'd be able to rest my arm on my desk, and wouldn't even really need the sling.

Thinking the conversation was over, I started to rise.

"One more thing," Highland said. I paused. "We are going to reassign CO Gardein to the library for the next two weeks."

I sat back down. *That* was unexpected. Over the course of the year that I had been working at the prison, I'd never had a CO in the library with me. The only times they were there was when the officer assigned to the Education building next door came on their once an hour rounds (or, depending on the officer, once every three hours), or when I needed them to come over and watch the inmates while I took a restroom break. The rest of the time, it was just me and the inmates.

That was sort of the *thing* when it came to the library. It was the reason I had inmates waiting outside before I opened, and the reason I had to force inmates out when I closed. The library was the one place on the camp that didn't have a guard. The one place the inmates could go and *not* feel like they were in prison.

"Gardein," I repeated. It was nothing personal, I liked Gardein. If I had to go so far as to pick a favorite correctional officer, she'd probably be at the top of the list. But I was also slightly territorial when it came to my library, and I was concerned that having an officer in there would disrupt the atmosphere I had carefully cultivated over the past fourteen months.

Highland nodded. "Just for the two weeks that your arm is in the splint. If something were to happen, you won't be able to defend yourself appropriately, and even with a panic button it might take too long for them to respond."

"Right. Okay, sure." I looked at her expectantly. "Anything else?"

With a wave of her hand she silently dismissed me.

By the time I got down to the Education building, my coworkers were finishing their lunches. I'd been absent for four work days, so there was a lot of business to catch up on as I quickly heated up my leftovers and joined them. Even then, though, most of the conversation focused on my arm, with me rehashing the experience and going over Highland's new rules.

A few minutes before 1 p.m., Gardein poked her head into the classroom we used as a cafeteria. "Hey, Ms. G. You ready?"

"Yup!" I stood then gave a heavy sigh. "I forgot to grab the newspapers from up front."

"No worries," she said. "I got them for you."

I gave her a grateful smile then followed her out of the building, remembering at the last second to remove my sling and tuck it into my bag.

The inmates had already started filing from their housing units down to the chow hall and Gardein positioned herself between me and the inmates for the duration of the short walk from the Education building to the library. Once inside, Gardein settled herself at my desk while I sat down at my computer behind her. True to her word, the stack of today's newspapers were sitting on top of the circulation desk.

Soon after our arrival the library door opened and my porters Lincoln and Carroll walked in. Apparently my request to have Lincoln reclassed was approved while I was out. They both nodded polite hellos to Gardein and started to walk behind the circulation desk but stopped short as soon as they saw me.

"Ms. G.!" Lincoln exclaimed, a wide grin on his face. "You're back!"

"I'm back," I replied and then, without missing a beat: "You need to tuck in your shirt."

Behind him, Carroll guffawed. "Damn, Ms. G.," Lincoln said, making a big show of tucking the tails of his state-issued light blue shirt into the elastic waistband of his pants. "You don't miss anything, do you?"

"I don't. And don't you forget it, either."

Carroll smiled. "Glad to have you back, Ms. G."

I smiled back at him. "Glad to be back, Carroll. Thanks."

Gardein walked over to the rack of magazines, eventually setting on *Entertainment Weekly*. She took it back to her spot at my desk at the door, and opened the cover to the first page. After over a year, I was finally going to learn what it was like to have a CO in here all the time. Admittedly I was not happy about it. Having an officer stationed in the prison library was going to make it feel like, well, a prison library. The success of this room depended on the absence of security. Or, perhaps more accurately, the *illusion* of a lack of security. An officer was always a phone call or panic button away, but it was easy to suppress that thought.

I sighed, resigned to my fate. I wouldn't be surprised if attendance dropped over the next two weeks once word got around that Gardein was going to be here every day.

But, as with every situation, there are silver linings. If nothing else, because Gardein *was* here and could handle most of the day-to-day elements that came with running the library, including making sure inmates followed the dress code and signed in, that gave me an excuse to focus entirely on my cataloging project.

I turned to the pile of books that had been left over from last week, before my decision to spend less than $4 on a pair of thrift store Rollerblades, and got started.

Two weeks later, my arm was free of the splint and Gardein was free from her mandated library post. In truth, I think she kind of liked her stint in the library. She got to read magazines all day and issues between inmates was minimal.

On one of the first Gardein-free days, I was continuing my never-ending cataloging project when an inmate approached my desk. "Hey, Ms. G.," he said, holding up a book. "Do you want this?"

Turning my head, I gaped at the familiar black cover. A pair of hands clasped a bright red apple. "Seriously?" I asked, taking the copy of *Twilight* from him. I cradled the thick paperback in my palms, as if he had just handed me a copy of the Gutenberg Bible, fresh off the printing press.

He shrugged. "Eh, my sister sends them to me. I don't read them."

"So you're just . . . donating it."

"If you think you can use it, sure."

Was he kidding? The library didn't own a copy of Stephenie Meyer's blockbuster supernatural romance, but it was one of the most frequently requested books through the ILL system. Every week I was putting in request after request for *Twilight* and the rest of the books in the series. This was a hot commodity.

"Yes," I said, smiling. "Yes, I can definitely use this. Thank you."

The inmate just turned with a small wave, not fully realizing the popularity of the book that he handed me.

Hoskins, who was sitting nearby, came over. "We're going to have to watch that one," he commented, nodding towards the book.

I agreed. Until I could get this cataloged and on the shelf, we were going to have to keep it locked up, so it didn't go missing. Even then, after it was out in circulation we were going to be vigilant about making sure it stayed in circulation and didn't go missing.

Still, it was a quiet afternoon and I quickly finished my daily book quota. I could keep going, get ahead on tomorrow's numbers, but there was that donated copy of *Twilight* just hanging out, locked in the bathroom until I could put it in our system. It had been a few years since I read the book, it wouldn't be *so* terrible to steal a few minutes reading it myself, right?

Chapter 21
The Spider and the Fly

All inmates shall be afforded access to institution library services. No inmate shall be restricted from the inmate library, unless approved by the managing officer or designee.

—ODRC Policy 58-LIB-01

Gardner slammed a piece of paper on top of the counter at my desk. "I need this notarized," he demanded.

So it was going to be one of *those* days with Gardner. Not that there was any other kind of day with Gardner, as he moved through the world like a tornado. A very angry tornado set on destroying anything and everything in his path. The guy had a lot of rage stored up, his veins pulsating beneath the skin of his bald head any time something didn't go his way. Some days, though, I got lucky and the tornado would completely bypass any interaction with me. On those days, he'd blow past my desk and camp out at one of the computers, banging furiously on the keyboard. When all the computers were full, he'd sit at a nearby table and wait, seething until it was his turn.

Today, unfortunately, was not one of those lucky days.

I pointed to the piece of paper taped to the top of the counter just a few inches to the left of his document. "I don't notarize on Thursdays. You'll have to come back tomorrow." My plastic, plastered smile took up the entire lower half of my face as I beamed politely.

"But I need this notarized right now." He jabbed his finger into the document, punctuating every word.

Dealing with Gardner was a lot like when I was a kid, and my younger sister and I would get into a fight. Amy was far more outwardly emotional than I was, so she would scream and yell with rage, and I would just sit there and not react because I knew that her end goal was to *get* a reaction from me. I certainly wasn't going to give her what she wanted—that would take all of the fun out of it. My non-reaction only infuriated her even more, so she'd scream and yell louder, eventually alerting our parents to the situation. Our dad would come down into the basement and find my sister screaming and me just playing silently with Barbies. Punishment was swift, with Amy being sent to her room, while I was left in the basement to play all by myself, just the way this introvert wanted it.

As the older of the two, sure, I was supposed to be the mature one and it was a little petty of me to be consistently setting a trap she was always destined to walk into, but I'd argue that, really, as the older sister it was my job to do such things.

(We'd both always scoff when he would tell us that we would grow up to be best friends. Twenty-five years later and well, okay, Dad. You won that one.)

I like to think that those years of passive-aggressive fighting with my sister served me well as I moved into the world of library service. Because anyone who has worked any kind of front-facing role can tell you that there are always *those* kinds of patrons or customers. The kind of customers who make you hate the "customer-is-always-right" philosophy. Patrons who want to get a reaction out of you, as long as you react the way they want you to that is. Customers just itching to start a fight.

Gardner was one of those kinds of customers.

With enough experience behind a counter or cash register, I knew that giving into a patron's frustration served no one, especially not me. Kill them with kindness, flies and honey, and all of that. Of course, the kindness applied was probably supposed to be genuine and authentic, and not a means of me pissing them off even further, but potayto-potahto.

I scrunched my shoulders up near my ears and gave an overly exaggerated shrug. "I'm sorry, but I don't notarize on Thursdays. You'll have to come back tomorrow."

"I don't think you understand."

"Oh, no," I said, mustering an overabundance of fake sympathy. "I understand. But, see, just an hour ago I had to turn away another inmate who wanted something notarized, and told him he'd also have to come back tomorrow. It wouldn't be fair for me to then turn around and notarize this for you when I wouldn't notarize his document."

Gardner stared at me with open hostility, his eyes drilling holes into me. It was so intense, that I imagined from his perspective, Gardner was glaring at me through a gun-sight trained right at my forehead. Fairness apparently didn't exist in his world, at least not unless it somehow always, and only, benefited him. "Fine. I'll just go next door and ask Kim."

I forced my eyes steady otherwise they'd roll back so far into my head I'd be staring at the interior of my skull. "She won't notarize for you, either. You know she only does it on Mondays."

"Yeah, well, we'll just see about that," he snapped.

As he snatched his document back up, I had a split-second epiphany. For most other inmates I'd have a moment of guilt-laden hesitation at the plan brewing in my head, but Gardner had pissed me off from day one, and if I had learned anything from my years listening to the musicals

360

of Stephen Sondheim, it's that opportunity is not a lengthy visitor.

That, and have enough talent with a razor and your victim will voluntarily sit right in your waiting barber chair.

Gardner didn't like me—that much was apparent—but he especially didn't like taking orders from me and I was 99.9 percent certain it was entirely because of my gender. Men like Gardner don't like taking orders from any woman, and they certainly don't approve of women being in any position of power. I knew from his file that he was in on a domestic abuse charge, his anger manifesting itself physically to the point that he landed in prison.

He couldn't lash out at me without risking extending his sentence at a higher-security prison, so he had to take his frustration out on me in other ways. Inmates had limited power within the prison walls, but they had still had some level of agency. By design, he was forced to hear what I had to say, but he didn't have to actually listen to me.

This meant that no matter what I told him to do, Gardner was guaranteed to do the exact opposite.

"Gardner!" I yelled after him. "Do not, under any circumstances, go next door and ask Kimberly to notarize that for you."

The door slammed shut behind him. I looked out the window and watched him stomp his way next door.

Welcome to my parlor, Mr. Gardner.

With a smile, I picked up the phone and dialed Kimberly's extension. "Hey," I said as soon as she answered. "So, Gardner was in here wanting to get something notarized and I told him no. He said he was going to come over there and talk to you."

"There's no way in hell I'm notarizing it for him. It's bad enough I have to do that shit on Mondays."

"No, I know that, and I told him that you weren't going to do it for him, but he doesn't care. As he was leaving I directly told him do not go over and ask you."

"Ohhhhhh," she said, catching on. "I see. Okay."

There is a fine art to writing incident reports. During orientation, it was repeated, over and over again, that incident reports were to contain facts and only facts. This served me well, because while we were to report only facts, we didn't necessarily have to report *all* of the facts.

The facts:

1. Gardner had come in wanting something notarized.
2. I said no because I only notarize on Thursdays as outlined by the schedule I keep taped to my desk.
3. Gardner insisted.

4. I repeated no.

5. Gardner said he was going to go ask Kimberly.

6. I directly ordered him not to do that and he did it anyway.

Those were the facts. They maybe weren't *all* of the facts, because I failed to mention that I had purposely directed him to not go ask Kimberly, knowing full well that was exactly what he was going to do. I also kinda fudged the conversation I had with Kimberly, where I mentioned the interaction with Gardner and she told me that he had disobeyed me by coming over to ask her to notarize his document. It wasn't *exactly* a lie: she and I did indeed have the conversation but only because we concocted it over the phone. It wasn't a spontaneous, casual conversation had over lunch, but a deliberate means of making sure I had the knowledge that he had come to Kim for notary work, in direct violation of my order. Was it petty? Sure. Was I following the spirit of the law? Probably not. But I also wasn't going to allow Gardner to circumvent the rules just because he thought he was above the rules. Nor was I going to react in any way that would also get me into hot water. As Don Corleone reminds us in *The Godfather*, "Revenge is a dish that tastes best when it is cold."

"Did you write me up?"

Gardner's face was flushed red with anger as he waved the piece of paper in my face. It was a few days later. From what I could glimpse, the piece of paper he was furiously waving was a note from his case worker requesting a meeting with him. I stood up from my seat to face him at eye level.

"Gardner."

"Did. You. Write. Me. Up?" The paper cut through the air as he shook it.

I sighed. "Gardner, I suggest you just go speak to your case worker."

"It's a simple question. Did you write me up?"

"Just go talk to your case worker, Gardner."

He narrowed his eyes, dark with rage. "Bitch," he spat as he turned and stomped out, bumping into Dr. Harald in the entryway.

"What was that about?" Dr. Harald asked, coming up to my desk.

Rolling my eyes, I shook my head. "I wrote Gardner up for disobedience of a direct order, and just now he called me a bitch."

Dr. Harald's head dropped in disappointment. He always had far more faith in the goodwill of the inmates than most other staff. Dr. Harald recognized Gardner as an annoyance, a pesky little fly who buzzed around incessantly, always trying to curry favor with the men in charge.

It's how he managed to get approval to use the computer from the Warden—a man—when the rest of us refused. For the rest of us, Gardner was an infestation.

"So, about Gardner?" Donnor asked. She was calling from her spot down in Segregation. In the background I could hear her shuffling papers, probably the incident reports I had written up. As head of the Rules Infraction Board, she had final say over punishments. "What do you want to see happen?"

Kim had given me a head's up that Donnor might want my opinion on repercussions, although I was still surprised to receive the call. For every other conduct report I'd written, as soon as I turned them in, they were out of my hands. I'd only know what happened if an inmate happened to mention it, or if the punishment was Segregation, in which case I'd see them when I went on my weekly visit. But other than that, I never knew what happened.

This time was different. This time I had swiftly written two different reports in close succession. Whatever punishment that would have been doled out for the original disobedience would probably have been fine, but this was probably the only time I can say that being called a "bitch" was a bonus.

"Can I have him temporarily banned?"

There was a pause. This was a big request. The library, by design and by law, was there for the availability of the inmates. But whatever punishment Gardner had been given in the past for his issues never seemed to deter him from misbehaving.

Even if Gardner was given bunk restriction and forced to wear a bright green jumpsuit, he'd still be allowed to visit the library for one hour every day. I needed something more severe to get the point across.

Honestly, though, I also just wanted a respite from having to deal with him.

"Yeah," Donnor finally said. "I think we can make that happen."

A few hours later, Kimberly triumphantly brought in a formal document outlining Gardner's punishment. "Thirty days," she proclaimed, handing it to me. "He can't come here for thirty days."

Damn. I'd been hoping for like, a week or two, but a whole month? It was going to be like a vacation. It was like Christmas in July.

Chapter 22
Check Mate

Board games may be purchased through approved vendors by recreation staff, unit staff, or through inmate [Industrial & Entertainment] funds. Dice must be removed and replaced with spinners or cards.

—ODRC Policy 77-REC-01

When I was in middle school, Field Day was both the best and the worst day of the year. It was the best because, well, it was spent outside. Despite being relatively intelligent, school was extremely boring to me.

Field Day, however, was a respite from all things academic. I could hang out with my friends outside, and we could stuff ourselves silly with hot dogs and chips, while we watched classmates make fools of themselves in ridiculous competitions like Hula-Hooping. Of course, Field Day could really be called *Track* and Field Day. So while, on the one hand, Field Day was a vacation from the classroom, on the other hand, it was kind of an all-day gym class, which was my least favorite of all classes. A day-long gym class that I would inevitably get a five-alarm sunburn from, regardless of how many applications of sunscreen I used.

Sometimes, everything is a tradeoff.

Yard Day is the prison equivalent of Field Day.

Yard Day is similarly structured: the inmates, excused from all other regularly scheduled activities, are able to participate in a variety of games. Activities are both physical, like baseball or basketball, but also mental, including board and card games. For lunch, staff fired up the grills and had a cookout, serving hot dogs and hamburgers to the inmates.

Yard Day was held on Wednesday that year and because it was an all-day event, my schedule changed for that day. Instead of working my usual 11 a.m. until 7:30 p.m. schedule, I got to come in early and leave after 4 p.m., along with the rest of my coworkers. Sure, it meant having to wake up early an extra day that week, but, at the other end, I had equally earned a bonus evening off. All about those tradeoffs.

In the days leading up to Yard Day, Highland came down to the Education department, clipboard in hand. "Grunenwald," she said, scanning down the list. "You will be supervising the chess tournament."

Chess? I get to spend the afternoon, presumably indoors, watching guys play chess? Apparently, as an adult, my sensibilities related to Field Day hadn't changed much. I'd gladly take it.

Yard Day was also a bonus dress-down day for staff. We were allowed to wear jeans and tennis shoes without having the pay the usual money for charity. Given the sunny forecast, I opted for denim capris and layered on as much sunscreen as possible, to hopefully mitigate any sunburn I would get while outside.

The library was closed for the day, so when I arrived, I headed down to Education and waited around with the rest of the Education and Recovery Resources departments until the official 8 a.m. start. The rest of the day's normal activities were maintained: breakfast and count happened on schedule, but the rest of the time the staff was out at our various posts monitoring the activities we'd been assigned.

For me, this meant the chow hall. Not only did I get to sit inside all day, I got to sit inside in air-conditioning.

My job was simple: keep track of the chess tournament bracket, and maintain order in case any disputes broke out. But I wasn't really too worried about any fights or disputes because these were chess players. To borrow a sentiment from the movie *Wet Hot American Summer*, they were indoor kids, like me. When given an option to go outside and play sports, or stay inside and play board games, they all opted to stay inside and play board games.

In other words: these were my people.

Many of them were also library regulars. The kind of regulars that showed up when the library opened and stayed all through first shift, only to return and do the same thing for second shift. Day in and day out. This shouldn't have surprised me. There is a certain overlap between the individuals who prefer to stay inside on bright sunny Saturdays, and the individuals who spend all their free time in the library.

But while I was excited to have been given the indoor post for the day, my expertise in board games didn't expand beyond CLUE. So a game as intricate as chess? Not my forte.

I had tried to teach myself years before, when my dad first brought home our personal desktop computer for the house. It was a Windows machine and while now the technology seems ancient, back then it blew my mind away. Included in the small collection of preinstalled games was an electronic version of chess. I knew how the pieces moved. I understood the Queen was the most powerful, the pawn the least. I understood the mechanics of chess.

What I always struggled with was seeing far enough ahead to predict any level of game play from my opponent. My brain just didn't work that way. I could easily puzzle out the logic of deciphering who killed with what weapon in which room of the mansion, but knowing where my companion would move their piece next? I couldn't see that far ahead.

Watching the inmates play their games of chess on Yard Day blew my mind, the same way that old computer did twenty years before. These were men who knew chess. They understood the mechanics and the techniques, their brains seeing every possible combination five, ten, twenty steps ahead.

The cavernous chow hall was silent except for the *click click click* of chess pieces as they maneuvered across the boards. The tournament started during the morning shift, with twenty inmates spread out across ten tables. The recreation coordinator had drafted the initial pairings based on who had signed up in advance, and my job was to write down the names of the winners and guide them to the next game as the players advanced.

One of the inmates playing chess was Tucker. Tucker was a library regular, one of the few inmates who had a long sentence: five years. Long for our prison, I should say. Most were in only for a year or two. Tucker had already cycled through all of the available job postings and the classes he was eligible to take. The Job Coordinator was constantly struggling to find something for Tucker to do. He was bright and not very talkative, and always looked as if he was seriously deep in thought. As if his mind never really stopped thinking.

His latest assignment was as one of the inmates involved in the Puppy Program. Since my first day, when I was greeted unceremoniously by a full-grown St. Bernard, I'd gotten used to the canine visitors that came with their handlers every day. I kept dog biscuits behind the desk for visitors and on really hot days, put out a bowl of water.

Tucker's dog was a black pug named Tug. Tug the pug loved me. *Loved* me—this dog would not leave me alone. When Tucker first kept bringing him in, Tug would run around the desk, tugging at his leash for more slack, so he could come over and say hi. Then Tucker would have to be the one to tug on the leash to redirect Tug back into the crowd of tables and chairs.

The dogs were supposed to stay with their handlers at all times, those were the rules. And Tucker always seemed to feel bad about Tug's behavior, often apologizing for the dog. However, I found it adorable, in fact, which is why, one day, when Tucker started to tug on the leash I said, "You know, he can just stay back here with me while you're in the library."

Tucker looked at me in disbelief. As if he didn't honestly believe that I sincerely wanted to watch a dog that wasn't my responsibility. But I did, which surprised me more than either of us. Tucker handed me the red leash and went and found a seat in the back of the room.

From that day on, anytime Tucker was visiting the library, Tug came and hung out with me. In the beginning, I'd hold on to the leash to make sure he didn't wander over to the circulation desk and risk getting accidentally run over by the wheels of the chairs, but after a while even that became unnecessary. The majority of the time, Tug just curled up at my feet and slept.

Which is what he was doing during Yard Day while Tucker played chess. I was so involved with watching the games, trying to pick up what minimal tips I could, that I completely lost track of time. It was only when Dutch walked in and motioned to the clock that I realized there was only about ten minutes left until the mid-morning break.

The inmates were dining alfresco today, which meant any in-progress games could be left alone until they could pick them back up after lunch. They went back to their houses for count, which was the cue for the staff to get our hot dogs and chips. After count, the inmates made their way through the line and settled in clusters around the yard, dining and chatting. Peals of laughter rang out across the expanse of green.

Once lunch was over, the inmates fanned out, resuming their activities from earlier. If, like the chess players who had been knocked out in one of the earlier rounds, they wanted to join a pickup game of basketball or baseball they could, or they could go down to the rec center where they could play ping-pong or checkers.

The afternoon felt slower than the morning, the number of inmates dwindling down with each successive game. By now, the inmates who had been knocked out didn't want to leave, they wanted to be there when a winner was crowned. I got the sense that at this stage in the game, the handful of inmates remaining were known around camp as the serious chess players. They were the grandmasters and, like every game of chess, the winner of the tournament was going to come down to who saw far enough ahead to know which steps to take to position himself on top.

Kinnear positioned his rook with a triumphant smile. "Check mate!"

Stanfield, fingers pinched on top of his King, examined the board carefully. Then he tipped his King over. He held out his right hand over the board. "Good game."

Kinnear nodded, shaking his hand. "Good game, good game."

I glanced up at the clock above the door. 3:30 p.m. We were done early. "Good job, guys," I said. I wrote *Kinnear* in the final box in the middle of the tournament bracket. "I'll turn this in, and they'll be eventually handing out prizes. Well done, Kinnear."

The tournament over, the men all stood up and

headed for the exit. I began boxing up the games of chess, carefully folding the board and counting the pieces to make sure all were accounted for.

After, I stepped outside, closing the door of the chow hall behind me. A baseball game was happening on the diamond, but I remained under the awning, safe from the harsh sun. The yard was covered with men in varying shades of blue, enjoying the fresh air and momentary freedom. For me, Field Day had been a break from the drudgery of academics and homework and teachers. For the men here at the prison, Yard Day was a similar break, it allowed them to momentarily forget where they were. It was a day of games and fun and friendship and food, a break from the drudgery of corrections and officers and rules. This temporary break from reality. I spent five hours watching chess that day, and for those five hours, the men were able to pretend they were someplace else.

I realize that advocates for harsher sentences may not agree with the sentiment of Yard Day. They may believe inmates *shouldn't* be allowed to have a break from reality. They should be forced to confront their crimes day after day after day.

I will allow them their opinion, but I vehemently disagree with it. At the same time, I'd also remind those that oppose any kind of flexibility or freedom in prison to remember that the men are still incarcerated. They are still paying their debt to society. A single day of hot dogs and ice cream doesn't change that. They still have to be counted several times every single day and be told where to go and what time to sleep and what time to wake up and follow the rules of prison life.

But they are still human beings with thoughts and feelings. Is it really so terrible to give them five hours every year where, at least for a short time, they can stay inside and play chess with friends?

A few days later, I was coming home from a very long day of work. All I wanted to do was get upstairs and watch some mindless reality television.

I tucked myself into the corner of the elevator and flipped open my phone, wanting to see if I had missed any text messages while at work.

The doors slid open and a twentysomething African American man got on. He stood next to me and reached over to push the button for the fourth floor. Tucked under his right arm was a basketball, matched by the white sleeveless shirt and navy blue basketball shorts.

At the time I didn't really pay attention to basketball, although I was aware enough to know that just a few weeks prior, LeBron James had broken up with the city of Cleveland on national television in an ESPN special that came to be known as "The Decision."

My apartment had a healthy mix of both new and old residents. My next-door neighbor had been there since the place had opened a decade before and I myself would go on to live there for eight years. But the low price tag for downtown living attracted young urban professionals unable to afford the fancier rents closer to the center of the city. There was a constant influx of incoming renters and while there were only about sixty units in the entire building, it was hard to keep track of turnover so I was used to constantly seeing new faces in the elevator.

I maintained my position, crouched in the corner, scrolling through texts. I didn't notice the guy had been staring at me before he said something.

"I know you," he said slowly, looking me up and down.

I turned to look at him. Scanning his dark face, I shook my head. "I don't think so."

"Yeah, yeah," he said, nodding. "I do. I know you."

He stood there, thinking, trying to place me.

It was just the two of us in the elevator, the silence awkward as he flipped through his mental Rolodex. "Did you go to school out in Lorain County?"

"Nope."

I don't do well at small talk, especially elevator small talk with strangers who were convinced they knew me when I was convinced they were imagining things. I slipped the phone into my purse and stared at the numbers above the elevator door, willing them to get to the fourth floor faster.

That seemed to trigger something and he took a tiny step back. It was subtle, but still significant enough that I noticed out of the corner of my eye. "But you *work* in Lorain County."

This caught my attention. "I do." I turned my gaze to him, scrutinizing him for some semblance of familiarity. Still nothing.

His head bobbed, once, twice. "You're a librarian." His index finger jabbed in my direction as he said this. Wherever he knew me from, he had finally figured it out, although I was still in the dark.

"I am."

"You work at the prison."

Ah. There it was. This was not the first time I had seen a formerly incarcerated individual that I had previously worked with outside after his release. But this was the first time I had ever interacted with a former inmate.

Before I could respond though, the doors opened and we both looked into the hallway. A crowd was gathered, trying to enter the elevator, but my new neighbor walked towards them, arms outstretched like wings. He said something to his group of waiting friends, although I couldn't hear over their chatter. A young woman with long, curly brown hair stood on her toes to get a better look at me over the wingspan of his arms.

He pushed them out in the hallway, giving himself just enough room that the elevator doors would close behind him leaving me alone in the metal box.

Apparently, they'd all just wait for the next one.

Chapter 23
Taking the Matter into Your Own Hands

Rule violation: (14) Seductive or obscene acts, including indecent exposure or masturbation; including, but not limited, to any word, action, gesture or other behavior that is sexual in nature and would be offensive to a reasonable person.
—Ohio Admin. Code 5120-9-06

Out of the corner of my eye, I spotted movement down the row of books. *Please not another bat. Please not another bat.* I shifted my head just enough and saw an inmate standing alone between the shelves, facing me.

He stood, silent and resolute. As I took him in, starting at his head and moving down his frame, my eyes followed the line of his arm. His left hand, dark against the navy blue pants, was settled at the fly of his pants making the subtlest of movements.

Through narrowed eyes I tried to decipher what I was seeing in front of me, analyzing the up and down movement of his hand. Is he . . . ?

Noticing my gaze, there was a flurry of

movement at his crotch while the inmate immediately turned 90 degrees to face the L section of Fiction. He plucked a book at random from the shelf right in front of him and hurriedly opened to the first page.

That was weird.

I turned back to the paperwork on my desk, shaking my head in an effort to shake the thoughts from my brain. See, because, I had this moment where I thought I saw the inmate masturbating. Just out in the open. While staring at me. But, that couldn't have been what I saw, right? I mean, there's no way an inmate would just stand there in the middle of the library book shelves and just jerk himself off right there where anyone could walk around the corner and see him. Hell, *I* could see him and I could make his life far more difficult than another inmate who had the unfortunate desire to want to read the next book in the *Left Behind* series.

Even that whole incident with Brown over a year and a half ago made far more sense. Brown had least had the sense to cut holes in the interior pockets of his pants so he could do it without being caught. But this guy . . .

I tried to focus on the form on my desk. It was September 2, which meant it was time to once again fill out my monthly statistics report. Every month I had to report back to Grace on how many books were checked out, how many hours the library was open that month, how many visitors I had in the library, that sort of thing. It was official documentation that got faxed down to Columbus and Grace could always be relied on to send mildly snarky follow-up emails to chase down any missing reports. Admittedly, I had, more than once, tried to blame technology: "Oh, gosh, Grace, that's so weird, I know I faxed it but it must have gotten lost in the ether. Oh technology. Let me refax that over right away."

Grace knew as well as I did that this was the modern day equivalent of "the check is in the mail," but as long as I refaxed it when I said I would, she would let it go.

But as I flipped through August's sign-in sheets to come up with a rough guestimate on how many inmates had visited the library over the past four weeks (knowing full well several had slipped in without signing in), I was once again distracted by movement out of the corner of my right eye.

The first time I was 95 percent sure I had imagined any shenanigans in the crotch area. This time I was 95 percent sure that was absolutely what I was seeing. The fact that the inmate once again pulled the ol' "Oh, HERE is the book I wanted to read" as a means of deflection sealed it for me. Still, this was a serious offense in regards to rule violations and I needed to be sure before making any kind of accusation.

According to Ohio Administrative Code

5120-9-06, masturbation was not allowed within the walls of a prison. The Inmate Rules of Conduct outlined the sixty-one rule violations all persons incarcerated at Ohio facilities could be written up for. When I wrote a conduct report, it needed to be in response to one of the rule violations in the OAC, and the number of the violation needed to be on the report.

Some rule violations were so frequent, I had the number memorized, such as twenty-one, Disobedience of a Direct Order. Others were rarely seen, at least by me, which is why I was always glad to have the filing cabinet of policies right next to my desk for those one-offs when I had to look the violation up.

Each facility also instituted their own policies and procedures that only applied to inmates at the facility. OAC thought ahead, knowing there would be inmates who would try to argue that because a facility-specific rule was not included in the Inmate Rules of Conduct it didn't count, but for those instances there was always *#61: Any violation of any published institutional rules, regulations, or procedures.*

Because the rules are numbered and run down a list, when I initially began to familiarize myself with them, I assumed the numbers were applied in a way so as to suggest severity level, like a scale of 1 to 10, with 1 being the worst, and 10 being the best (or, well, least worst, I guess).

In that way, it makes sense that *Causing or attempting to cause the death of another* is rule violation #1 while the aforementioned published rules is at the very bottom, #61. *Any violation of any published institutional rules, regulations, or procedures* is basically the correctional version of "Additional duties as assigned."

Yet, OAC 5120-9-06 states that the numbers do not indicate severity but, instead, are there as a way to itemize violations in a grouping system. So, assault and related acts were rule violations 1 through 7, threats 8 through 10, and so on.

Sure. Okay.

What makes it a little tricky is "sexual misconduct" makes up rules 11 through 14. Maybe it is just a grouping system and the numbers don't mean much beyond that, but *some* order had to be applied when they put the list of rule violations together, right? Because, honestly, I have a hard time looking at a list that has CAUSING OR ATTEMPTING TO CAUSE THE DEATH OF ANOTHER at the top spot and *not* believe there is some ethical or moral reasoning behind the order of the rule violations. That's pretty much the worst thing you can do, right? Kill (or attempt) to kill another human being. Across time, cultures, religious factions, we may disagree on most things but that is one thing we can all usually agree on.

Even then, even if I were to believe the

numbers are applied without thought to severity the groupings themselves must be in some order, correct?

My point to all of this is that having masturbation at #14 shows just how serious the Ohio Department of Rehabilitation and Correction took sexual impropriety among the men in its charge.

By now I had effectively given up on finishing the monthly report that day, and Grace was just going to have to deal with it. But I still turned my gaze and focus back to the form, because it was the only thing in front of me that provided any means of distraction.

Thankfully, four years of marching band wherein I had to be able to march downfield without running into either flautist to the left or right of me, while also maintaining the very straight line across the entire back row of the three hundred-person band, provided me with superb peripheral vision. This meant that from his vantage point in the stacks, the inmate probably thought I had turned my attention, and gaze, back to whatever was on my desk. In reality, however, I watching him out with just the slightest tilt of my head.

Watching and waiting.

Once assured that I wasn't looking at him, he put the book back on the shelf and shifted his body back in my direction. And the activity at the fly of his pants began again.

Fuck.

I picked up the phone and held it low, putting it up against my ear closest to the window and furthest from the inmate. I tilted my head to hide the receiver. He was new, and I had no idea who he was, and if he left I had no way of finding him again unless I got lucky, or unlucky as it were, and he decided to return to the scene of the crime and take another whack. I had to keep this call on the down low.

"Fordham here."

"Heyyyyyyyy," I whispered. "Can you come over here real quick?"

"What is it?" he asked. Fordham wasn't known for being one of the fastest moving officers. Those that were assigned to Education fell into two camps. There were the ones who approached the job as if they had the same security risk as in the houses, and always responded quickly to my calls, and were consistent and timely in their hourly rounds to the library.

Then there were the ones who saw Education as an opportunity to spend eight hours sitting at a desk in a relatively quiet environment with little interaction with the inmates, who were always in class. Those COs would always come when I called, although it usually took some finagling on my part to convince them, and their so called "hourly" rounds were sporadic at best. They'd mosey on over when they felt like it, and because so few people visited the library or signed the log, they could easily just match the time from their last visit to make it appear as though they were more accurate in their time management skills.

Fordham fell into the latter category.

"Uh . . . Can you just come over? I'll explain when you're here."

With a heavy, reluctant sigh, he hung up the phone.

The inmate, realizing I was on the phone, quickly hurried over to the exit. "I gotta, uh, go to, um—"

I smiled and held up my index finger. "Yeah, if you wouldn't mind just waiting right there for one teeny tiny second, that would be great, thanks."

He might not be great at keeping it in his pants, but he was good at following orders.

After what felt like forever, Fordham's figure appeared in the window as he made the very short walk from Education to the library. When he opened the door and came in, it was like watching molasses move.

"What's up?" he asked.

"I wasn't doing nothing!" the inmate cried. His naturally dark face had gone ashen.

Up until that moment, I don't think Fordham

had even noticed the inmate standing there, let alone thought he had anything to do with my call. Now, I watched as Fordham's entire demeanor changed. He raised his body up straight like a marionette doll whose strings had been pulled taut. Taking a short sidestep to the left, he positioned himself between the inmate and the exit.

"Oh, really?" Fordham asked. "And what *didn't* you do?"

The inmate's eyes shifted quickly around the room, bouncing off the walls and shelves of books. It was like watching a person attempting to find that one solid spot to stare at, while at the same time attempting to catch their balance. If a person could flail while standing absolutely still, this inmate was doing exactly that.

"I was . . . well, I just . . . it's not what it looked like!" he stuttered. His eyes turned glassy, a veil of tears threatening at the corners.

"Uh-huh." Fordham turned to me for clarification.

Great, so I was going to have to be the one to say it. Out loud. I took a deep breath. "He was . . . masturbating," I finally announced. I could feel the heat in my cheeks rise.

Caught, the inmate's whole body crumbled, like the bones of his body just sunk into themselves.

Fordham raised an eyebrow. Whatever he was expecting me to say, it was not that.

"Write the conduct report," Fordham instructed. "I'll take it up front."

I raised my eyebrows. This was unusual: with the exception of Jackson's last evening, every other conduct report I'd written was just dropped at the captain's office as I was leaving at the end of the day. Hell, some of them I forgot about and didn't take until the next day. Then, again, every other conduct report I had written were minor infractions, nothing compared to this.

"Okay. I'll let you know when it's ready."

Fordham gave me a nod and exited, leading the guilty inmate by his elbow. As he did, Inmate Franklin got up from his seat at one of the tables and followed him out.

Franklin returned within seconds. "I told Fordham I seen it, too," he explained. He scrunched his face as if smelling something particularly foul. "Nasty."

I nodded in agreement, thanking him for speaking up.

After that, the rest of my morning was spent drafting my conduct report. Facts, I kept reminding myself. Just the facts. Don't embellish or add feelings or conjecture. Just state the facts.

Shortly before the library was to close for lunch, I rang Fordham up next door. He picked up my conduct report and delivered it straightaway up front in Administration.

The phone at Stephanie's elbow rang and we both paused in our eating. She answered, gave me a glance, then handed me the phone. "Coleman," she mouthed.

Huh. That was unexpected. My interaction with Lt. Coleman had always been limited to exchanging polite conversation as we passed each other on the walkway.

I took the phone from Stephanie. "Hello?"

"Ms. G. Coleman here. Tell me exactly what happened."

My eyes met Stephanie's and I held her gaze as I went over the story. It was easier to pretend I was telling it to her rather than Coleman. It was mortifying enough to have to tell it all, so I might as well make believe it was just two women gossiping.

"So you actually saw his—" Coleman stopped.

I nodded, even though he couldn't see me. "Yes."

There was a pause and Coleman's voice dropped low as he conferred with Captain Freeman. "This isn't the first time he's done this," Coleman said. "There are similar incidents at other facilities. He has a history of gross indecency."

My eyes widened. On the other side of the table, Stephanie was antsy with anticipation. "Really?" I asked.

I could practically hear Coleman nodding on the other end of the line. "Yeah, he shouldn't have been sent here because of that; he somehow slipped through the cracks.

"Okay, thanks. That's enough for us."

Hanging up the phone, I gave Stephanie a shrug and relayed the conversation.

This wasn't my first guy masturbating in the library, but this was the first time I was so *aware* of it when it was happening. Not just aware, but knowing the guy was looking at me while he did it. I felt violated and exposed. Graduate school had left me totally unprepared for this part of librarianship. I wondered if this is how Alice felt when she stepped through the looking glass, and discovered everything had turned topsy-turvy. Oh, and there was also that dark shadow of threat lurking around every corner, jaws snapping, claws scratching. Beware the Jabberwock, indeed.

Secrets in prison don't say secret for long, and by the next day word had already gotten around.

"There was a masturbator in here, Ms. G.? And you caught him?" someone asked me the next day.

"Caught him? He was *staring* at me."

I had to deal with this same exchange multiple times that day.

On Friday, I went down to Segregation for my usual visit. As soon as I got in, I ran my eyes down the whiteboard above the officer's desk, looking for Jenkins's cell number.

I began on the other side of the room, wanting to avoid the inevitable for as long as possible. Cell to cell I went, asking if the inmate or inmates inside wanted anything from the library. Every few feet I'd throw a glance in the direction of Jenkins's cell. That was his name: Jenkins, habitual masturbator. Unless an inmate was a library regular, the only other reason I'd usually learn an inmate's name was if I had to write up a conduct report, such as the case with Jenkins.

When I first started going around the Segregation unit, Jenkins was asleep on the top bunk but as I rounded the corner and began working on his side of the room, it seemed that he had woken up.

"Mr. Jenkins," I called into the cell. Regardless of what had happened, politeness needed to be maintained. "Is there anything you'd like from the library?" I kept my eyes trained on the notepad in front of me. When he didn't answer, I looked up.

His entire face took up the porthole window, his mouth turned up into the widest grin I'd ever seen. All of his teeth were bared, a brick wall of white. It was by far the creepiest grin I had ever seen, like jack-o'-lantern level. Suddenly I knew how Little Red Riding Hood felt when she first came upon the wolf deep in the woods.

Despite there being a solid steel door between us, I took a step back.

"Know who I am?" he asked.

"Yes, Jenkins. I know who you are." I looked down at the notebook in my hand, pen poised. I avoided his gaze but I could still feel it boring into me. "Are there any books you want from the library that I can bring you?"

He didn't answer. My eyes darted up then back down, just long enough to see him still staring at me with that grin on his face. "Yeah," he said. "Bring me some James Patterson."

I scribbled *Patterson* next to his cell number on my notepad, then quickly stepped to the side to get to the cell next to his and finish my rounds, wanting to put as much distance between me and him as possible.

The next day, I was due to return to Segregation with the books. During the morning break, I loaded up my basket with the appropriate titles, or as close as I could get, and headed down the walkway hoping I'd run into someone with a Segregation key along the way, saving me from having to awkwardly loiter around the exterior door.

"Captain!" I called out, quickening my pace as I hurried up the sidewalk of the Education building to catch the person exiting. Above, the darkening sky was full of clouds heavy with impending rain.

Up ahead, a man in a crisp black uniform

turned his bald white head in my direction. Despite his short stature, Captain Freeman was an intimidating force across the prison yard, garnering the respect of inmates and staff alike through his fixed, yet fair, rule of law and order.

Falling directly below the major in the chain of command, the captain had authority over the lieutenants and correctional officers, while also acting as a sort of liaison between the civilian employees working out in the yard and the brass up in the Administrative offices.

It also meant he was one of the few individuals in the camp who had a key to let me into the Segregation unit.

The yard was empty except for the two of us, and I fell in step beside him as he led me down the walkway towards the heavy steel door that led to Seg. "One thing," he said, putting the key into the lock. "You should stay away from Jenkins's cell."

"Oh?"

Freeman held the door open and waved me in. "He was caught doing it again in his bed here in Seg."

"Oh."

He offered me a sympathetic smile as he shut the door, leaving me alone in the long, empty corridor.

Bolton stood up from his seat when I entered the cell block, keys at the ready. He followed me from cell to cell, unlocking the trap door in front of each one as I dropped off the books the inmates had asked for.

Right before we got to Jenkins, I stopped short. "Here." I thrust the requested James Patterson book into Bolton's hands. "I'm not going anywhere near that cell."

Without a word, Bolton took the book and slid it into the trap door. "Jenkins! Your library book."

I heard movement inside the cell, a rustle of metal upon brick as he jumped down from his bunk and it hit the cinder block wall behind him. "She out there?"

Bolton shifted a slight look in my direction before turning back to him. "Just take the book, Jenkins."

The worn James Patterson title disappeared into the cell and Bolton clapped the trap door back up, locking it tight. The sound of metal meeting metal echoed through the cavernous room. I breathed a sigh of relief, boundaries solidified.

By the following week, when I returned to Segregation, Jenkins was gone. Shipped off to some higher security prison due to his history of "gross indecency."

Chapter 24
Ink Art Serrated

Rule Violation: (57) Self-mutilation, including tattooing.
Rule Violation: (58) Possession of devices or material used for tattooing.
—Ohio Admin. Code 5120-9-06

Officer Klein walked into the library, thumbs tucked into the belt loops of his pants. He was tall and lanky, a local boy from right here in Grafton. "Alright!" he shouted into the quiet library, startling us all. "Everybody up and out. Back to the dorms. Emergency count."

The inmates grumbled as they stood up from the tables and shuffled to the circulation desk, newspapers in hand. "This is some bullshit," I overheard one of them say as he traded the paper for his badge.

"Emergency count?" I asked Klein as he waited, watching the room clear. The inmates were already counted several times a day, like clockwork. Emergency counts, spontaneous situations where everyone had to rush back to the dorms and stand by their bunks to be counted, were rare.

He nodded, gaze trained on the inmates as they

filed past him and outside. "Inmate from next door possibly escaped."

"Escaped," I repeated skeptically, knitting my brows together.

The yard closing down was far more common than emergency count. Yard closing could be handled one of two ways: first, everyone was to stay exactly where they were, no inmate movement at all. So if the inmate was in the library when the yard closed, the inmate had to stay in the library. The second option was that the inmates were herded back to their dorms like sheep, and had to stay there, and weren't allowed to leave the dorms until the yard reopened. This was often what happened with imminent weather. More than once the library had been shut down early because severe lightning was headed our way and the Captain ordered all inmates back to the dorms before it struck.

The worst instance of yard closure was when Mr. Hooper, GED teacher, lost his keys.

Yes, you read that right: Lost. His. Keys. Inside. The. Prison.

Keeping your keys secure is, like, Prison Employment 101. But somehow Hooper managed to lose them. Not only lose them, but he had no idea where he had lost them. In this instance, the inmates were forbidden from leaving whatever area of the prison they were in at the time of yard closing. Security didn't want to give them any opportunities to dump the keys, if they had them. So until the keys were found, nobody could leave, including staff. School was done for the day, as were the AA and NA meetings, so the Education staff and the Recovery Resources staff aided in the hunt. At one point during the search, I looked out the window of the library and saw Stephanie precariously squatting over a drain, attempting to peer inside to see if the keys had fallen down there.

Correctional officers scoured the yard while others tore the dorms apart. Eventually, 4:00 count rolled around and an officer came to the library to escort the inmates back to the dorms.

By dinner, Hooper's keys still hadn't been found, much to the frustration of those of us who were supposed to have left hours before. I was posted in the chow hall that evening, along with Dr. Harald, directing inmates on where to sit for dinner.

Finally, around 6:30 p.m., Hooper's keys were finally found out in the yard and the staff were free to go home. Because of Hooper's incompetence, I had to stay late for three nights that week, which annoyed me to no end.

That wasn't the first time Hooper had shown himself to be a security risk. One day, after the library had closed for the morning, I was in the Education department and saw Hooper in a classroom with some of his students. Class was over, so these inmates were dawdling until they had to head back to their dorms for count.

Whatever Hooper was teaching them was so captivating, they decided to stay behind.

From my vantage point by the copier, I was able to stare through the classroom windows and saw that Hooper was teaching them how to write in code. To Hooper, this was just a novelty. A fun and interesting thing to teach his students. But to his students, this was a way to skirt the security of the prison.

How he still had a job after that, I have no idea.

But as far as security threats went, the key thing was just a closing of the yard. Emergency counts were different. With emergency counts, the yard gets shut down and inmates are sent back to the dorms, where they stand and are, well, counted.

Of course, most of the time, the officers are looking to make sure we don't have too few inmates. In this instance, the prison was making sure we didn't have too *many* inmates.

Although, why you would escape one prison just to enter another made zero sense to me. But protocol is protocol.

I closed up the library and headed next door to await instructions.

False alarm, it turned out. The inmate from next door was found and we had the correct number in ours.

A few days later, I was back in Segregation for my weekly visit. My eyes ran down the

Segregation whiteboard, the furrow in my brow deepening the further down my gaze went. I referenced the notebook in my hand then looked back up at the board. "What happened to Doyle?"

I had been surprised to see his name on the board to begin with. Doyle, while perhaps not the brightest crayon in the box, was not known for getting into trouble. Certainly not Segregation levels of trouble that is, often relying on his boyish charm to talk himself out of any situation. Nevertheless, he had been in Seg for the past few days, although currently, according to the whiteboard, he was in the medical unit.

Bolton and Lopez exchanged a quick glance, smiles dancing on both of their mouths. Neither answered, but Bolton's belly jiggled as he attempted to contain his laughter.

"What?" I asked, looking back and forth between the two of them. "What's so funny?"

Lopez looked to Bolton before continuing, but Bolton shook his head and waved him off. His laughter was so tightly contained that if he opened his mouth even for a breath, he'd completely burst into hysterics.

"Uh, well." Lopez gestured for me to come closer to his desk. "There was a bit of a situation." He looked to his partner for help, but Bolton, while no longer on the verge of bursting out into laughter was still not ready to contribute to the conversation. Lopez rolled his eyes. "It seems that Doyle got a hold of an ink pen. Gave himself a tattoo."

"Come on."

Bolton, wiping tears from his eyes, nodded. "We still don't know how, but he had the pen hiding in his bunk."

"How bad was it?"

"Got infected," Lopez answered. "We had to send him next door to Medical."

Their laughter no longer seemed appropriate, and the look on my face must have given my concern away because both of them snapped to attention. "No, no," Bolton finally said. "He's fine. He just needs to stay there for a day or two so they can keep an eye on it."

Admittedly, my curiosity outweighed my concern. "What happened?"

They both shrugged. "We don't know how he got the pen," Lopez said. "But somehow he got it in and broke it open, used the shards to poke holes and then put in the ink."

Prison tattoos are not uncommon, and for those inmates with an entrepreneurial spirit, it can even offer a side hustle while inside. Payment for ink in the clink works on a barter system, as inmates are forbidden to possess money. This is why envelopes coming in and going out of the facility had to be pre-stamped, a special class of envelopes purchased directly from the post office, since stamps could be traded in lieu of cash. Prior to the smoking ban, cigarettes would have been the payment of choice, although there were still other options, usually food and sundry items purchased through commissary.

That said, most inmates who possessed that same entrepreneurial spirit of turning prison tattooing into an inside job are also intelligent enough to know it was best to fashion some kind of motorized tattoo gun from contraband items and not just use some random ink pen.

"And it got infected?"

"He tried to hide it," Bolton answered, picking up where Lopez left off. "But it got so bad that his bunkmate finally alerted us."

"Jesus."

"Wanna see a picture?" Bolton's eyes lit up. Both he and Lopez looked at me like overeager puppies.

"Um . . . " *Did* I want to see a picture? I already had one tattoo myself, but I was itching for more. In an ideal world (and with an unlimited bank account) I'd have two full sleeves, both of my arms technicolor tapestries. Seeing a tattoo job gone horribly wrong might ruin all interest in further ink adventures (though my finances would certainly appreciate that outcome).

Not waiting for an answer, Bolton pulled open his desk drawer and produced a digital camera. Technology of any kind was so limited inside that the digital camera looked like some object from an alien planet when compared against the stark white walls of Segregation.

I leaned over his shoulder as Bolton clicked through the photos on the camera's memory card of evidence. Finally, he stopped on one photo and handed me the camera.

Based on the angle of the photo, my best guess was that Doyle had tattooed the side of his calf. Correction: Doyle had tattooed *most* of his calf. The tattoo was huge, at least by the standards of a homemade ink job done on the sly. It appeared to be a sun of some kind.

A very red, very painful, very angry-looking sun that burned bright against his pale skin.

"That idiot," I said.

Bolton burst out laughing.

The following week, Doyle was back in Segregation. His attempt at homegrown ink had earned him an additional length of stay in Segregation. By the time I got to the third cell, Doyle was already waiting for me. "Hey, Ms. G."

"Doyle." I paused a beat, then: "What the ever-loving hell were you thinking?"

He grinned and ducked his head, his white blonde hair falling into his eyes. "Y'know, Ms. G., I knew there was a reason we didn't use ink pens back in the house."

"Uh, yeah. You think?" I gave a quick shake of my head. "Can I get you any books?"

He tilted his head to one side, thinking. "Can

you bring me some sexy books? You know, *sexy* books?"

Ah, yes. The "sexy" books. A frequent request. "Sure thing, Doyle."

"Thanks, Ms. G.!"

Nora Roberts was about as steamy as our books got, but it didn't stop inmates from reading them for, ahem, *personal* reasons. Romance novels were a bustling industry in prison and while the really descriptive books weren't allowed in, some of the softer romances were.

Whatever. If they wanted to jack off to a romance novel within the privacy of their cell or bunk and away from the library, I wasn't going to stop them. I became a librarian for many reasons, the main one being giving people access to the books and information they want. If that meant sometimes peddling the prison equivalent of porn, then so be it. Despite my own personal interactions with masturbating inmates, I don't really have a problem with men jerking off in prison. Just don't jerk off *at* me.

Fall had come again, the flourish of reds and golds lining my drive to work every day. I'd officially been at the prison for twenty months. In that time, the library had checked out thousands of books, and I'd cataloged just as many. I'd seen inmates come and go, and come again.

I was now headed back down to Columbus for

the next meeting of the prison librarian minds.

This time I was allowed to drive myself in my own car. No big behemoth of a white van that required waking up an hour earlier than normal.

"We won't reimburse you for gas," Highland warned me when I first asked if I could be allowed to take my own vehicle down and back and skip the extra step of coming to the prison first.

"That's fine!" I exclaimed. Between sacrificing the extra hour, or paying for my own gas, I was more than happy to pay for my own gas.

This time around, I felt more comfortable finding my way to Columbus and selecting a seat among the other librarians. I'd been at work for almost two years, I understood how things functioned and operated. I sat in the large meeting room, listened to Grace discuss recent policy changes and once again remind us about the importance of turning our monthly stats report in on time. At the end, I got back in my car and drove home. The whole day felt routine. Boring, even. Sitting in a room listening to someone else drone on for eight hours made me realize how much I missed the constant flow of men in and out of the library, and more than once during the day my mind drifted, wondering how things were going back at the prison.

The following week, Dr. Harald pulled me into his office. "I want you to give a presentation," he said, "about your recent visit down to Columbus. Tell us all about what's been going on with the library and all of that."

"Oh, okay, sure."

"We'll have Highland and some of the other Admin staff sit in. Oh, and select two inmate workers to join us. You know, one black and one white, so it's balanced."

Internally, I cringed. I understood the point he was making but it just felt like tokenism to express it in such, well, black-and-white terms.

"Sure thing."

That afternoon, I pulled Lincoln and Webb aside. "Would you guys be interested in sitting in on a meeting about library services next week? It'll be up in Admin, and you'll be excused from count."

Lincoln and Webb shared a glance. Whatever passed between them was agreed upon by both, because they each in turn looked at me and nodded. "Sure, Ms. G."

The day of the meeting, Lincoln was on duty, but Webb wasn't. Lincoln hung around while the library was closing and while we were waiting for Webb, I wrote up passes for them to have when we arrived at Administration, showing they had permission from a staff member (me) to be up there.

After the library was closed and Webb had arrived, they followed me up the pathway to Administration. When we walked through the door of Admin, we were stopped by the correctional officer.

"Did you let their houses know?" the officer asked, reading the slips of paper that Webb and Lincoln had handed him.

"Uhhhh. . ." in his instructions for the day, for getting Webb and Lincoln permission to be up here, Dr. Harald had not mentioned anything about needing to call their houses. Not for the first time, I was frustrated and flustered by the lack of information provided by my supervisor.

"What are they here for?" he asked.

"The library advisory meeting," I said.

He continued to look back and forth between the permission slips, as if undecided on whether or not to allow me back there with the two men standing behind me. Captain Freeman poked his head out of his office.

The officer conferred with him, finally Freeman waved us through. "Just call the houses next time so they know their count number will be off."

I nodded, "No, I get it. Dr. Harald didn't—"

Freeman nodded. "It's okay. Go on back."

I turned to Webb and Lincoln and gestured for them to follow me.

Highland and Dr. Harald were already seated in the room, and we were soon joined by Stephanie, along with two of the women who worked up in Admin, Driver and Madison. Webb and Lincoln took their seats around the table.

"Well," I said, calling the meeting to order. "I can start with the cataloging project, which is going well. I've made a good dent in the books, although there is a long way to go. But I think once the books are all in the system, and the inmates are also in and can be checked out by their ID number, the library will become a lot more efficient."

Honestly, I don't know if anyone was even really that interested in listening to me talk about the software I was, for lack of a better word, obsessed with. Since getting it set up a few months ago, I had been breezing past all of my cataloging quotas for the day. Granted, they were self-imposed quotas, but still.

Of course, during this process I had discovered just how disorganized the library really was. So many nonfiction books had been classified as fiction and vice versa. It was frustrating, but explained why I had a hard time finding books I knew we owned.

After I went through the recent stats, average number of books checked out each month, average number of visitors, and that sort of thing, the team turned to Webb and Lincoln.

"What do *you* think about the library?" Driver asked.

Webb and Lincoln confirmed what I already knew: the library was a favorite location among all of the inmates at the prison. It was one of the few places where they felt they were treated like adults and could just *be,* without constantly being reminded they were in prison.

If nothing else, my takeaway from the meeting was that I had done good with the little library I was given.

What I left out of my presentation, the key piece of information I was still keeping to myself, was that I was starting to plan my escape.

It was little things, adding up over the course of twenty months. The dread that came every morning when I woke up and realized I had to go back to the prison. The oppressive feeling that came with a job that required me to sacrifice two major pillars of librarianship: patron privacy and access to information.

I loved working with the men I got to see every single day. I loved helping them find books and discover new authors. They were funny men, who kept me entertained with their banter and I was going to miss that.

But I was tired and burned out from the environment. It was exhausting, mentally and emotionally, to work in a prison every day. Correctional officers get into it understanding what they were signing up for. As a librarian, I didn't, and while I was grateful for the opportunity I had been given, this was not a long-term career for me.

Stephanie was the only one who knew I was

applying for jobs, the only one I trusted to not tell anyone. Some of the worst gossips were among the staff and I didn't want to give them any ammunition prior to my landing a new position.

The day before my twenty-ninth birthday, I was offered a job at a local career college. I would be their new librarian, overseeing a library that focused on the academic needs of the students. The schedule was four ten-hour days, Monday through Thursday. Not only did I no longer have to work Saturdays, but I'd have Fridays off, too.

I celebrated both the new job and another year around the sun by sitting in a chair and having a scruffy man permanently inject ink into my inner right wrist. Unlike Doyle, I had the advantage of having access to licensed tattoo artists. The words—defy gravity—were a call back to the musical *Wicked*, based on the book by Gregory Maguire, about the Wicked Witch of the West.

Twenty months ago, I had started my journey as a prison librarian feeling like Dorothy Gale, lost and alone in an unknown and unfamiliar world. But now, sitting in the chair in the tattoo studio, the sound of the gun buzzing in my ears, I knew it was time to grab my broom and soar.

This jailbird was ready to fly the coop.

"Is it true, Ms. G.?" Woodson asked a few days after I'd put in my notice, eyes forlorn. "Are you leaving us?"

Word had gotten around.

"It's true," I said. "I found a new job at a college."

He looked thoughtful. "Before you go . . . would you be willing to write me a letter of recommendation? When I get out, I want to try and find a job at the library and I thought if I had a letter from you . . ."

"Of course!" I said. "I think that's a great idea."

Woodson beamed, satisfied. He took the stack of books sitting on the edge of the circulation desk and headed into the book shelves to put them away.

I glanced at the calendar. Seven sleeps left.

My last day of work, I woke up without a voice.

I don't know what happened, I hadn't done anything over the past few days to strain it, but I couldn't talk. If I couldn't talk, I couldn't be effective at my job. So much of what I did on a daily basis included instructing inmates. Tuck in your shirt. Sign in. Remove your hat. Not only could I not do my job, because I didn't have a voice, I couldn't even call in and explain the situation to Dr. Harald or Highland.

The first shift was a struggle, my voice low and raspy. I did a lot of gesturing with my hands or writing things out on a piece of paper that I would flash at the inmate. Things like *Tuck in your shirt. Sign in. Remove your hat.* Ms. G might not be able to talk and it might be her last day, but the rules of the library were still going to be enforced.

During the break at count, I went into Dr. Harald's office and asked if I could finish my last shift early. I felt bad, with Thanksgiving around the corner, I'd already given a shortened notice period and not a full two weeks. But while at the beginning of the day I could kind of speak, by the end of the shift I was completely voiceless.

Dr. Harald nodded and stood up. He put out his hand, which I shook, as he thanked me for a job well done.

I gathered my belongings and went around the department, saying my good-byes and wishing everyone well. After I'd seen everyone I needed to see, I made my way out the door and started up the long walk up to the entryway.

The yard was quiet, the inmates and officers back at the house for count. I walked quickly, the air cold with winter on the horizon. When I got up to the entry, I pulled my keys and chits out of my pocket and dropped them into the drawer. Next went the panic button. Finally, I unclipped my badge and dropped it in beside the other items.

"It's my last day," I struggled to say into the voice box. "I'm all done."

The shaded head on the other side of the window silently nodded in response.

I took a step back and waited for the familiar buzzer.

With a deep breath, I pulled open the heavy door and walked through the gate for the last time.

Epilogue

Out of the corner of my eye, a flash of familiarity breezes past the window in my door.

I've been at my new position for several months, this time as the sole librarian at a career college also on the west side of Cleveland. I had finally made it to academia. No, it wasn't as flashy a position as one at Case Western Reserve University or any of the other halls of learning in the area, but it would do for now. The college's location of North Olmsted, as compared to Grafton, also had the benefit of being surrounded by a shopping mall and restaurants. Lunch breaks were spent running errands and eating way too much Chipotle (I could *walk there*), and no longer was I chained to my desk and required to call for someone to watch the library when I just needed to go use the restroom.

The habits of prison had been so ingrained that after I'd been there for a week or so, my manager, the campus president, came to me and said, "You know you're allowed to get up and leave and walk around, right?"

It seems even employees can become institutionalized after a while.

The library in the school was small, really not that much different in size from the prison library, but it was open and airy. The entire back wall was lined with windows, bringing in a day's worth of natural light. Tables and chairs crowded the blue carpet, a small selection of dark wood bookshelves pressed to the wall.

That was another remarkable difference: the majority of the library's collection could be found online and students were encouraged to do their research through the digital collection, not the physical collection. A row of computers lined the wall, free for the students to use whenever they wanted.

My desk sat at the front of the room, so no longer was I crushed into the back corner. Granted, this time the windows were clear on the other side of the room but the door had a small window, like a porthole into the hallway. A window through which I just saw someone I thought looked familiar. But there was no way, right? I mean, what were the chances that—

The door popped open. "Ms. G.!"

Welp. That answers that question.

"I thought that was you," he exclaimed, grinning from ear to ear.

"It's me!" I was stalling for time because while I recognized his face and distinctly remembered him from the dog program, I could not, for the life of me, remember his name. "So, you go to school here now?"

Bashful, he shoved his hands into the pockets

of his jeans and nodded. "Yup, yup. I'm doing the computer science program." When he looked back up at me he was beaming.

"That's great!" I said, and it was. Gainful employment was a struggle for former inmates, their guilty conviction a black mark against them on applications. The economy was still struggling and jobs were scarce. While it was hard for formerly incarcerated individuals before the Great Recession, it was even more difficult now. When a hiring manager was presented with more applications and resumes then he knew what to do with and only one job to fill, why would he risk it on a man who had been in prison, when there were hundreds of other qualified candidates without that on their background history?

Education was the only other option for a man who didn't want to make the same mistakes and end up back behind bars. But that came with its own challenges, trying to pay for it being one. Reliable transportation could also be an issue and after a while, school just became another obstacle that suddenly wasn't worth the energy and time.

After that one visit, I never saw him again. I never even relearned his name. I don't know what happened to him and could only hope he had found another alternative means of survival.

In February 2016, after my maternal grandmother died, my parents, sister, and I traveled to Houston to clean out her room at the nursing facility that had been her home for the past year or so. Those belongings that remained back at the house she had shared with my late grandfather had been divided up among family members or donated to Goodwill when she first went into the home, all of us knowing she wouldn't be returning to the house. Here, she kept a few mementos in her room, mostly photographs of her grandchildren spread out across her dresser so she was better able to see us from her hospital bed.

While going through her bedside table I came across a box of older keepsakes including her wedding album and photos from her childhood. Black-and-white vignettes of a little girl and a blushing bride.

Among the photos were newspaper clippings, one dating back to the Tuesday, October 26, 1948 edition of *The North Adams Massachusetts Transcript*. It was an obituary for a Mrs. Andrew N. Thorington—ah, yes, my great-great-grandmother on my mother's father's side reduced to her marital status even in death. Growing up, I had known about Andrew, a Civil War soldier. Through my own personal deep dive into my ancestry over the years, I knew that he had been twenty years older than his wife, Clara L. Cooley, when they had married. This was her obituary.

As my parents and aunt and uncle went through

the drawers, I sat on the edge of the now empty bed and read through the obituary. Most of what I already knew about Clara had been pulled years ago when I first fell down the rabbit hole of Ancestry.com. Hours were spent following her trail: she had been a member of the Daughters of Revolution and through her applications I had traced my own history back to New England in the late 1600s. Clara had been an amateur genealogist, which is close to being a librarian, and through her I have four ancestors who fought in the Revolutionary War, in addition to her late Civil War veteran husband.

But I didn't know much about Clara herself so, perhaps a bit morbid, her obituary seemed like a good place to start.

She was born in Hawley, Aug. 29, 1863, the daughter of Calvin E. and Olive (Crittenden) Cooley. She was married to Mr. Thorington on Aug. 4, 1885. He was an officer at the Hampden county jail in Northampton and she—

Huh. My great-great-grandfather Andrew had worked in a jail.

I continued reading. *He was an officer at the Hampden county jail in Northampton and she was a matron in the same institution for 30 years.*

Wait. Rewind.

Both of my great-great-grandparents had worked in a jail?

Seven years prior, I stepped out into the prison

418

yard for the first time as a prison librarian. I had no idea what to expect and I really had no idea what I was doing. When I tell the story of how I got there, I usually do mention the state of the economy, the struggle to find a job, and that I was willing to work just about anywhere to pay rent, including working at a prison.

But maybe, just maybe, something else had guided me there, too. Maybe, passed down through the generations, there was something in my blood that told me that for that brief period of time, I needed to be working there at that prison.

At this point in my life, I've been working in libraries for over twenty years. I've worked at public libraries and academic libraries and research libraries and, yes, a prison library. But none of the patrons I have met along the way have had as big of an impact on me than the men I met during the twenty-one months I was employed at that prison. Every single day I think of them, by name, and wonder how they are and what they are doing. I wonder if Woodson got that job at the library, and if Conway enjoyed his green beer.

But more than anything, I hoped their experience with me instilled in them a love for the library as an institution. Because even out in the big wide world of life after prison, the library is a neutral space. The library doesn't care who you are or where you come from. The library just wants you to be there, enjoying the books and reading the newspapers, and checking your email on the computers. The library is a space for everyone, regardless of background and history.

Public libraries as we know them today are due, in large part, to industrialist and philanthropist Andrew Carnegie. Over the course of three decades, Carnegie provided funds for nearly 2,900 public libraries including 1,700 in the United States. Prior to Carnegie's investment in America's literacy, libraries were guarded by fierce gatekeeping techniques, most often monetary: for a fee, you could access the books inside. There were private clubs that reserved books only for members, or students at an academic institution. Local libraries that provided free titles for a city or town were virtually nonexistent, and those that did exist were often treated as an afterthought by the local bureaucracy.

A lifelong reader, Carnegie wanted to change the elite trappings of libraries. As these free libraries began to sprout up around the country, and around the world, libraries and the books inside stopped being merely for the privileged and wealthy, but were now available to everyone, regardless of income or status. It wasn't just about having access to books, either, but the knowledge and information that could be gleaned from them, as evidenced in a quote attributed to

Carnegie: "A library outranks any other one thing a community can do to benefit its people. It is a never-failing spring in the desert."

It's a refreshing image, the pool of glistening water in the middle of an arid wasteland, the life and vitality that can come from drinking. Carnegie spoke of public libraries, of course, but the idea that a library can reinvigorate a person is true for all libraries, including, and perhaps especially, prison libraries. Surrounded by guards and bars and razor wire, the library always proved to be the one place at camp where the men could just exist.

This is true for all of us: the library is, and hopefully always will be, a place where we can just be free.

Acknowledgments

First and foremost, I have to thank my editor, Veronica Alvarado, for championing this book. I initially mentioned "my prison librarian memoir" to Ronnie as a potential topic back in November 2016, so it's taken almost three years for us to get here. I told her that I wanted to do this story justice, and thanks to her patience and hard work, I like to think that I have.

Major kudos to the entire team at Skyhorse Publishing, especially production editor Jen Houle, and Tom Lau for once again giving me a fantastic cover. Along with them, thanks to sales team members Steven Sussman, Rachel Bloom, and Anna Brill.

So much love goes to my Beta Readers, Sydney, Alexa, and Claudine, for their comments and support. And, of course, to my OG Beta Reader, Jenn. Next margarita date is on me.

The research process for this book included documents, reports, and rules made publicly available online by Cornell University, the Ohio Department of Rehabilitation and Correction, the University of Michigan, and the Correctional Institution Inspection Committee. This includes the regulations I frequently cite throughout the text.

To Team OverDrive, thank you for the support, and for being the best company a librarian writer could ask for.

To Ben, my husband and partner in crime. I'm so happy you are the music to my words.

To my family for never, ever doubting my dreams of being a published writer.

On August 22, 2018, I returned to the Hudson Library & Historical Society and gave a presentation on the art and craft of memoir writing. My mom was in attendance, and I used the story of our mismatched memories regarding my original employment at that library as an example of the challenges that can come with writing in this genre.

Seven weeks later, she passed away after a hard fight with cancer.

I'm still convinced my version of events is correct, but on the off-chance that she was right all these years, and because she really pushed me into getting a job at the library, all I can say is, thanks Mom.

Books are
produced in the
United States
using U.S.-based
materials

Paper is
sourced using
environmentally
responsible
foresting methods
and the
paper is acid-free

Books are
produced using
top-of-the-line
digital binding
processes

Center Point Large Print
600 Brooks Road / PO Box 1
Thorndike, ME 04986-0001 USA

(207) 568-3717

US & Canada:
1 800 929-9108
www.centerpointlargeprint.com